Pacific End

Notes for a Novel

By

Thomas Mengert

The Victorian Gentlemen's Press™

Pacific End
First edition, published 2023

By Thomas Mengert

Copyright © 2023, Thomas Mengert

Cover photo by Thomas Mengert

ISBN-13: 978-1-942661-46-7

The Victorian Gentlemen's Press
P.O. Box 876
Keyport, WA 98345

Epigraph

"The House of Dust"
by Conrad Aiken

The sun goes down in a cold pale flare of light.

The trees grow dark: the shadows lean to the east:

And lights wink out through the windows, one by one.

A clamor of frosty sirens mourns at the night.

Pale slate-grey clouds whirl up from the sunken sun.

And the wandering one, the inquisitive dreamer of dreams,

The eternal asker of answers, stands in the street,

And lifts his palms for the first cold ghost of rain.

The purple lights leap down the hill before him.

The gorgeous night has begun again.

'I will ask them all, I will ask them all their dreams,

I will hold my light above them and seek their faces.

I will hear them whisper, invisible in their veins . . .'

The eternal asker of answers becomes as the darkness,

Or as a wind blown over a myriad forest,

Or as the numberless voices of long-drawn rains.

We hear him and take him among us, like a wind of music,

Like the ghost of a music we have somewhere heard;

We crowd through the streets in a dazzle of pallid lamplight,

We pour in a sinister wave, ascend a stair,

With laughter and cry, and word upon murmured word;

We flow, we descend, we turn . . . and the eternal dreamer

Moves among us like light, like evening air . . .

Good-night! Good-night! Good-night! We go our ways,
The rain runs over the pavement before our feet,
The cold rain falls, the rain sings.
We walk, we run, we ride. We turn our faces
To what the eternal evening brings.
Our hands are hot and raw with the stones we have laid,
We have built a tower of stone high into the sky,
We have built a city of towers.
Our hands are light, they are singing with emptiness.
Our souls are light; they have shaken a burden of hours
What did we build it for? Was it all a dream?

Table of Contents

Pacific End

Scene:

The American Empire circa 2016

Dramatis Personae:

A novelist

She who cannot be named

A varied cast of people who show up in passing

Various novels of many times and seasons

Method:

Experimental and spontaneous prose

The Seeds are planted...

I know that your love was as real as what you are feeling now. I honor them both because they are parts of you.

***

Don't try and rescue this. You always like things to be so nice and neat and clear, as though life can ever be caught, copied, and sealed up in a book. Well it just isn't that way.

***

(Soto voce) Is life an interruption to the act of composition or is composition an interruption of life? (Then aloud) If I ever write about us it will only be to make you look good.

***

Do whatever you want, just don't pretend that you understand me or that you ever cared. I know there was always somebody else.

***

There was nobody who mattered but you; that was the trouble. If you ever wanted me at all it was because I could be so easily cast in a scenario where I would be just the latest in a string of villains in your private tragedy.

***

You were the worst of them because with you I almost believed that I could be loved completely. You hurt me more than I ever hurt you. You just don't know it and that's why I'm leaving. You wanted this to happen. You planned it all along. Everything good that you ever did was just playing me for a fool. Why didn't you care enough to choke me; that kind of love I would have understood!

***

I always wanted you to come with me down to the coast. It's where I feel most truly alive. As for understanding you, what I am writing may serve to explain things ... for both of us.

Part One
Things Break Apart

In the year 2016, at a point now far enough into the 21st century that my own deep mid-century roots in the eventful 20th century were beginning to seem distant and part of that cold and static reservoir that is history, things of longstanding solace and serenity in my life began to break apart. Even literature, that resource that is still living because of the perennial relevance of its ideas, seemed inadequate to bridge the gaps and crevasses that were beginning to open up all around me. I felt the need for change yet simultaneously felt that a new beginning would only increase my present distress. I was unwilling to begin again the long process of forming new associations, of growing familiar enough to call a changed environment home. In reality I hungered more for some reinstatement of what had been rather than to resume the gypsy existence that had once seemed to me the only way to avoid stasis and routine; predictability savored too much of our final decline and dissolution.

In 2016 I also felt forces gathering on the horizon that had always been present in some form but that my own relative youth and optimism had always seemed adequate to confront. Now for the first time I felt deep within my being that this reservoir of inner resources would not always be available on demand. So it seemed the perfect time to follow the example of one of my heroes, Emile Zola, and to write my own version of an experimental novel, to make my accusation of the times, and to discover a way to reinstate if possible the élan vital within me. We turn to books to either confirm what we already believe about life or to help us escape our prior ideas by giving us our world back again as seen from a different angle. In our print and image saturated environment of course the problem may not be to acquire more information but rather to find a way to return to silence and darkness. Maybe there we can find peace.

When I am most sad or distressed I seek out the ocean because it still speaks that lost and forgotten language that Thomas Wolfe spoke about in his first novel, "Look Homeward Angel." When we can't control what happens to us in life death begins to beckon to us. We imagine that it offers a portal of relief. It doesn't. Instead it offers us the same elemental dissolution that I feel whenever I go online and am promptly overwhelmed by the sheer volume of what everybody thinks about everything. It is then that I return to the classics of literature to regain a point of fundamental orientation, a moral North Star. I turn by preference to what is already over one hundred years past and hence in the public domain.

It was once possible to achieve by arduous study a fair approximation to the totality of all that was knowable. Samuel Johnson could feel that he possessed the bulk of human knowledge at his finger's ends. That is not possible now. We are adrift in a sea of conflicting beliefs without guide or arbiter and no assurance that any land remains towards which we can set our course and trim our sails. We live in a state of constant transition. We are all advised to establish a presence out there in what is now called cyberspace if only in order to exist. We may not be icons who can trade their names or images for money in endorsements or the media, but we will if we sign on to the post-modern imperative at least play some marginal role in the incessant data stream, lost among the multiplying gigabytes. By the spring of 2016 I wanted to escape backwards into my own lost dreams. I wanted to ask if what had once been dear to me still mattered. I needed to put myself back together or at least to gather the wreckage out of the spindrift and pile it up on the shore.

○

The habit of book browsing, once it has been acquired, is one not easily lost. I recall in particular a thick paperback by the Italian novelist Elsa Morante entitled simply, "History," that intrigued me. I have always enjoyed mixing genres and it seemed a grand economy to be able to boil everything that has ever happened down into one book that would, like Hegel's phenomenology, explain everything that had ever happened or ever would happen. I never intended to fall prey to that great anaconda literature that once having grasped its victim never lets him go. I aspired in those long ago days to be a scientist. I liked a discipline that is constantly engaged in self-renewing but that at any period can be reduced to a few basic underlying principles. Certainty is the ultimate economy and once acquired it is possible I imagined to plunge into life with no hesitations or doubt. Best of all faith is not required. Young people like to rush as quickly as possible through preliminaries and get to the meat of any issue. Only time and experience reveal how difficult it is to find the center-point of anything and how generalizations immediately reveal questions of methodology and bias that immediately place conclusions in doubt.

I have a vast nodding acquaintance in my personal library with an ocean of unread books that far surpasses in extent the small reservoir of books that I have actually read or rather absorbed because to read a book properly it should enter us at every pore. "History," is alas one item of the former category. In spite of its evident excellence it has been pushed aside until now by the deluge of later candidates for my attention. One of the reasons for this indefinite deferral is that with the exception of "Finnegans Wake" that I have read three times now no single book is able to look through all human events to find one underlying theme unless it is the Bible.

Comprehensiveness robs the novel of the charms of individuality and specific locality. We turn to novels to provide a unique point of view to what we all share – the experience of living our lives. Over time a dialectic relationship develops between living and reading; time spent in one pursuit is subtracted from the other. At last a point is reached when it becomes evident that it is impossible for one person to ever live long enough to fully encompass either pursuit in their totality. This means that it becomes necessary to admit into any comfortably closed system an element of indeterminacy and chance. Worse, the grim specters of error and probability as opposed to certainty rear their Cyclopean heads. A sufficient retrospective will finally reveal that the life that we have in fact lived is not the same as the one that we had charted out with equanimity so many years ago.

In a few brief words this is the problem that is addressed in what with uncharacteristic resignation I am characterizing here as mere, "notes for a novel." In a more expansive sense I am trying to do what I once imagined Elsa Morante had been about in any book with such an intriguing title as, "History." I am trying to boil down into one "novel," the term is only an approximation, a period of storm and stress in my life that happened to coincide with one of the periodic gentle revolutions when our nation "elects" a new President. In this year it finally became undeniably clear that chance was the sole unifying factor in my life. I had never been in control of my life narrative. Covering all options is to choose none. We are doomed to the particular. We unfurl trembling leaves and hope that they are not scorched by the brutal sun of reality. As sunset nears it becomes all too evident that closure is unattainable. Everything is characterized by novelty. It is for this reason that I call what follows a novel and not something else.

○

One of the great mythic pursuits along with the Secret of the Lost Dutchman's Mine in the Superstition Mountains of Arizona and the search for a completely honest man has been the search for what has been called, The Great American Novel. Many people have assigned that title to Herman Melville's, "Moby Dick," while others prefer Mark Twain's, "Huckleberry Finn." The present effort that I have chosen to entitle, "Pacific End," is an unlikely contender for such an exalted status for two reasons. The first is that with due humility I have chosen to qualify it by claiming no more than that it contains notes for a novel rather than the novel itself. This habit of deferring the day of reckoning is one of the habits that I retain from my youth and one that I share with our exalted nation, one that has amassed the largest national debt in world history. The second reason that this work of mine is unlikely to grasp the coveted laurels of a generally accepted national discourse is that I am not particularly pleased by our history and thus presumably not a real patriot.

Eight hundred years from now, if we are still around as a species,

I am convinced that the American experiment will be catalogued as a late period entrant in the race for empires rather than under the section describing the struggle to found democratic states. At that distant date in the future a minor entry may refer to the obscure year of 2016 as the one where America broke free from its former pretences of being a government of the people and for the people and became a low-grade theocratic state characterized by religious intolerance and violence with a simmering core of fears, resentments, and discontents, all of them manifest in that year of choice when America reconsidered the wisdom of allowing a liberal and gentle hand to guide "the sole remaining superpower."

The year 2016 did offer some rather interesting initial choices though: a genuine populist in the form of Bernie Sanders, a woman candidate from a major party, and a mouthy billionaire tycoon with populist rhetoric and with nails ready in hand to hammer down the coffin long prepared for the middle-classes and plans to allow the corporations to run amuck. A comparison of the various presidencies in terms of clemency and pardons shows a sharp contrast between the mercy of the Obama years and the grim Levitical legacy of the two Bush regimes. As America flirts with the outer limits of its new pauper status it has grown increasingly intolerant of individual homelessness, of diversity, and of anything less than a mentality that is strongly rooted in the Old Testament and with only a selective reading of the gospels. The likelihood of finding any aesthetic or critical consensus about The Great American Novel for the foreseeable future in such a country means that a monument to our national collective identity in novel form is unlikely to emerge. Instead what we are likely to see is books like the present one that seek to explore new beginnings with little encouragement by looking for new ways to package their verbiage through formal experimentation with the form of the novel. These efforts will no doubt have a certain fin de siècle quality and may at times sound like the lyrical lamentations of the great poet of the Tang Dynasty, Li Po. Plot may occasionally swim to the surface but the predominant mode will be one of reflection.

In this way the novel may begin to resemble a loose collection of essays rather than an extended version of the short story. I am not without preceding models in this manner of writing. There are vast lyrical sections in Thomas Wolfe's masterpiece, "Of Time and the River," that come immediately to mind; then there are the writings of the great German novelists: Mann, Musil, Kafka, and Broch. Even the wanderings of that forlorn knight of the woeful countenance, Don Quixote de la Mancha display an essay-like quality. Novels help us to find a point of orientation amidst the uncharted seas of experience. It was for this reason that I decided to spend vast quantities of time in reflection in a year, when more than is usual even for me, I felt myself to be lost, disoriented, and with no lighthouse to beckon or to warn me of the reefs and shoals ahead.

○

The art of the novel has been until relatively recently been story-based, plot dependent, and only secondarily concerned with the form that the novel may take as a primary subject for the narrative. The new novel in contrast is introspective, concerned with language as such, and may either have multiple narrators or none at all. The pressure that drives the flow of language may come from within the expressive format and drag the reluctant author behind it. The traditional model of the novelist as a cool and distant designer or architect has been altered in many recent narratives and replaced by texts that appear to be writing themselves obedient to the evanescent impulse to create that is distributed at random among the inhabitants of any historical age. Such novels savor of the concept of emergence, a primary principle in what is now called General Systems Theory where results are non-predictable and often of a radically different nature than might have been expected from a knowledge of the inputs. This may give the text a quality that appears to be tentative as though the author, unable to reach a definitive conclusion, is simply recording hypothetical constructs that may need modification in the light of subsequent events. The novel becomes more like an augur drilling into the hard-pan of experience in exploration of meaning rather than the stern pronouncements of an oracle who is presumed to know all things even prior to writing anything at all. Augur or augury is the question. How shall the novelist justify or explain what he intends to do prior to setting forth? Should some advance permit granted by sovereign authority be required of the prospective novelist so that he or she will not mislead the masses or is the mere asking of this question indelible proof of the vanity of authors and their presumption that anyone will ever care to read what they write? Every science of course must begin with a postulate that is accepted without proof so for the purposes of all that follows we will assume that writing matters.

Literature is not, as far too many people suppose, the mere trimming to life; it is the essential basis for culture and civilization. Without the witness to the human condition provided by our writers human beings would be placed in the moral quandary of rediscovering in each age the full dimensions of thought and feeling, an equivalent of constantly needing to reinvent the wheel. The astonishing thing is that even the earliest writings of the Greeks, the Hebrews, and the Romans already show not merely a sophisticated outlook but a formal perfection as though literature sprang fully formed from the brow of Zeus. After reading Aeschylus, Plato, Dante, Shakespeare, and Milton what more can psychology add to our essential grasp of human nature? The broad parameters of our emotional life never change. Which of us would ever wish to waken from the silence that preceded our birth to face love, loss, and terror without knowing how the great writers of the past have traced their causes and permutations in a form of outstanding aesthetic virtue? It is this insight that draws a select few in each generation to join the unending dialog of the mind when that conversation takes place in words rather than in musical notes or images.

At a certain point in life it suddenly dawns upon us that the vast and uncounted legions of the dead were in their time not substantially different from ourselves. For a certain length of time the world was theirs and we who now pride ourselves on our wisdom and control of nature were then only the distant trajectory of a genetic stream utterly dependent upon the fevered meeting of complementary organs and the luck of one individual sperm to propel us along the path of gestation and birth. The stories of the dead seem quaint and limited by the simple fact that their stories are already determined whereas ours are not. We can still alter the flow of circumstances and take positions towards contingent events.

It is only with age that it suddenly dawns upon us that only a few uncertain decades remain to us to complete whatever summation we desire to make of our one life's course and meaning. Like a swiftly closing shutter on a camera our film is exposed and on the basis of this short duration the complete picture must be developed. The voluminous resources of the past become irrelevant as we run out of time to consult them and the future remains as it always has been, surprising and inscrutable. All of what I have just said may be summed up by saying that life suddenly becomes a serious matter rather than a moveable feast.

Rather than be surprised by such unpleasant truths I purchased two books years ago dealing with what theologians once called "the four last things." When the life expectancy in even the advanced nations of Europe coincided with the first two decades of human adulthood and Christian belief was normative if not universal death and all of its panoply of sepulchral display was a normal concomitant to life. Today we simply note that such and such a celebrity will not be eating caviar and brie at this year's post-Oscars party. The rest of us must be content to pass with little notice or acclaim and enter that realm mocked by zombie movies and sanitized by an efficient cremation industry.

Gone are the poet's corners in gothic cathedrals or the picturesque and moss-shrouded gravestones around the country chapel. Death is a sanitized inconvenience and an occasion for the marvelous legal devices thought up by estate planners to painlessly and efficiently distribute assets. The small cache of personal treasures that are left now shorn of sentiment find their way to antique shops or thrift stores and the pageantry of the great procession continues without us.

One of the books that I purchased had the comforting title of "Sin and Fear." It appears that the ancients, not satisfied with the lugubrious details of bodily decay insisted further upon contemplating an almost universal damnation feeding upon graphic horrors that would make the paintings of Goya seem frivolous in comparison. Our current impatience with a rigorous theology may be seen as a reaction to the former habit of our ancestors to revel in what we alternately despise or seek to ignore – that we possess but a limited leasehold on life and our future state is beset with fears and the slow cauldron bubbling with our shame, our resentments, and our regrets.

The other volume that I purchased dealt with the funerary customs of the ages. Its title temporarily escapes me but I can see its black cover with its picture of the grim reaper in my mind. I confess that I have yet to finish either of these books. They are the type of reading that invites deferral to a more propitious time. No doubt my heirs will find them amusing and instructive. Instead of these I am in the habit of reading novels brimming with life. I am just getting around to reading George Elliot's, "Middlemarch" and I intend to begin a study of Trollope when opportunity permits.

Having attempted it on various occasions I am unlikely to take another stab at George Meredith's "The Ordeal of Richard Feverell." The books that I read these days are as likely to be chosen by chance as by careful decision. My library is so extensive that some of my most favored volumes are buried beyond the possibility of easy retrieval in the depths of a storage unit. I have spent years paring my life down to the minimum of space and expense. There are no priceless paintings on the wall, no patio surrounds a swimming pool in California, and I am unlikely to fly to Cannes to escape the chill of winters in Paris. I have foregone all of the usual accompaniments that go with the life of fantasy and prosperity the better to concentrate upon essentials and in spite of this I am as unprepared for my last end as a guest at Poe's "Masque of the Red Death." I take comfort from those gentle lines in Shakespeare's, "The Tempest." "We are such stuff as dreams are made on and our little life is rounded with a sleep."

One of the most disastrous things that can occur to us, frail creatures that we are condemned to existence in space and time is to lose track of the narrative that we tell ourselves in order to survive. The same cause that creates vertigo in the realm of position and locomotion, the conflict between two or more diverging frames of reference, can create moral vertigo when it occurs in a life narrative. Deprived of a central theme or storyline we find that we can no longer make decisions because our former criteria for decision are now in question. Suddenly it is a matter of indifference where we are, how we act, and where our life is tending. We are reduced to the purely sensory realm for comfort and security and relative absence of pain becomes the best we can manage as we drag ourselves through the ensuing days and weeks. It is not uncommon for a significant loss or a shaming event to disrupt the manner in which we orient ourselves. Without the mirroring, the echo effect from an unyielding surface, or the reflection of light from surfaces we would be caught in a vacuum. There have been experiments in sensory deprivation where the subject begins to hallucinate to create a new world to replace the one that has been lost through the absence of impressions. Sometimes it is not necessary to produce a sense of moral vertigo to muffle all impressions; instead it is sufficient if only a few of life's constants are altered to leech our days of their customary meaning and significance. Writers tend to be more vulnerable in this regard because the necessity to create has over time become essential to maintaining their balance in the world.

It is a common observation that one of the prerequisites to produce an artist is sensitivity to impressions. This sensitivity is such that absent a proper context provided by expression the artists among us, perhaps because they have a deficiency in precisely the rooted habits and ready faith in the received truths of their time and place, cycle into various forms of madness and addiction. The significance of this observation is that novelists feel compelled to formalize fictional worlds to keep their everyday world intact. Novelists with a moralistic bent not content to simply portray our societal inadequacies will dream of a world that would be adequate to our human needs and aspirations. It is such as these who may be appalled by history as though it could be altered by their singular will. This is of course a form of inverted megalomania where it is the very insignificance of the writer that increases his sense that somehow he alone is responsible for all that is. This raises the question of the place of the writer in society. Can any literary creation hope to alter history or are we only witnesses called by the prosecution to indict the cruelty and meaninglessness of events without any real prospect to change them?

I was born six years after the world said no to the two great attempts to set up secular empires, one under the sign of the swastika and the other beneath the rising sun flag of Japan. The victories left only two contenders for hegemony each with a smattering of the old nations appended to their spheres of influence, nations that were traceable back to the Treaty of Westphalia that ended the Thirty Years War. One of these powers persisted in calling itself "the leader of the free world" while the other claimed to speak for world-socialism. Neither side was committed to peace because both claimed that power means nothing if it is not backed up by the force of arms. Ethical norms were only the concern of philosophers and theologians; when it comes to power exercised between nations, threat and duplicity are normative. There are winners and losers and the losers are dead. There in a nutshell is the background against which my generation must be viewed. At midlife I decided to write a novel sequence that traced the death of America to the America that emerged during the Presidency of William McKinley. It was then that we decided to join the world's elder empires and make a bid for supremacy.

In my youth I recall thinking that by my mid-life and the simultaneous turn of the millennium the world would have been fine-tuned on the big questions and human progress would shift into overdrive. Imagine my surprise when America proved the perennial power of feudal rule as the intellectually and morally vacuous reign of the Bush-Cheney regime placed America firmly in the ranks of petty-profit, legal torture, and the cynical exploitation of the attacks on the World Trade Center. After that I saw that I could hope for no salvation by political means and that meaning must be sought elsewhere. Even the laws were malleable and subject to expropriation as the Bush v Gore case proved when five "justices" decided that it was sufficiently important to be sure that a Republican won to distort the high ideals of the 14th Amendment and appoint a President of their choosing. America had always been a byword for greed and violence but with the Bush era America had finally been enshrined in history as the patron of duplicity and vulgarity as our new national identity.

It is said that character and identity formation are the result of every decision that we have ever made. Decade by decade we pile up memories and weave associations until by our fifth or sixth decades we realize that we are in danger of running out of file space to absorb new data. The result is that we are forced to lump vast aspects of discrete experience into categories. We are more likely to resort to generalized and summary treatment of cases rather than to view them as deserving a de novo hearing. Doubt becomes a costly thing when it becomes not merely useful but essential to appear before ourselves as resourceful, wise, and terminally competent. Our later years are not the time to have an identity crisis. We are supposed to know how to handle things and to accept losses with grace and dignity. A brief look back over our shoulders should suffice to demonstrate how far along we are and how numerous are the new entrants on the field of play. A lateral view will show us that many of our contemporaries have already fallen away, the ranks thinned by cancers, heart disease, or at their own hands. When our vision becomes sufficiently clear we realize that the former strategies that we have adopted are inadequate to the need to do more with less. It becomes necessary to adjust, to minimize, and to reduce our scale of expectations. It is at precisely this time that escape beckons. Is it possible to start over again elsewhere while retaining at least some of the assurances and relationships that tell us not only that we exist but that we have made a good record in our lives and are entitled to at least some of the claims and dignity appertaining to one who has managed to face and survive what we have in fact faced and survived? Or are we predestined to be diminished until at last we realize that we are only a caricature rather than a portrait, our life no longer a grand pageant or procession but a harlequinade? In a tale told by an idiot full of sound and fury what role shall we assume?

I set out in the year 2016 to find an answer to questions such as these by seeing if I could make a new life on the Oregon coast.

○

The road down into Oregon from Washington to the great bridge over the Columbia River first passes through the tide flats and estuaries of Willapa Bay where the sweetest oysters in the world grow. The town of Raymond soon merges with South Bend the county seat before the road swerves off to skirt the bay whose waters catch the late afternoon sun off of the Pacific. The tiny coastal towns of Ilwaco and Long Beach are west of here as are Westport and Ocean Shores. The road that I take follows the tsunami menaced lands of the Pacific County tidal sloughs before it breaks through at the Columbia and one catches a first glimpse of Astoria across the river's broad margin where it enters the sea over the treacherous Columbia River Bar. From the height of the bridge everything shines below me in the late summer afternoon. The waters of the Pacific stretch south from the bridge to Warrenton and you can see the dunes that begin there before reaching down to the towns of Gearhart and Seaside.

It is always a great feeling to enter Oregon and to think that this was the dream at the end of the questing followers of the Oregon Trail. Our endings are in our beginnings and our beginnings are in our end. For the novelist revisions are a rule of life; even when we think that the novel is finished and ready to submit a new slant may be possible to apply to the finished text. Life in contrast allows for no revisions but only for what was once called a list of errata that would appear in the book with reverence to pages and lines where misprints might be found. As artists in all forms know, the desire for perfection can freeze the act of composition in its tracks. Perhaps this was part of the problem between us – that she thought I was seeking perfection in life rather than in the mere reflection of life as processed into the medium of words. Not that I am proof to the temptation to wish to isolate form from substance; this is as natural to the artist as breathing. Art begins in intuitions that a form may be possible to express what would otherwise merely exist as silent and self-enclosed experience. The artist is always looking for a way to get behind raw experience so as to extract some essential quality and then fix it into permanence so that it will neither perish nor decay. Artists are enemies of the universal law of entropy. It is not that we oppose alteration because in change there is much beauty; what we fear is the marring and dislocation that destroys perspective, that breaks the line, leaves lacunae when continuity is required.

My thoughts were along these lines as I looked across the room on that bitterly cold afternoon and watched a perfect example of the best that the new age has to offer as she read the latest version of a first draft of a writing project to be called "Pacific End.' She read it with all of the attention that writers hope will be devoted to the hours that are lost to simply living by reason of their unique urge to create. There is perfection in anything still untried that we lose by actually taking pen in hand and setting ink to flowing onto paper. To write at all is to experience loss through the necessary limitations imposed by the partial realization of an idea. Diamonds exist in the earth compacted by the years into crystalline substance but the separate facets only emerge after being subjected to the artistry of the jeweler who will descry precisely where the various planes may be brought forth by cutting and polishing. Yet for all of that some tiny thing askew may invite a deeper admiration where the mind alone would simply affirm a general design. Value is in many ways subject to all of the idiosyncratic qualities of the human. Perfection defeats itself by being inadaptable to the defacing impacts of a most imperfect world. Just as nature abhors a vacuum it also resists perfection in any form and immediately begins to apply pressure to deface it, to wear the edges down, to restore the omnipresent rule of disorder. But just for a moment sometimes there is a still room, an urgent text, and a discerning reader and then sometimes art happens.

○

Of course the problem is to reach general truths by means of what is recognizable and topical, even contemporary and regional. So it was that I decided that rather than joining the crew of the doomed Pequod that I would record the march to doom of our own ship of state in the election year of 2016 , one on which the delicate balance of a dying world may depend to tip the scale of fate in a decided and definitive direction. In doing so I thought that I could also discuss the strange impulse that leads various persons to write what are called novels.

Every age desires to add some new codicil to the last will and testament of the human race but only our age has the actual power to preclude further additions to the weary epic of human life. To take extinction and its prospects as a point of origin for a novel is hardly inspiring but then far too many novels are written in the morning of life rather than at twilight. It seemed high time to give equal weight to the region when the outlines of familiar objects begin to blur and the evening seems to have arrived suddenly and unannounced. The time of letting go is as inevitable as puberty but is far less formalized. Instead the ills and sorrows of the latter days are confined to plays like King Lear and The Tempest and the various farewells and elegies that grace the final days of poets. Sunset novels, novels that diminish the sense that we have that our powers are forever self-renewing are rare. Epitaphs are usually confined to a few lines on marble or stone but it might be possible, for such was to be my vain design, to write an elegiac novel.

O

Certain years in my past stand out because they served as pivot points either for my particular life or for the nation as a whole. Early on it seemed to me that the year 2016 might be a prime example of the latter, a watershed year, a year that would pose the question of whether our nation might adopt a stance that favors the benefits of peace over the arrogance that leads to wars. Our local playhouse had just finished staging a play that raised the question of whether it might have been possible for the scientists that were part of the Manhattan Project to have simply presented a united front and said unequivocally that atomic devices when used as weapons posed no marginal advantage to survival for the human species and as such could not be entrusted to the rulers of any nation whatsoever. As the representatives of all of humankind they could have pointed out that even the greatest conflicts such as the Thirty Years War of the 17th century appeared from the perspective of later history to have had little real relevance, that all of the resulting deaths had left certain long established natural borders between racial and linguistic groups more or less unaltered.

Now with the advent of world-trade and cyberspace the very concept of sovereignty and national interest has become in many ways an anachronism. If the economy of Greece falters the stock prices in Singapore fall. How much better then to adopt a policy that preserves the vast mass of the human race until a sustainable level is negotiated and the vast differences between peoples are at least partially leveled. Would this not be the proper preliminary act to usher in the return of the Christ rather than to provoke an artificial Armageddon, a sort of second sin of Cain, and face the grim prospect that the few possible survivors of any nuclear exchange would be too maimed and genetically damaged to rebuild a New Jerusalem from the smoldering ruins of a desolate planet? But try and tell that to people whose entire faith in Christianity has grown to be posited on the presumption that we are the last generation.

I grew up with a friend like this, one who planned to leave a set of letters with me for all the people whom he had determined had no chance of being caught up in the air in the twinkling of an eye as one of the saved as determined by his marginal sect. It met in a rented building a few miles from our high school. Of course all of this was before a post-Nixon America was to forget the lessons of Viet Nam and started electing Republicans who each promised to make America great again by increases in military spending. Of course America has never really stopped waging various proxy wars while preparing for the big one; after all, it's what we do.

O

The years that I recall best were ones that held promise rather than menace. They were times when I felt a solid base beginning to form beneath our wandering family, one that was always seeking the higher hill before building a castle adequate to the dreams I shared with them. It took me years to develop a more sardonic approach to vanished fairy tales, a more Edith-Sitwell-like point of view. I was raised with aristocratic pretensions without the means for securing them.

I am immune to the appeal of most pageantry but can be bowled over by an apt turn of phrase like, "I have been faithful to thee Cynara in my fashion." We cannot pick the era when we live out this, our brief sojourn on what Thomas Wolfe called "this most weary un-bright cinder;" therefore we write novels. I have lived a life mediated by literature so it was perhaps foreordained that

I would wish in time to throw a few words onto paper, more a suggestion than the realization of my design. If I am accused of mixing genres here my excuse is that in an age of shifting ideas and styles of composition greater latitude is allowed to what purports to be a novel. Writing is in many ways a private activity and who would be so presumptuous as to limit the ways that we may talk to ourselves. If I am overheard as I write to please myself and to satisfy my own aesthetic protocols what harm is done?

○

I began this day by reading a selection drawn from the year 1896 in the journal of Arnold Bennett and I also began the belated reading of Oliver Goldsmith's, "The Vicar of Wakefield," certainly as good a start for the day as most. What can be better than to prime the pump of language and to turn the mind to what were once called improving thoughts? From thence I ventured out into the world but without the comfort that I might meet Samuel Johnson and his friend Boswell later over coffee or ale to discuss whether reason or passions rule the world. I would not even have the advantage of animated mutual monologues with a dear friend who has recently opted for a move to New Mexico where no doubt he will soon be made the whole legislature as he seeks gold in the mountains around Taos or becomes an arbiter of Pueblo culture in Santa Fe.

I have not yet abandoned a sense that my life should form an aesthetic whole, one that will always press along the borders of the reality of my insignificance and demand to be heard or at least realized in some marginal way so that I at least may see the way in which this or that experience or meeting or relationship was essential and has led me onwards to whatever new delusion will obsess me in the future. It is in just this way that a sense of story emerges from what are otherwise unconnected events. Years stand out as pivot points and before long the web of one more individual life is formed. We wear our scars so that our bodies finally become not merely a residue of abuse but a palimpsest where an acute observer can read a legacy of every place we have ever lived, of every dream we have ever entertained that someday our lives would all come out right and at least one other person would look at us and think, "How marvelous it is that you have survived to the present moment when I have the honor of meeting you."

O

Many people harbor the secret aspiration to write a novel someday. Even more people have all of the requisite life-experience to provide the content for a novel but they never actually write one. Some feel inadequate to write convincing dialogue or fear that they cannot create convincing characters. Other potential novelists wonder about questions of plot or point-of-view. Then there is the problem with the sheer flow of words, with description, or with the tension between selective revelations so as to build a sense of suspense in the reader. There is a flow in the novel between expectation and fulfillment. The novelist must provide a point of rest after each partial plot plateau so that the theme is realized and a final resolution takes place, one that leaves the reader somehow changed for engaging in the reading experience.

Even considering these many obstacles to a novel's realization many novels do in fact get written. Some are prosaic and predictable and others like the one in your hands ask questions that go to the heart of the function that literature and the novel in particular perform in a busy world with a surfeit of information. The work in question at this present moment is called "Pacific End," a book written largely in a single year on the Oregon Coast dealing with (why not be frank here) the vastly under-reported feelings of those who have reached the advanced age of sixty-four and are about to join the vast ranks of the superfluous aged in a culture dedicated to the idolatry of youth.

I am no stranger to the sea having lived upon it for the past twenty-years on two vessels that have been moored in Puget Sound. I have through those years also been a frequent visitor to the Oregon Coast and I am at the present moment a part-time resident here with an established domicile. Of course where I live is less essential than the deeper meanings to be extracted from the twin seas of the vast Pacific Ocean and the vast sea of all pre-existing novels. From these two sources I have hoped to extract, such is the sanguine nature of one who has actually written a novel, a unique effort, one that will probe the nature of experience whenever it is reduced to form in a novel. Is the novel part of life, an addition to life, or even a distortion to the sequence of random events that occur prior to being ordered by the intrusive intellect into a novel form? The novelist's life is not an easy one; it requires a sort of *apologia pro vita sua;* I hope to provide one here.

The first problem that confronts the aspiring novelist is the same problem that confronts us all in the act of living; we must choose from a huge array of possibilities the one authoritative version of our life and then proceed to fill in the gaps by means of a series of successive choices. There is a name for this; it is called "self-determination." Each of us is engaged in recording an unwritten text in the form of events whether we record them later verbally or not. The writer differs from others largely by virtue of a greater compulsion to exercise his peripheral vision in observing others and then reflecting upon their motives. Observation alone of course would be insufficient without the gift of expression that we call verbal artistry. Combine the two with persistence and determination and the result is a manuscript that will later undergo the indignity of being filtered through a person called an editor, hopefully one possessed of good taste and with the requisite aesthetic distance as well to judge another's work and make valuable suggestions or excisions.

From this point various market-driven forces come into play from dust jackets to advance review copies. These are sent to makers of public opinion and into the vast maw of untutored public opinion as the book emerges into the light and finds its way to various bookstores. After that the book's life may be as short as a single season, a brief snowfall amidst the vast avalanche of print media. This ephemeral existence must in turn justify the novelist in his assessment of the wisdom of writing in the first place and will undoubtedly influence his choice of whether to ever write a second novel.

As for life, do we ever get the life that we wanted so that at the end we will not end up as strangers to ourselves? I ask myself this question daily and it may have led to my desire to compose a hymn to disappointed hopes. My confessional mode may be designed simply to infer intimacy and to persuade the reader of the author's sincerity. If authors knew themselves completely they would not possess the complexity and contradictoriness that are required elements of our profession. It is not impossible that authors, and by extension me as well, insofar as I claim to be a novelist, have long since kissed pragmatism goodbye. The writer may for instance have chosen literature for a major in college or even attained an advanced degree only to discover that communication although valuable is usually only remunerative in marketing, advertising, or the drafting of complex contracts. To simply express important ideas beautifully must fall back for justification on the perverse instinct of some people to desire that life be meaningful as well as simply productive and remunerative.

These people read books and are drawn to novels in preference to other life activities. They may be found under beach umbrellas on a summer day or reading in a state of semi-trance as they wait for a bus. They may be found in the proverbial comfy armchair or standing in a line (the British insist that it is really called a queue). The writer and the reader will probably never meet and each may entertain a radically different picture of the other. The writer cannot screen his readers to eliminate those who should never have opened his particular book and as a result is subject to being a victim of prejudice or misunderstanding. To anticipate preferences and to curry favor with people whom we do not know or to force the issue by blatantly asking for their love and approval is as pointless as it is unprofessional. The author must believe that his "self-talk" may be worth being overheard and then simply proceed to write as though people were already clamoring at bookstores to see if the new shipment of his latest novel has arrived.

○

It is the business of literature to record and comment upon life and by doing so to give it meaning. Of course this raises the question of whether that meaning is to be found in life or is primarily a creation of the writer. His or her individuality and habits of perception and expression can be so pervasive that the world looks different depending upon the author. Life is enriched to the degree that we approach events with the tools that being well-read may provide for us or at least I have always thought so. But then I am biased by virtue of having been fascinated from my earliest years by books. It is not enough to say that they were iconic objects that seemed to possess their own fascination and power before I could even read them, because it was my desire to penetrate to the text and the story that led me to request that I be read to on so many occasions that the reading became superfluous because I already knew the books by heart.

A discerning adult might have seen the early warning signs and warned my parents that a child who might have progressed in the world of corporate illiteracy and political intransigence was being early-on ruined by ideas. Andrew Carnegie may have built libraries but their relation to the steel industry is problematic and Jay Gould and the Big Four could have built railroad empires without seeing them reflected in "The Octopus," by Frank Norris.

At the present hour when the fate of the novel is questionable by the mere fact that it is not alterable through constant rewrites and because it aspires to permanence it has seemed advisable to compose a novel that questions the very being of the novel using one year of my life as the source of its content and to provide a very loose vertebra or framework to support the structure and supply a rudimentary if transient form to guide its composition and to act as a criterion for inclusion or exclusion of the various contending elements that may present themselves to me by chance or by inscrutable design.

Of course mere experience is inadequate for a novel. It helps to have a theme which in the case at hand is the impact made by change, age, and death on one who has always viewed life as in some manner always available because like many writers the author wants to include everything and be around to witness the changing fashions that condemn most books to oblivion. Flesh at least has the advantage over words by being undeniably real and being available to experience. A book is not a child but a mere occasion for an interchange between writer and reader. It must seduce because it cannot command and whatever love it obtains must be purchased by hours of earnest perusal to the exclusion of other activities; how one is to be worthy of this sacrifice is the problem of artistic technique.

○

In a way this book is a long farewell letter addressed to one who will probably never read it. Though I think she is quite unique she will remain unidentifiable and nameless here. I think she would be pleased that after spending the requisite time to try to understand her and weaving her into this narrative she is by her own request unaware of its composition. Portraits are always selective and the medium is bound to affect coloration and alter profiles. For this reason my real subject here is to explore the novel itself as an art form and to confess what I happened to think about in the year 2016 in the vast nation of America in its decline.

But before I proceed further in what may prove to be a vain and inscrutable quest, my modern "Tristram Shandy," I want to say something more about this search for an abiding theme. Many people turn to various oracles under the belief that guides exist who are better in tune with how events should or will shape themselves. I am not immune to this need to find a framework, a tradition, or a scaffold to support my efforts and to guide my choices. I used to always take three fortune cookies whenever I went to a Chinese restaurant in the years that we shared from various distances: the first was my fortune, the second cookie was her fortune, and the third was where we were together as a unit. By averaging out the messages in all three messages I would try and figure out where we were going.

I was reading the "I-Ching" "as well during those years, the edition put out by Princeton in the Bollingen Series. I kept looking for ways to harmonize her incessant changes of mood and to look for hints of what might be coming next. The Chinese are comfortable with the way that things tend to change into their opposites and I thought I would find in the "I-Ching" a way of navigating her world, a world where storms could blow up at any time to raise waves in the usually quiet tidal inlets where the writer-part of me seeks to discover patterns in time's grand estuary. There, that sounds sufficiently pretentious to justify what will require many months of sustained effort to justify in the form of a novel.

○

Beginnings and endings are always the toughest part of an endeavor whether in life or in novels. Are they the same thing, life and novel, beginning and end? It was in the year of 2016 that I tried to resolve this question for the simple reason that it wasn't yet 2017. Who can say what years will be viewed as watersheds? History is always stalled for a moment in the present. Everything has either happened already or is part of the hopes and fears of tomorrow. The novelist comes to the intersection and looks carefully in both directions before seeking to cross the road that lies between them.

It will of course take time to write this particular novel and the author can only hope that his initial conception will retain some relevance when he reaches the end. Even then it will take some time to do alternate versions and to re-write chapters or sections with various amendments and all the while the world will be altering around the author. He may succumb to some illness; he may die; he may run out of ideas or fail to find a publisher; or the whole enterprise may seem futile or too costly in terms of discipline and commitment so that it may remain forever but another example of frozen intentions. If none of these factors has terminated the process of creation then it may be possible for some future reader to seek out a comfortable position, clear his mind of distractions and begin to read. The novel only begins to really exist when that interaction of minds happens.

Suddenly the novel steps forth like an actor on the stage and hours of solitude wrought laboriously into form reach their stated goal. Novelists, like those who love, never lose sight of other hearts and minds and to that degree are not as self-involved as might be supposed by virtue of their desire to impose their version of events upon the crafted object called a novel. If in addition to this the novelist is an American it may be assumed that some of the ethos and dreams of that nation and region will find their place in his efforts. Americans who are not native all share in common that their progenitors were sufficiently dissatisfied with their home countries to leave them. Some of that fractious and discontented spirit is inherent in Americans. We want something that we are either failing to receive or are getting in insufficient quantities.

The native people of these shores finally realized this innate disposition of ours and went into the casino business. Gaming and banking, which is sort of the same thing along with real estate in various forms, combine with the service economy to keep most Americans alive. Other people make things or cross borders to harvest our crops. We want them to do their business and leave so we can get back to living the American dream: to buy cheap goods of foreign manufacture while staying massively entertained so that we will not have to think too much.

○

The one clear thing in this year of 2016 is that many Americans are mad at each other. The fabled recovery since the great recession of 2008 has not been uniform. Lots of Americans have failed to win the lottery of their dreams with the result that real happiness remains out of reach, at least for now. We want more than we used to think possible and class questions are off the table since of course we are all equal as Americans; we all hope to emerge as winners in life's greater lottery.

In 2016 we are all backed up against the Pacific Ocean and we hope that the Japanese and the Chinese won't mind it that we send lots of I.O.U's to them in exchange for real things. We are vaguely impatient and a little uneasy as the election approaches. It isn't change that we desire but the final fulfillment to which we feel we are entitled. It is precisely at this season that a stray novelist, one committed to novelty and riding the crest of our present confusion and polarization may decide to write "Pacific End," as a sort of unguided exploration of the writing process, of values, and of the slack period between tidal changes as old-age and death become present concerns rather than remote contingencies.

○

The years of change between Presidential administrations are times of transition in the great amorphous body politic where ordinary people are engaged in the countless daily inconveniences entailed in making a living, educating their children, and providing for the aged. The rest of the world is just beginning to imagine a world existing without a clear American predominance in inventions, trade, and military might. Each of these factors makes the year 2016 significant and if we survive long enough perhaps historically memorable.

We have lived so long on the edge of the apocalypse that it has become normal to entertain expectations in the face of the real possibility of nuclear annihilation. As I write this I am aware that my home is only five miles from the vast Bangor nuclear submarine complex. A tiny thread of land separates my quiet vessel on Liberty Bay from the deep fiord called Hood Canal that hosts the quaintly named Boomer Class of submarines each of which carries the total firepower equivalent of the entire Second World War. The irony of our geographical proximity had not escaped me through the years; I the powerless novelist dreaming of peace while the minions of Dick Cheney dream up new ways to involve us in wars. Our vast national security apparatus accustomed as it is to the limited influence of novelists will no doubt show little concern with whatever I will write here.

The Russians at least feared writers during the years of Soviet rule while our rulers place the highest possible faith in the generally unread status of most Americans. We are a nation of gamesters and passive participants in various arranged spectacles. Critical reasoning is irrelevant when we are far more likely to give credence to mere blustering self-assurance than to logical processions from premises to conclusions. For this reason the writing of "Pacific End" is not a revolutionary act for all of its efforts to discuss questions of form as opposed to substance and to embody its own aesthetic stance. It is all good clean fun; the novelist as music hall entertainer. But was it always so?

○

To write at all is to shake one's fist at fate. The first words set the pace for all that follows in a novel to sound the clarion call and capture the reader for the next 200 or 800 pages while the author tells the reader something about life that he didn't know he believed. Even gospel narratives follow this rule. When John the Evangelist says, "In the beginning was the Word and the Word was with God and the Word was God," he has the reader in his hands because he has just summed up the biggest Christian mystery and the essence of Christology in a formula that can be recited in ten seconds. This passage explodes like the first neutrons speeding away from a shattered nucleus in a fission reaction. St. John doesn't propose this sentence for consideration or debate but rather slams it into our consciousness as conviction, as truth itself, as the truth that is prior to all other truths on which truth their own existence depends.

Of course the gospels although they are narratives are not novels. It takes something different to make a novel. Novels convey truth through selection and construction rather than simply reporting what happened because the actual events in a novel never really occurred as they are related. Even if real-life models were used they are transformed in the act of writing the novel. All of this is to say that novels are not real life. But having said this I must immediately qualify what I have said by adding that life events have conditioned the author as have various conventions and the examples of other writers of novels so that an experiential reservoir exists and on this the author draws.

Novelists are part of an old profession, not perhaps the oldest of all, but then who is to say whether the bard or the baud provided the best option for an evening of entertainment in the fire-lit caves of prehistory? What is known for certain is that out of hazy beginnings and some false starts the word exists and dwells among us to this day in what are called novels. Novels can bring things together, break things apart, transform our consciousness, and may even redeem our hope that life has a meaning after all. Novelists by the nature of their pursuit are guilty of presumption. They make claims, they take our time, they distract us from other things, and they ask that we pay them for deliberately imagining a world that they lay before us as though they are gods and not the poor scribblers that must push and shove to find a publisher and muscle aside other books on the shelves of booksellers.

But then we all make presumptions and novelists give us the opportunity to test them. At the beginning of a novel the author must decide just who is speaking when a passage is present that is clearly not meant to be dialogue. The question of the gender of the narrator's voice is also seen as important as though the male and the female version of existence were hermetically sealed realms with no bleed-over from one to the other. Males may not menstruate but they do bleed and many a woman knows about rape and pillage from the point of view of the Vandal and the Hun because she at times partakes of both. The authorial voice may be most accurate and general when it refuses to declare a realm of sexual allegiance to one sex rather than the other. An author confined to a single sex would by definition find the other half of humanity inaccessible. This means that the author must presume a sort of omniscience whether writing a third person narrative or not. This is only one of the presumptions that ground the novel but one of the most significant if often overlooked.

○

So to continue I feel that I must dispose of one preliminary question here: why write at all?

To be a writer does not occur to most people when they choose a vocation. There is a good reason for this: writers seldom lead happy lives and most are read little or even if they are it is for a short season of popularity before their books fade into neglect and begin to follow the long slope that ends in the public domain.

Writing is right up there with acting, sky-diving, and surfing along the California coast in spite of sharks, risky and foolish ventures. Maybe it will be discovered someday that the urge to write is a genetic flaw or some sort of auto-immune defect leading to the desire to churn up emotions and thoughts that most people learn to gently forget and to turn these transient materials into words. In any case, I am among the unfortunate afflicted. I found a local bookstore in the same way that some kids wander into pool halls. I spent my time in youth with bad companions: Dickens, Conrad, Thoreau, and Hesse and what have I got to show for it now but a lot of underlined volumes and a desire to toss a few years into the stew of words that has been bubbling merrily away since the composition of Beowulf and Piers Plowman.

○

We like to imagine that to be a distinguished author is to have escaped many of "the thousand shocks that flesh is heir to;" unfortunately this is not the case. The testimony of the lives of countless authors shows that the lot of the men and women of letters and reflective thought is one of sorrows. The muses bring sorrow in their train. Writers are not plagued by neglect alone but by the indignity reserved for those whose best powers are those of intuitive understanding and holistic expression as the witnesses to an age that often pays them little regard. Honors are often delayed until the remedy of deferred regard can do little to reverse the results of the previous years of scorn and neglect. Immortality brings little solace to those who have watched as their hopes and the ideals of their youth have been systemically brought to naught. The clarity of their visions are as nothing when applied to a world that rewards duplicity, cupidity, and bullying, the very means by which fortunes are gathered and vulgar power is retained. The notorious empathy for the lower orders that so many writers manifest is due to the fact that writers often break bread and drink their cheap and sour vintage in the same places as the impoverished classes. Some attempt to eke out a living by leading the unwilling minds of youth to contemplate what has already been written. Others write in those hours that they can set aside from those dull labors that blunt the mind's finer perceptions. The overall result is that an international and perpetually renewed caste of observers is created, one nurtured by reading of the sufferings of those who have preceded them.

A sort of grim initiation is waiting for those who would wish to follow Hawthorne, Poe, Baudelaire, and all of the others whose witness alone remains to sum up an age when all who possessed wealth and power and the amenities that these can bestow are empty names and silenced voices. Yesterday's petty tyrant has perished with the system that once exalted him while the author and his works finds honor in the emulation of those who alas risk sharing the fate of their models. No truer words were ever spoken than those of Jesus the scorned Nazarene when he said that a prophet is without honor in his own country.

The act of writing quite simply asks from the prospective author all that is within him. It is not merely in order to hone style, to polish descriptions, and to refine his grasp of character and motivation that authors read what others have done before them; rather it is to see how the author's own work can reinforce and extend the long sustained witness of articulate humanity in its shared pursuit of meaning that the author seeks to follow along the storied halls of literature with his compatriots and peers. Despite the neglect that is often his lot in life, even to fail in this massive pursuit is to escape the squalor that attends the progress of the mighty when that progress is unworthy of celebration by the poet or elaboration into epic prose. This is the revenge of the writer.

This is not to say that writers may always be spurned at will with impunity. The rapier of satire is always available to leave the great surrounded in perpetuity by an aura of ridicule as was Lord Chesterton after his presumptuous implications that he had acted the part of a patron to Dr. Samuel Johnson as he prepared his great dictionary. The author's labors remain his unique patrimony even while editors, publishers, and booksellers feed like so many harpies at the product of his heart and mind. Long effort to find and express the hitherto unordered sequences of mere events by fixing them in a formal medium of expression makes the mind of writers acute in a way not often granted to mere mortal flesh.

○

My own set of presumptions has had a long gestation. I began to write early in life at that restless and bewildering time that was once called youth and today is called young adulthood. I encountered the novels of Thomas Wolfe and found in him a brother of the soul. I too felt within me the surging tides of the blood and the desire to see all places and to know all things. At the time I felt that these feelings were exceptional – this lost feeling of celestial abandonment and aloneness. Later I was to realize that they are the human condition and I was less exceptional than I supposed I was. A little less concentration on the exceptional would have given me a happier life, but in those days happiness itself seemed insipid when compared to my glorious visions that one lifetime could somehow contain all times and places as though cultures, civilizations, and religions and all else awaited a final proofreading by me before being assembled into a definitive form by my own mind.

Not that I thought I was special in an august and exalted way. I did not aspire to an emperor's robes or even to be on some board of directors of a medium-sized corporation. If anything I was overwhelmed in those days as I am still by my insignificance. No, it was merely that I felt the legacy of the ages pressing upon me and signaling that with proper application a final integration might emerge through an unbiased evaluation. I think that Thomas Wolfe felt this same pressure to exceed his own era and nation and that this pressure drove him to his early death by exhausting what a single human body could bear. He died just before what would have been his thirty-eighth birthday of a massive tubercular lesion of the brain caused by an old tubercular infection that was reactivated after an exhausting summer of travel to the west. He planned to write it all up someday in a novel to be called of all things "Pacific End."

○

Thomas Wolfe's quest ended in Seattle where my own quest began in the 1970's. It was a time when America was seeking to define an alternate vision of its destiny in the shadow of the beat generation and its preeminent voice, Jack Kerouac. Now from the point of view of the post Bush-Cheney era I can see how vain those early visions were and how great was the ensuing betrayal of our highest aspirations.

My own bout of tuberculosis, the disease of artists, came in 1980 but by then there was INH and Rifampin to treat it, so I lived. I was treated in the local health clinic alongside of the Cambodian refugees who had just witnessed the greatest horrors since the Nazi era. We crossed paths and took the same weekly sputum tests, took our medication, and waited for our strength to return. When I was strong enough to travel I took my copy of Ezra Pound's "The Cantos" and Joyce's Finnegans Wake and set off on a quest that has brought me to an age when literary quests seem the final witness to a fatal vanity. Today I dream only of escaping following the trail of memories that dogs our steps, wishing that I could recreate a self that simply greeted the day with gratitude and left history to record its own story by other hands than mine.

I have reached that season of life when recollection is less an occasional occupation than it is a necessity, one imposed by the fact that an entirely new beginning is impracticable. Instead novelists tend to reach a time when they simply rework old material. There have been too many prior times when I thought that I had found my own personal version of that perfect beach on the French Riviera where like Scott Fitzgerald I could regain that energy that once seemed so plentiful only a decade before. Idealism is cheap to those who do not know the costs. If we can only be happy when released from bondage then nothing can be worse than excessive leisure. As we age leisure is imposed upon us because there is less in us to exploit and less beauty to make it worthwhile to seduce us. The end result is that we writers tend to simply wander about in various regions of the world if our means allow us to do so looking for a familiar face, knowing all the while that many of our friends are already dead at home and the others are simply waiting to be called into some medical clinic to be presented with a selection of various unpalatable options each of which can only make vague promises, not of recovery but only of what is called life-extension, as though life can be measured in quantity alone.

I think that all of us know that we are really seeking that one perennial magic moment when everything is just right, when all the planes and facets line up and a single ray of light serves to illuminate the whole world assembled at last. Sometimes when we were very young we glimpsed this magic form for just a moment as Keats did on the face of a Grecian urn or in hearing a nightingale. In those fortunate hours it is not necessary to tell over the few treasured coins that will remain of the once infinite years – everything was before us and the burdens of regret and folly only read in the passing faces of those inscrutable older faces that seemed never to have ever been young.

The problem with most writers as they age is that they know that most stories worth telling have already been told, if not in their own prior works then by someone else. Shakespeare knew this also but he had no problem borrowing his plots knowing that he could still use his marvelous facility to bring out all of the hidden dimensions that others had missed and in doing so to make something eternally new.

Too much introspection destroys literary art with the single exception of the poets. Novelists and writers in the short story format must turn outward or sink into the quicksand of the single soul there to gaze into that endless hall of mirrors that led Franz Kafka to instruct his friend Max Brod to promise to destroy all of his manuscripts at his death. The writer who hates his creations must first loathe himself – as did Lautreamont and Baudelaire. The people who really live it seems to me have no time for reflection. It isn't that they are shallow or are even ill-informed; it is that they inhabit a web of relations and obligations that demand quick responses.

Politicians know this so they keep their messages simple and their lies concise. A true psychic engineer could probably predict all of future history by simply applying the principles of fluid dynamics to events. Even professional comedians know that a certain proportion of their audience will laugh if the signal is given that a laugh is expected just as an orchestra will respond to the baton of the conductor. History is based on nothing more than this same expectation communicated to the vast yielding tides of oblivious humanity by those who claim to be leaders.

Writers are contrarians in this regard. It takes a madman or a malcontent to hold up a parade. Considering how obnoxious writers and artists often are, it is surprising that their performances can still on occasion draw a crowd. All things considered a clown or a juggler will always be more popular. Nothing is more disturbing than an original thought: it is either incomprehensible to most people or if finally understood it is deemed to be a truism or a circular argument. Even the Nazi death camps seemed routine in their operations after the first few weeks. It takes a lot to really surprise or shock human nature once its routine is established. To this fact all atrocities may be referred.

○

So considering all that I have said so far, why am I writing these notes for a novel; have all of my assertions thus far been mere preamble? Bring on the show!

But you see dear friends, I may so address you may I not? I have deduced that the surest way to ensure attention is to delay the payoff – every casino in the world knows this principle. Nothing ensures compliance more than to make a vague promise the fulfillment of which will be infinitely delayed; meanwhile the audience is held captive. Would you test this assertion? Just get three or more people to stand on a street corner and look up in an indefinite direction and point. A crowd will gather in no time and they will still be looking and pointing fifteen minutes later if you quietly slip away. Some reactions are self-sustaining as Europe learned in the Great War of 1914-1918.

The Buddha told us that life is suffering and all these years later millions of people still think that he was telling them something new. I discovered as much by simply stubbing my toe on a couch one day going out to the kitchen for a beer. Still need proof? Confucius told the Chinese to take orders was a good idea. Lao Tse told them that the ultimate was inexpressible and could not be comprehended. Three spiritual leaders with a message that can be summed up in the phrase "Why try?"

But then maybe I am just being a pessimist. You might think that I have read too much of Cioran but I am just starting beginning to read him, seeking to confirm my own intuitions. Isn't that the way of it? We read people who confirm what we already think. Ann Coulter does this all the time, but then who is Ann Coulter? I don't want to be too contemporary here; it is fatal to a writer who only writes works that he has predestined to be classics of a sort. Historical novels only work if they deal with events from a prior century, otherwise they are deemed too topical. The present moment always seems too trivial to be a worthy subject for the writer's art, but then tell that to Balzac.

The liberals say that the earth is warming but the conservatives know that a rumor like that is bad for business so they say that we are all doing just fine and the reports of a shark on the beach may hurt the tourist season. The best advice to a presidential candidate today is to look earnest but to know when to shut up; unless you are Donald Trump and having a motor mouth is just what put you high on the polls in the first place. The other Republican candidates should have learned earlier that simply looking terminally outraged can only take you so far. National debts and melting glaciers are really only symbols after all and symbols are meaningless to the uninitiated – a good punch line is so much better! So we whirl along into the millennial century and somewhere in Texas George Bush spends his time painting – no trips planned to Europe any time soon where universal jurisdiction over war crimes might cause an embarrassment. As for the old World-trade Center, New York was ripe for a little urban renewal and Dick Cheney happened to be on hand. Someday he may explain it all to George. Halliburton needed a little price stimulus. But I don't want to appear cynical; we will leave that to the French. The British and the Americans can always explain imperial rule as being in the best interests of human progress. As for the Germans, as the European Community looks to them for bailout money, some are asking why they ever needed to fight a world war to achieve eventual hegemony. History is strange: just wait around and everything comes full circle.

○

To reflect the present time is to reflect not progress but rather stasis, the calm before the storm. This feeling is not an unfamiliar one. We have seen it before in the calm variously termed the belle époque and the Edwardian era – that period just before the fateful year of 1914. It is difficult to imagine the sheer nullity and ignorance of the present era continuing without a break or course change into some other direction. The sails of history are already beginning to luff as the great vessel begins to turn. It is more than mere terrorism that is in question here; it is the sheer load of meanings that can find no common interpretive norm to sustain them.

We lack a universal hermeneutic and lacking it we are simply overwhelmed with discourses if we are thinking people with the great deluge of sheer unrelated data. When the equivalent of a power-surge comes the primitive synapses of the majority of minds will simply melt-down and the screen will go blank. Call it mind-crash. It is coming; in fact it may already be here.

○

Of course the year that I am recording has already witnessed my own mind-crash for what do you call it when your life cascades down around you, when everything that you had built out of empty castles in the air are finally revealed as exactly what they are?

The funny thing is that we both shared the same desire, to be like two atoms in a particle accelerator, to crash into each other which such force that we would both be annihilated in a single burst of energy or fused into a common molten mass that neither of us would ever again escape and by that means know that neither could abandon the other even if it worked to our mutual destruction. Each of us had woven a separate dream starring the other, a starring role in a play that it was too late to re-cast. We had gone too far and invested too much. The script was so involved and convoluted that outsiders could never hope to understand its theme since it brought us each so much unhappiness. We couldn't get any closer without mutual panic and still we could not imagine letting go without ceasing to exist.

Some people call this love; we called it a beautiful torment or midnight madness.

○

So this summer I set off again to rediscover at least some of the old places.

The perimeter of my aspirations had once enclosed all of the places that other writers had already made magic – Key West, Corfu, Trieste – now it seemed futile to sell a new generation on an expansiveness that could be embraced in an afternoon on a computer screen. Nothing is exotic if you can get your body there in twenty-four hours. But why make the effort if goggles and earphones can recreate the experience? Will we someday be fitted with our own USB port and simply bi-pass the senses entirely, brains in a jar?

It is only in the particular in the unique that we can love. We celebrate in each other what is irreducible because it is our own. Anyway, I always thought so. I have left a little piece of myself everywhere I have ever been. But lately, I am reduced to memories like a tire that has fragmented into ribbons each unconnected with the others, no longer part of a single rotating circle. Each of us is a zone of references, a neural network, one flavored and scented by time and places long past. But Proust has already explained this phenomenon down to the ground. Nothing has become more boring than to probe into our common core of perception. We are like small devouring insects or crabs in a tidal pool simply moving about while our separate jaws glean whatever circumstances have placed before us. To emerge as an individual is to be accused of narcissism while to aspire to universal truths is to be a monomaniac. The result is that we are now a collection of faces in ever expanding webs of private reference like molecules dispersed through a solution in a flask, networks accessing other networks, one vast inquiring total mind gazing at itself. Will the Internet suddenly wake-up and intone like Rene Descartes, "I think therefore I am?"

○

Meanwhile at the micro-level of our individuality we desire to continue whatever unique perseverance drives us from day to day – to buy a Lexus, to get a face-lift, to buy a condo on the gulf coast, or to hear "I love you" from whoever we currently covet. It would be nice (I once thought) to be so much the gypsy that I could answer any offhand reference to a place by saying, "Of course I have been there. I must say that like the off-season best. I wrote my third novel there in a little hotel by the bay."

How nice it would be to have missed nothing that life had to offer, to look forward to greeting death without saying, "You know I never got back to that little village in northern Italy where I stayed at the pensione. There were flowers blooming in the window and carts brought the produce into the square just below my hotel window each morning." Instead there is only a string of strip-malls across a sterile America and a string of unsavory people who needed to be placated if I was to survive. Life has been filled it seems to me with all the wrong people, with chance collisions where I was searched like a refugee at a border for the contraband of an original idea so that it could be impounded and a commercial slogan substituted.

So it was that as the summer of 2016 began I started paring everything down to an essential core, to return to where I had been, to see what might remain there still redolent of that past vision that had once made it sparkle with promise and infinite desire – each hope a gateway to a perpetual happiness, a secret that could be reduced to a phrase in a tidy notebook and then passed on.

Someone should have told me that words are overrated; a cheese sampler or a chicken salad in a wide ceramic bowl with the right mixture of walnuts and cranberries has more immediate appeal. The works of every Victorian novelist can be held today on a thumb-drive. This summer I woke up to the fact that publishing was a dying industry like a resort in Deauville where Churchill might once have stayed but has not been famous or frequented since by the great and powerful. We no longer value the particular nettles of another's mind sufficiently to wrestle through their thoughts. What moral dilemma is worth what it cost Orestes? Why return to Ithaca at all? As for Sophocles: everyone feels like you buddy, so get over it already! Factor any equation out and you reach zero.

○

They say that whoever wishes to write a novel must first master character, motivation, and point of view. Henry James did all of these but forgot that language should possess flow like a river and not move in fits and starts, modifying every assertion with hesitations and qualifications. Finally, a thing is what it is and that is how non-novelists experience life. Motivation and closure as in novels are not often present in life because in any life there are too many cross-currents. Even lovers are distractions from the continuing monologue that we wage with an indifferent world that flows about us as though we were an obstruction and not as we presume the very purpose of the flow. Everything comes towards us, is noticed or ignored, and then passes on. We interact with far more people who, after a brief transaction, will fade from our memories as just so many adjuncts to a typical day. But if our lives are made primarily from inconsequential and transient interactions then why should the novelist concentrate such vast energies to sustain the pretence that he knows why his particular characters act as they do and to imagine a plot that will trace those actions towards some ultimate revelation or moral end? Even the so-called "new novel" is didactic simply by its avowed purpose to eliminate any anthropomorphism, forgetting all along that novels do not sprout like mushrooms from a rotting log but must be composed, directed, and centered upon some anonymous hypothetical reader who will take a book down from a dusty shelf and allow it to speak at some indefinite future date.

But then this is less a novel than it is a memoir of sorts, the only difference being that the writer presumably tells the truth about events that actually happened in a memoir. It is precisely here though that the problem of point of view rears its ugly head. The memoirist asks us to believe that his present self has somehow managed to create closure and to contain the poor bewildered bastard that he once was in his now celestial comprehension of all that has happened to him. In other words he begins by lying to himself at least. Unless he is dead the most that is possible to him as writer is retrospection while still in transit. What he produces is a slice of film commenting on another slice of film while the projector is still going. Only at the end of a life with the film flapping about (as it used to do) would it be possible to say, "There! Now let me tell you what my life was."

This means that everything we say is an approximation to some elusive final text and even that is an alien medium to life itself. Selection as a principle already distorts life, dams it into various successive reservoirs, and tries to extract energy from a lifeless succession of memories. And what of commentary, that is preservation twice-removed? Who can be trusted to bear witness in his own behalf even if his life bore few surprises and his intentions met few frustrations? It would take a panel of judges with vast subpoena powers to do justice in any particular case.

This all adds up to a preliminary defense for impressionism in the novel or memoir, a necessary one you will agree. Without it every subjective response would be considered as possibly biased or inaccurate whereas by pleading guilty from the start anything in the way of authorial latitude will be allowed. The impressionist need not say whether even his present voice is the real one; it may only be one assumed for the occasion.

And what is that occasion? What if no one ever opens the book? What if the whole thing has been one long exposition of vanity? Imagine the book of Ecclesiastes if the manuscript had been lost, just a bit of parchment lost in the reeds along the Jordan? That would indeed be a vanity of vanities! In fact why write at all if everything is arbitrary or personal? By all of the above I mean to assert that in an impressionistic work such as this nothing is a digression.

○

So to get back to what I in essence never left, this summer I tried to start everything over, to perform a mopping-up operation on a life that I judged to be incomplete, at variance with a set of standards never quite articulated but felt along the blood. I had intimations that some inscrutable timekeeper might be looking nervously at his watch. Each year the stage of this multifarious world was growing more crowded.

As an example just now down below on the lawn below me a wedding is taking place. The wind has come up over the mountains to dispel the heat of the day and under the aspen trees a girl in white stands like some sort of symbol of what she is every day. The feminine principle is incarnate in her not because she is unique but because so many others have stood in turn in the place that she currently occupies, each one making a gamble on the future with a slim young man at her side. The wedding dress takes her body to its form so that she is once and forever a bride. She is ceremony. She is offering. She is the human race renewing itself. How can one day contain so many tomorrows? But then I was writing of the past wasn't I so from whence comes this present tense? Can it be that time sufficiently remembered is always experienced as present? What difference does it make if an event is recorded in so-called real-time or ten minutes after the fact – or ten years? Already it is encrusted with modifications, adjectives, and expletives have gathered like so many wolves about the corpse of the moment.

To probe the nature of experience is inevitably to be plunged into metaphysics – only a sponge lives in one eternal present filtering plankton without effort; even a bi-valve must make decisions of a sort. So it is that we distort and alter what flows past us each day trying to impose meaning on what we do in pursuit of our ideal end, that vast matrix that tries to order the will as it places its pieces in the vast puzzle that lies before us. We start with a frame and an idea and everything else is accident. So it is that if a book would be true it must not be forged like Hemingway's illustrious sentences but rather discovered in an act of uncontrolled but directional composition. The real truths of experience are always interstitial. It is between utterances in the silence of reflective thought that truth emerges if it is to be found at all, not in the forged links in a chain but in the widening circles from a stone that disturbs the surface of a blackened pool and then disappears into the depths.

○

Life is a series of interruptions of the essential narrative. We push aside the veil of intention and gaze into the darkness beyond. The ship of our security is forever taking water over the stern. Menace! That is the word for life's beleaguered course! But to say so is to deny all those tiny reassurances without which we could not face the day but would remain forever abed, tremulous and afraid. Like the bats of night, one of every two hundred is freighted with the virus of madness. Things fly at us and we duck our heads but we cannot elude them should they decide to sink their fangs into us.

Phobias are always symbolic. It is not the thing itself that we fear but what it represents in our inner world. We carry about with us our own Dead Sea Scrolls inscribed with our vision of a serene and perfect world, one that we will never inhabit; stoic or epicurean we try and fill the intervening hours with distractions and dream of good-fortune with all of the avidity of a Chinese astrologer casting his yarrow sticks. We trade tales of our various ailments, each of us the diagnostician of the other's ills. No human problem but someone has endured it before us. A partial chart exists for very voyage. It is up to us as novelists to extend the known world into terra incognita.

The alternative of course is not to think at all, not to communicate our fears because too much candor is bad form and may depress the company. We only dare to face our ultimate fears over a cocktail glass or in the seedy detritus of our dreams when our conscious mind falls away and leaves us prey to undigested issues now clothed in the strange garb assembled by the unconscious author of our dreams for an audience of one. Our dreams are finally incommunicable even to ourselves. We flee before their hidden messages like sandpipers from the waves on tiny bird-feet. We play a game of approach and retreat, playing tag with that which can submerge us while ever and again we hear the boom and whisper of the surf on the distant reef of death.

***

How long should an author play with an image or an idea? That is the question that defines craftsmanship, but in a work with few rules any liberty can be taken. If we consult the reader's patience every other sentence would be one of apology, "Excuse me for saying this but..." If authors are egotists it is because they write as bailiffs in the Court of the Eternal Truths calling all to order before the judge of all things enters. But what if the courtroom is an illusion of the mind? Well, then it will hardly matter will it if a few stray neural patterns are reduced to print. Intimate communications are rare among family and friends let alone between strangers; this is why the confession is perhaps the primal origin of all literature: "Bless me father for I have sinned..." We fear to say I love you to another because we hang from a dreadful ledge when we do so. Camouflage, persiflage, and silence are our screen from truths we cannot bear to utter. Somewhere there is an ideal listener, a reader who will recognize a thought as parallel to his own. It is such as this reader that we seek. Ideas are the commonwealth of the human race. Shakespeare's phrase, "When to the sessions of sweet silent thought" contains the essence of all reflection.

Not since the writings of Montaigne were followed by the triumph of the novel though have we wished to confine literature to an unabashed psychology probing the unuttered truths that we speak to ourselves alone. Time has enhanced the novel's appeal. We are an introspective age and all of us wish that someone could be found who would care to read our confessions and extent to us forgiveness and compassion. We are all in competition for space in the grocery tabloids.

"Look what a mess my life became (be sure and read the next installment.)" The predominant current art-form is the image because its grasp must be instantaneous or forever elusive. To be discursive is to court dismissal by the impatient reader. Post-modernism has become a series of signifiers without an object. The work of art must never comment upon itself, least of all in the process of its initial composition. Objectivity demands that the author be impervious to his own text. A poem must exist in splendid isolation as though it wrote itself. There is a blatant Puritanical streak in the reader who demands that the author disappear from his work. Some achieve a semblance of this but only because of a virtuosity of technique. The best of writers like the devil may truly say, "My name is legion."

✶✶✶

Objectivity is an illusion born of superior craftsmanship. To penetrate the opaque surface of a pool of circumstance, to record a unique trek over rough-ground towards a mist-shrouded mountain on the horizon is to advance the cause of recorded thought. Great writers do this by daring to embrace their own subjectivity as equally real as the ground beneath our feet while keeping the faith that words would not exist if they were ours alone and not a bridge to other minds. To trust that what we think and feel is not ours alone is to put a terminus to our contemporary fad of solipsism. We make of literature an object rather than an address to awaken a response through an unnatural severance as though no placenta of thought united the author with his text. We prefer to wear masks like anarchists in a crowd of protestors to avoid the possibility of arrest, to be personally identified with what we say as writers.

These were some of the thoughts that beset me this summer as I began to write the formless something that I dared to call, after

Thomas Wolfe's planned novel of the west, "Pacific End." Not that I thought that I could imagine what he might have written had he lived; it was only that I wished to honor what might have been his thematic intent. Thomas Wolfe had always manifested a certain 17th century turn of mind. Perhaps, this was why I enjoyed him – we were both creatures existing out of our proper time. This phrase, proper time, implies that history has a shape beyond being simply a succession of events as it is experienced. The recent decline of the novel as an art form compared with what it was in the 19th century stems from the loss of a complex plot with its neat causes and effects, its synchronicities, and the sense that some abiding presence witnesses our actions and judges our motives. As a lawyer I have begun to realize that we live in a strict liability universe that exacts damages not on the basis of our intentions but according to how our acts play out against multiple dimensions only some of which are foreseeable or even visible.

Books emerge onto best-seller lists because they resonate with some cOmmon source of that inscrutable decision to buy. After a time authors develop a following not so much based on excellence as on brand recognition like soft-drinks. Of what use are subtle turns of phrase or poetic sensibility when what mediocrity desires in to have its banalities confirmed and to be told that there is a way out of the quest for the full stature of our moral being by being like everyone who is equally dissatisfied with the particular trap into which they blundered after high school. To the non-discerning no promise is so cheaply gilded that it will awaken skepticism if it is wrapped in some form of assumed sincerity. The current formula for bestsellers is: "I was a mess, then I got better, you can too and here is where you can send your check. If you do so today you get a matching set of steak knives."

It works and who can quarrel with success, just ask anyone throwing money into a slot machine. The contemporary American mind has such a short attention span that in less than two hundred years we forgot from whom we stole the land that makes up most of America. So why attempt to write the great American novel when we could simply steal its equivalent from some other national epic? Our national ethos is after all one of universal entitlement – to want is to possess, to simply define a need is to anticipate that it will be fulfilled.

The idea that a poem's meaning is irrelevant to the author's intentions arose among what were once called "the new critics" – the central insight was that nothing is contextual – a thing is a thing is a thing. It refined the critic out of his own subjectivity by imagining that the poem could articulate not only itself but the criteria by which it would be judged. Imagine my surprise then when as I wrote "Pacific End" I discovered that I was hoping to do the same thing! I who always hated the false objectivism of the new critics had inadvertently adopted their model.

Perhaps I was drawn in this direction because I was attempting to be contemporary – to write a novel that could survive the tiny pin-pricks of being "tweeted" to death by people who never read novels. Incomprehensibility is a virtue when a book becomes merely another fashion accessory, a counter-cultural statement that one is a reader. Besides if all texts exist in isolation then meaning is always tautological and who is to care if a novel has no characters, no plot, and makes no progress – simply describe, enunciate with conviction … ensure belief. The book is over when it is over. Marcel Proust began this trend in novels and brought it to perfection. Who cares about a search for time lost when time never seems to cease? When everything is simultaneous there is no history – you wake to a life and simply start moving again like a beetle that has been placed on its back – it isn't going anywhere in particular but it is in an evidently great hurry to get there.

We are living today in a data-stream; worse, we are living on a data flood-plain derived from no mountains but welling-up from some dark subterranean source in the collective unconscious. It is no longer the id that is unconscious; we celebrate all of the wet corpuscles of the brain. It is the ego that is now unconscious. We are blank screens played upon by overlapping lasers of conviction as these are beamed at us by media sponsors or the owners of familiar trademarks. But to say as much is to unthaw old media commentators. The war between mind and media is over and the media has won a victory over anyone who would now deplore it. We are the media and the audience simultaneously.

I was about to add an exclamation point here, but that would be so anthropocentric of me. The text should exist on a page as though it was self-generated to avoid accusations of bias – unless it takes the form of a confession. Nothing is a greater instigation to credibility than to admit forthrightly that one has always been totally subjective or better still mendacious. What can be more refreshing than for an author to admit that he will betray you? It is like a woman who explains on a first date that she is incapable of fidelity or a man whose primary attraction is his love of inflicting pain. Such things currently get lots of play-time.

Hitler knew this: only tell the world that you will plunge it into chaos and it will let you do it. Stalin used a different technique. He simply played the insecurities of his subordinates off against each other. No one will ever know what Stalin really thought about anything since his only real genius was that nothing was beyond him. I may as well mention Mao here as well. Mao knew that the Chinese would follow him because individually they had never been told that they had a right to exist; they were accustomed to being reckoned in units of a thousand.

But what of we Americans, can we be reckoned as individuals? We are told that we are individuals and are startled to discover that we are really a vast amorphous mass like a great pulsing jellyfish with its tentacles reaching in all directions and our stinging cells alert to any alien presence in our midst. Americans thrive on the fear that people from other nations may be laughing at them. The pre-emptive strike is as American as apple pie – the real wonder is that we have never used it. But then low-grade anxiety is so much more preferable to disarmament and it provides a healthy stimulus to the arms trade. In practical America good business practice always carries the day even at the risk of survival. We are all far too busy to mount a good revolution. The result is that everything simply continues towards an apocalypse indefinitely delayed.

✶✶✶

An anti-narrative is one that calls into question the common assumptions that create a national mythos. As a marketing strategy it is not as foolish as it looks. For instance, just as a paranoid is engaged in constantly scanning the world for evidence of duplicity and betrayal, our national security society is always looking about for signs of anti-American sentiments. It is usually possible to gage the naturalness and legitimacy of national pride by the spontaneous and variable ways that patriotism manifests itself among the citizenry. A correlative of this is that we can recognize tyranny by the degree that patriotic displays are staged, managed, or even compelled.

The American responses to the events of September 11, 2001 are emblematic of our collective desire to clasp insults to our collective bosom as evidence that we are a misunderstood and victimized people rather than what is far more likely, that we are meddlesome, arrogant, ill-informed, callous, and uncultivated in our awareness of other nations and people and that as a result we manifest a readiness to use military force to answer all questions.

The attacks on the World Trade Center were essentially symbolic, an effort to get the attention of a people that only comprehends the language of power and effectively exerted force. All the scholarship or persuasive rhetoric in the world would have been confined to the back pages of the nation's newspapers; but show an image of these two pristine edifices burning and people scurrying about like ants in the streets below and even the mass of amoral and lethargic suburbanites will take note of what their nation's policies have meant in the daily lives of other nations. It is too simple of course to say that we deserved the attacks; they were after all attacks. It is even more important though to understand that these attacks were not unprovoked. The daily existence of America is a drain upon the world's resources and a trial of their patience with our national penchant for delusion and mendacity.

But it is the way that we have responded that proves that what I have just said is an accurate assessment. Our first action was for Congress to write a blank check to the President to form the equivalent of a national posse and to go riding out into the hills in search of the desperados. Even after the revelation that America had been led to war with Iraq on false pretenses the American people basically took it all in stride, "At least we kicked somebody's butt; that will teach any outsiders not to mess with us. We are still the man!"

Worse still we have made that bright September day a twin image of American innocence with the Japanese attack on Pearl Harbor. In other words we have institutionalized these events as symbols as a sort of treasury of justification that can be drawn on at will in case we want to go after anybody who opposes our interests. The sites of the attacks pay a daily dividend in cultivated outrage in the people who visit them and take their children there. "Just look at the price of freedom. Someday you can join the armed forces and kill those who disrespect our rule and our right to impose that will beyond our shores in our own national interest, one that is now global." In other words, we want what we want and other people better want it too or suffer the consequences. How does this differ from German nationalism gone berserk under the Nazi regime?

***

Of course to say the above sentiments anywhere but in a novel, which of course is fictional by definition, would be to court America's version of a fatwa calling for the author's death. But an anti-narrative of course has as its purpose the desire to oppose the dominant narrative of self-congratulation and complacency that is presumed to be our signature national legacy; after all, *we are Americans and can do no wrong*. As a minor art-form the novel may be more outspoken than the editorial.

The successful candidate for our largely symbolic office of the Presidency will not adopt an anti-narrative. He or she will of necessity cast the agenda of the party that he or she represents as emblematic of the national will so that the individual voter will believe that he is getting what he wants. What Americans want now of course is change and they desire change because Americans never really get enough of anything and it is high time that they got more of whatever it is that they currently desire. Does this sound like anyone we know who is running for office?

This year of 2016 is more than just a hinge between two administrations. It is also the year when as an omniscient author I have been sensing other endings everywhere. The tectonic plates are shifting, many of them plates the ones upon which my own security has long rested. I am not free of a desire for a narrative with a happy ending. Romance and epic are my preferred forms of literature. I like the vast sweeping saga of nation and family. My very nature is land-conscious and I cannot imagine anything more welcome than my own version of a family estate with its high walls, a substantial drawing room, and a kennel of baying hounds to accompany me as I visit the outlying districts on errands of mercy to grateful cottagers. In other words my natural bent is one of benevolent conservatism.

How then did I end up writing an anti-narrative rather than cozying up as best I could to any personal power and privilege that may pass to me through fortunate descent? Why instead opt for a life of dissent and discontent? Do I perhaps like being a victim? Or perhaps I am still under the mistaken impression that novelists are celebrities with sex, fame, riches, and power as essential modalities of the vocation? Did I leave anything out? Yes I did, maybe the two most important of all: I left out having a cultivated mind and the time to employ it. I would have included good luck as well, but then no one knows whether he or she has been lucky until they die. All evaluation is retrospective. Culture and the time to enjoy it have always seemed to me the mark of a civilized life with the result that sooner or later I would naturally gravitate towards the great novelists who have attempted to sum up an age on parchment, vellum, or only in paperback classics.

This is cold comfort though as I age because the classical novelist though remembered is also long dead and past collecting royalties, recognition, and acclaim. I wanted to be a novelist of sorts but with my perception that America wasn't turning out to be what I had once supposed it to be I necessarily developed the fatal habit of irony and its attendant attitude of sarcasm. I began to look to the discontented rather than those who approved of things as they are. I became fond of the minor keys and grew fond of the rogue and rascal as long as he existed on the margins of society and was confined to the quest for survival and perhaps a little fun along the way. By contrast I saw respectability as essentially pharisaical and evil. As time passed I learned that respect is most often afforded to bullies and phonies. I read "Catcher in the Rye" with vast approval. Holden Caulfield was on to something. O course this probably proves no more than that I am a creature of my own privileged generation when this novel developed a huge following.

I grew up in an age when people were paid big money just for being personalities. Is it any wonder then that I wanted to be a star of sorts, in fact a prima donna? The prima donna can only be definitively recognized when she has begun her descent; as long as she is till rising she can still pose as a beautiful and promising ingénue. The only way to prevent failure is to defer success indefinitely. The denizens of the bar featured in Eugene O'Neill's greatest play, "The Iceman Cometh" manifested this truth. Americans always feel that they have missed something precisely because their expectations are so high initially.

***

I began writing "Pacific End" when it suddenly occurred to me that I was running short on time and that narrative or anti-narrative I had better get something down or I would end up like Poncho Villa on his deathbed saying, "It can't end like this; tell them that I said something." Here I was with my back up against the Pacific Ocean and the summer ahead looking pretty dark because she who cannot be named said that I was a heartless and emotionally void creature who should throw the twin stones that I carry about with me always to remind of her into the sea. So I started writing a formless thing that would question the very meaning of the novel form as a good medicine to my bleeding wounds.

Last night I dreamed that Edith Wharton, whose prose seems to provide instant insight into the deepest of the mysteries of the human heart, was gazing into a mirror and lamenting the dead whom she had once known in the full flower of their youth. Now she alone remained of all that gallant company to face what time does to make us strangers to ourselves. I recalled on waking her dismay in the dream as she traced the various lines traced by our customary expressions on faces, the very lines that cause our faces to shatter along new planes as we age. Should we seek to adopt a new set of emotions we create facial chaos. Those who habitually smile often must continue to smile or look like their new simian selves or like a ventriloquist's dummy waiting for a knee on which to sit. For all of its sadness it was a beautiful dream and I awoke to still see the young men of her vision visible in my mind. I tried to quickly memorize the details but knew that I would only retain a brief thematic summary of the dream an hour hence and a fading daguerreotype image of the slim figures and youthful faces with their laughing eyes.

It seems to be a great truth that beauty must be unconscious of itself if it is to remain beauty. It must be discovered by a certain cast of light on a face that does not know it has been observed. Later on we enter that period of artifice when we consult various technicians saying, "Kill me if you must but make me beautiful." We each aspire to the condition of the ocean that by remaining in constant activity is still always primordially itself. Who could tolerate a frozen eternity? So it is that art which seeks to freeze beauty's image in fact betrays it because what is beautiful is never still. It exists in that time which is stasis but not static, our breath is arrested in contemplating it but we do not perish. When change overwhelms us we seek for something that we can imagine as existing out of time, yet beauty of all things is the most fragile and transient. Why then do we pursue it so avidly?

✳✳✳

The Newport Oracle says, "I treat time the way that most people treat money."

I stumbled upon her at a friend's recommendation when I complained about feeling so disconnected.

"You must meet … no I will not name her for she resists identification. She will be less likely to speak her truths if you ask her questions – like nature itself she must be approached quietly and allowed to speak in her own language."

"And what is that language?" I asked. "No doubt she has lived in many places."

"She lives only in today."

"No past? Then how can she be an oracle?"

"The truest oracle knows that change is the most potent of illusions. She told me once that we must always guard our thoughts because the Amen Bird is perpetually flying over our heads and if we think dark or wicked things it will say Amen and they shall then be ours for always."

"But we all have such thoughts," I replied smiling.

"It is not the thoughts but the ways that we brood upon them and nurture them that puts us at risk."

"Then I have much to fear," I thought, because like most writers I am accustomed to brooding; it is part of my craft."

***

I had brooded much in recent summers. I felt like I was running short of time. I had finally arrived at the point where I was ready to read "In Search of Time Lost" by Marcel Proust and "The Ambassadors," the last novel of Henry James, the one that he considered to be the most perfect product of his elliptic later style. Both books put me in mind of the task that every novelist must face – to so render experience that it is both preserved and intensified while being simultaneously recognizable by less aware minds with a less delicate sensorium. By 2016 I thought that it might be amusing to record notes for a novel in the very process of its own genesis and to use my customary summer excursion in a manner akin to Wordsworth and his long poem, "The Prelude" by describing the genesis of a work by recording its preconditions.

As I once told my publisher in answer to his question of what a previous book was about – a book is about itself. It is in the realization of design that the author creates something new – change the form and you change the outcome. This is as obvious as the assertion that an event does not exist until it happens. It is impossible to judge a book as though it was the realization of a pre-existing blueprint rather than the surprising coming together of diverse elements that is implied in any creative act. We often forget this.

***

As the summer progressed I looked for guidance wherever chance might intervene and provide insights. I was like a planet looking for an orbit as it plunged through space without a star.

The vacuum of her absence was as intense as her presence had once been. I needed to connect again to life but was uncertain where to seek out my own version of Thomas Wolfe's mythic sense of personal security. I like him was accustomed to seeing my life in universal terms as though I was in the process of providing a pattern for all human lives rather than simply manifesting one tiny shattered version of a sub-text to the vast volume of humanity. Isolation allows for inflation of our sense of personal importance. Only those who feel securely loved can readily tolerate crowds without feeling that they are about to dissolve into the seething mass. The act of writing may substitute for the everyday experience that most people find adequate to prevent this sense of dissolution.

***

I learned an important thing about a mother's love from the Newport Oracle on that first afternoon when I met her at her shop.

"When my son was born I spent the first three months alone with him, overcome by the wonder of his being. I would not allow others to see him because our own communication was so intense that I knew that they would prove a distraction. It was not mere maternal possessiveness, you see. It was that I was still learning the language of his eyes and gestures, a language that had been formed in silence while he was inside of me but that could now be spoken openly between us."

"Do you recall that language?" I asked.

"No because it was a language for that period only. For me each day stands alone."

"Then what becomes of memories?"

"Oh they exist but they must not be allowed to be more than they are and infect the present."

"Then how will you write them all down?" I asked. "When you write your memoirs, I mean."

"I do not think that I will write memoirs as you say. I will write one line and I will think about it and perhaps the next day I will write another line."

"But of course, you are after all an oracle and the pronouncements of oracles are always short and mysterious."

"Oh do not suppose that of me; I merely live and listen to those who come to me. They find beautiful things here and they leave happy with a little gift."

"So do you sell things or give wisdom?"

"Wisdom is not mine to give. I would not presume so much. Do you?"

"Well the writer must presume something or there would be no writing."

"Then perhaps you should write of those presumptions and why you require them so."

"Perhaps I will."

***

In the nineteen-seventies, the age of the mass availability of classics with gaudy covers in paperback editions I naturally assumed that somehow these creative minds had been engaged in describing the world as it really was and that my reading of them would give me a head-start on the perpetual struggle for survival. I had yet to learn that true power is often virtually illiterate and that writers live hardscrabble existences as the prey of editors and publishers. The lucky ones find an audience and through a series of fellowships or awards they manage to afford to live the reckless lives out of which they distill their moral tales of failed artists or perhaps the cocktail society that they are allowed to glimpse now and again while imagining the rest.

But that was the seventies and America was still suffering from a post-sixties blues. It was a nervous time of inflation and oil shocks and I played my small part by working for a time seeking oil cars out of Gulfport, Mississippi or the Quaker state as the purchasing agent for an oil company. I still hoped to return to graduate school because I had yet to shake the illusion that Americans give a damn about culture in any real sense or wish to advance in any way the debate about life's essential issues. I used to read daily from the complex prose of "Absalom, Absalom," by William

Faulkner and imagine returning to Europe because that was what the authors of my grandfather's era had always done to hone their craft. I was slowly but surely working my way towards a voice for my own generation, one that must be a lost one because it has yet to produce many names that will still be read in a hundred years. New ideas derive from crisis and the long post-war peace since 1945 has left us hungry for some great watershed while realizing that we can no longer survive as a species if we have one. Instead all we can do is to sit still and watch the polar ice melt and the ocean levels slowly inundate the low-lying nations, an apocalypse in slow motion.

***

It was at precisely this time that I found myself suddenly that summer writing "Pacific End."

"What do you mean by Pacific," my father asked me one morning as I announced my intentions?

I told him it was a novel about the difficulties involved in writing a novel called, "Pacific End."

I had in mind a mirror facing another mirror, facing another mirror – a sense of realism to be confounded by itself. What is subject and what is object or are they two sides of the same thing, an integral perception?

It was a goal of the modernist artists to be comprehensible only to a select few aficionados who would be sufficiently well-placed that they could proclaim that a new genius had arisen. Joyce, Beckett, Genet, Burgess - all stressed forms to the breaking-point the better to articulate a view of the old earth as seen from Pluto. Anyway, that was what I had in mind though it was hardly matter for breakfast time banter in the mountains with my father.

That day the clouds had come up over the pass from the coast and it was actually chilly. I had yet to hear from she who cannot be named. I had decided to skip a conference in Seattle and to hang onto the ragged edge of a summer that like all summers would not return. I knew that I would look back on its dispersed energies and remember a succession of faces and scenes un-plotted and pacific moving towards no particular goal because all of my prior goals were unraveling like the line that had kept me anchored for so long to the tiny port town where I had been living for the past twenty years waiting for something to happen, something to return me to a road that I had lost somewhere around the Reagan-Thatcher era when the twin empires gave one last tug and won the Cold War while forgetting that empires define their identity in opposition to their enemies. Victories are always hollow. Even in private life we remember our ex-lovers far longer than our current relationships – we are all of us faithful to Cynara, in our fashion. The only real pacific end is death.

∗∗∗

I have no doubt that some billionaire Chinese conquistador will someday soon land on the west coast of America in a plumed helmet and announce that he has discovered a new land. He will proudly claim it for old Cathay and proceed over time to rid it of its pesky savages parading around in feathers and animal skins. If history repeats itself why is this conceit such a far-fetched notion? Maybe there is some justice in the world after all. In any case a few years ago I started reading the "I-Ching" to familiarize myself with the basis for Chinese conceptions just in case. In this ancient book of changes an apotheosis is always followed by a reversal of fortune.

Applying this perspective to our present position American culture will soon be recalled if at all as characterized by a failed attempt at democracy and the invention of the ubiquitous hamburger. Our descendents will inhabit the Asia-East Provinces then and learn Mandarin or Hindustani rather than English. The autumn leaves are falling on what Abraham Lincoln once tried to preserve; hegemony is rotating as it always does. Throughout the year of 2016 I felt that everything was being ground down into dust. Each political party was engaged in making their final promises: the Republicans promised the well-off that they could keep their property and the Democrats had promised to spread the wealth around. Neither party seemed to realize that it was Chinese money that was being spent for defense or for welfare and not our own. America is like a bank in default to its depositors with a lot of nervous tellers looking forward to locking the doors

in good order and losing themselves in the streets before any
violence breaks out. It was a good time to write a book about
death and the pacific end of all our American dreams.

Not that I wanted to be right about anything. Believe it or not I
like comedies in the old Aristotelian definition of the term. I like
it when the universe gives us a break and the fool or rogue gets by
on charm alone like Tom Jones or Tristram Shandy and escapes
the retribution that his actions might have invited. . Human
nature at its best rejoices in mercy and loathes strict justice; such
a pity that physics does not follow our desires or chemistry our
aspirations. I think it's time that we realize that this planet is
it; we just aren't going anywhere. Taking the equivalent of what
are currently called "selfies" of the solar system is fine but really
merely an exercise in futile aspirations. We are stuck with this
one earth, wrinkles and all: one sun, one moon, the panoply
of stars overhead to awaken wonder and instill humility, and a
blessed canopy of air to sustain us. As for the practicability of
wars, even if only using conventional weapons, I would point out
that we are roughly in the same position as persons in a tightly-
packed elevator who must avoid any unsavory exhalations.

I have a friend who assures me though that physicists have
discovered that what is happening isn't really happening as proved
by a thing called the double-slit experiment as applied to photons
or particles. Our expectations of reality according to this point
of view can influence what are otherwise assumed to be merely
physical outcomes that should be independent of mind. The
result of allowing mere expectation to change outcomes is that we
need no longer feel that we are alone in a mindless universe; the
world pulses along with us and shares our passions and desires. If
reduced to the practical order we might imagine someday galaxies
as mere reflections in the quiet pond of a universal comprehension
and one that we might share. It would be funny if Leibnitz with
his monads or Berkeley's idealism was the correct view after
all. But if the world that we observe is in reality an idea then
who is the original thinker? Are we merely holograms of some
distant and underlying reality? Or is what we find surprising the
influence that other dimensions perhaps have upon the four that
we already know? Perhaps, all thought is a metaphor for some

other presently ungraspable reality. The conundrum is that we are seeking the answer to a question that we have not thought to ask because we have yet to invent the words in which to pose the question in the first place?

***

Of course the novelist is supposed to deal with the world as we find it but then what if that is the very issue: how few of us ever really find the world. At every instant and in every place some event is happening that will remain un-witnessed simply because we are not there to observe it. In the kaleidoscope of events our choices are constantly applying a filter not only to impressions but to the very possibility of impressions so that the novel written today, if it is to be true at all, will be different to the novel that might be written tomorrow under whatever influences are operative at that time.

All of life is like a Rorschach test to interpret random patterns as best we may. But where is the interpreter to be found? Does providence arrange chance meetings or is it that we read significance into past events based upon our prior preconceptions of what categories of judgment should be applied. The paranoid knows that he is being spied upon because his very existence is based upon a preconception of opposition. This opposition is less fearsome than what is the more likely case: that the world views his existence with sublime indifference. His true fear is that no one is noticing the signs of his pain and the loneliness that would make him cry-out to another if he thought that anyone would ever really understand him.

We leave it to the writers and musicians to decipher us by first deciphering themselves. We demand truth from art so as not to be misled. Yet novels, or so my father says, deal with what never happened. On the contrary I would tell him, in a good novel the author deals with what happens every day because human experience is a constant. We read fiction in order to confirm our conclusions or to expand our own range of emotional experience. The language of fiction adds new instruments to our internal orchestra so that more complex musical scores may be played. Even the atonal elements speak to those oblique sentiments that perplex us.

It is part of the heartache of two people who love each other for instance that they are often like visitors to a prison speaking through a wall of impenetrable glass to each other. Each sees the other speaking but the sound does not convey the private meanings attached to each phrase so that each drowns in associations that the other does not possess. "Why do you not hear me, hear me, hear me?"

Poets on the other hand so often deal in private associations that we deem them to be profound merely because they do not provide us with a lexicon to their private meanings. I was converted to prose when I realized what the writers of the seventeenth century in England could do with it. I also grew to admire the way that a novel could become a complete world unto itself so that the willing reader would often prefer not to escape from its spell but to wander endlessly in the new environment of the author's interpreted world.

***

Each day I continued writing "Pacific End" knowing all the while that the time that I could afford to expend was limited. Dealing with a writer without frustration often means watching as he calmly pours a cup to overflowing indifferent as a pool forms and runs off onto the floor. To an aphoristic mind a complex and nuanced presentation must by its very nature be false. To list all of the preconceptions and references prior to making any statement is simply impracticable for writers. The result is that our conclusions seem to appear out of thin air and if they have never been encountered before they are as alarming as objects that appear suddenly on a radar screen and then as instantly disappear. Nothing is as alarming as an effect that appears causeless and not merely spontaneous.

I believe that this is the reason why my father guards himself against me and why I in turn regret that guardedness. "How," he must ask himself, "Did this person come from me?"

If I speak of "a widening gyre" he does not register William Butler Yeats. If I say *"la belle dame sans merci"* he does not think

John Keats. I in turn do not know last season's basketball victors or how skillful trading can build a fortune. Trading requires the ability to let go of the formerly possessed and that is an ability that I lack. Like an ever growing snowball I no sooner finish one book but I buy five others. The day before I left the mountains for the coast I purchased four books on embodied experience and one on how clothing influences social perception – doesn't everyone care about such things? After all, everyone has a body! But then embodiment for me is a conundrum and for my sister a vocation – each molecule weighed for its likely organic effect when incorporated into the pro-biotic solar system over which she presides with all of the oversight of a Tsarina. Everything is doled out and measured in tiny spoonfuls and only in feeding her dog does she err in unmeasured quantities. The moments of her day are similarly filled so that no interstitial time is unused. She and I share a desire to let nothing escape us. Were we then jointly-deprived of some essential nutrient of the spirit as we matured? We orbit around our father's silences. What do they contain? Why does he seek solitude so avidly like a sun that would prefer to exist without its circling planets? It is at times as though he would prefer to cast his light into endless space without reflecting off of those near objects that turn to him from warmth? Or is it that he is already entering into that slow fade-out like a dying star that besets everyone with the aging process, something that we cannot know until we get there? We tend to end each visit with a joint effort to repair the injuries wrought by too-close association after long absence and my own desire to seek connection while there is still time. But then I am time-haunted in a way that perhaps he is not, thus this strange novel that is less a novel than a confession of what it would be to write one with no other framework than the daily onrush of unrelated events.

I saw two boys today on the beach, one white and one black, who had improvised a teeter-totter out of two pieces of driftwood. They looked up at me and smiled in six-year-old triumph as I walked by completely unaware that they had just solved the race problem in America. I notice things like this. The day before I had joined a discussion group of retired businessmen and professors who meet weekly simply to talk about things, a rich symposium of minds no less profound than these two children but from a more sophisticated assessment. We cooperate because we must in order to survive. Money purchases the leisure to reflect and all that the two boys possess is time. Time is the one essential irreplaceable commodity. Who is richer the boys or the retirees? You know you are old when the young appear to be a separate species like playful dolphins sporting in the waves.

***

The calculation of wealth is in the last analysis the calculation of residual possibility. Money can make events occur but between transactions money is essentially static. This is because money is actually an idea and not a thing in itself. It is only when money is reduced to property that it becomes actually embodied and takes form as a thing or an event.

The power of ideas was represented in graphic form for me today as I walked along the beach. Two men were engaged in balancing stones into improbable constructed pyramids. The art objects that resulted were strangely disturbing in their temporal suspension and I am sure that others coming upon them would find them so as well because they represented in their sheer immovability a violation of the normal expectation for stones: that absent mortar to make them adhere they do not retain this seemingly law of gravity defying relationship. It was as though they represented a frozen instant in time. They should topple over momently but they did not do so but rather remained defiantly in place. This resistance to expectations is encountered whenever we encounter a new idea. Ideas have this same quality of static definition in a world of change. The waves on the headland in turn could not have made this more manifest: each wave appeared to be acting from a sense of individual urgency as though it entertained an expectation that in its unique encounter with the headland some lasting effect would be produced instead of the usual vanity of spray suspended for an instant in the sunlight and then diffusing itself by merging with the tidal surge at its base.

In the usual fashion of a writer's tendency to associate disparate fancies I could not help but compare my uneasiness with the static spectacle of the balanced stones with my dismay that my father believes that a home preserves its value best by being surrounded by rules that prevent as if by magic the dispersal of its being that would be represented by too much shared experience. Visitors are in this sense invaders and it is nor surprising that the metaphors characteristic of the Donald Trump campaign are those of threats to property and security. Immigrants are not additions to the valuable labor force of the nation but drains upon the tax-base through educational and medical entitlements.

The nation, to the Republican mind, is an idea and one that is under threat. The Constitution is reduced to an iconic document of original intent rather than the embodiment of forces to be interpreted according to needs as they arise in a systematic fashion. It is not surprising that when the conservative mentality speaks of family-values they are really celebrating the idea of patriarchal control by static ideas. The real threat of a woman president is that from this mindset a woman president is an oxymoron, a violation of the sage Pauline advice that women should submit not merely to their husbands but to the sovereignty represented by established ideas. If women must submit than children must even more readily acknowledge that a predestined order exists that does not take its origin from the flow of nature as manifest in wind and wave but from rocks piled in defiance and carefully balanced so as to remain unchanged unless they are deliberately dismantled by the artisans' male successors.

This raises the same question that an unbiased observer might conceivably raise coming upon these momentary monoliths – who did this thing? The authority of the objects is presumably derived from the right of the artificer to decree that this arrangement of stones is to be indefinitely preserved. The stones themselves of course proclaim nothing but themselves – there they are! It is the idea behind their arrangement that determines whether this set of relations must be allowed to stand because of the effort involved in thus displacing the usual rules of diffusion and entropy. Natural disorder should eventually restore these stones to a purposeless and elemental state of simply lying about on the beach.

Scrambling appears to be the first law of nature and randomness to be the will of whatever God rules the usual course of events;

but then how are we account for dissipative structures and for living things that, for a time at least, can even write novels?

Should not this same principle of the inherent disorder of events influence the composition of novels? Is "Pacific End" to be merely a brief arrangement of unrelated ideas or should it follow a plot, a predetermined course according to a predetermined plan that exists outside the form of the novel as such and is imposed upon it by the conscious author so that when it is finished it stands there balanced improbably like just so many stones on a beach? Is the novel primarily an object or an unpredictable dialogue with an unnamed interlocutor, the future reader?

✳✳✳

But let us not remain obsessed by the novel-as-form. Novelists after all are a rare and effete breed and novels a rare effusion; let us rather speak of the larger questions of property arrangements. After all, it is still undecided whether it is in the best interests of property as such to destroy this living planet. The earth shows an uncontrollable bias towards cohabitation. To many religiously-inclined people this is the real problem with ecologists and other bleeding-heart liberals: that these insist upon promiscuous cohabitation with the soulless elementals of the earth. The prerogative to rule is the very essence of their ideas. The scope of future use must follow origin and the power to engender children is presumptively accompanied by the entitlement to control what ideas they in turn may manifest so that no judgment once rendered by competent patriarchal norms may be overturned: to do so is by its very nature an act of impertinence to the original stackers of stones.

Property from this point of view is best characterized by the right to exclude rather than to invite. Any use may inadvertently engender the disorder that was opposed and reduced to form by the initial idea that created the object in the first place. Use diminishes value because it implies that the primary artificer must remain in sole possession and control or suffer personal diminishment as a result. Only repeated affirmation of its origins makes hospitality tolerable. Rituals must constantly reaffirm their basis by returning to origins in a primal cause. What Jesus referred to familiarly as "Abba" was for minds such as that of St. Thomas Aquinas "the unmoved mover." Has something in Christianity perhaps been lost along the way?

Is woman merely an envelopment of the growing human seed so that a life process once begun must be allowed to reach its proper conclusion? Or is human life once embodied an indwelling of something that even if not pre-existent is at least self-subsistent by its very uniqueness and thus entitled to preservation? The traditional patriarchal view has in effect suspended the teleological goal of life by insisting upon a legal solution based on the mere declaration that the fetus as substance is or is not to be accorded the rights of a person. By approaching the issue in this manner the patriarchal mind, obsessed by property concepts as it is, has made abortion-on-demand a virtual certainty even when it supposedly opposes it.

By denying the role of woman except as providing an environment for the fetus the whole matter has become gender-specific and polarized. The fetus has been characterized as an invader of the womb rather than an enrichment and fulfillment of the procreative function of the woman. Who has the right to exercise control has become the essence of the argument and the answer has become a "who-question" rather than focusing upon what abortion is when considered in its essence – a termination of a unique and irreplaceable event to serve a preconceived idea. The whole issue is approached from a property perspective as opposed to a process analysis.

✶✶✶

Processes cannot be reduced to static ideas about process without distorting them – this is the essential lesson of quantum mechanics and one that stands Aristotle on his head! A novel is not a thing but a process and as such in the process of writing "Pacific End" I came to realize that it must be written so as to conform with and to confirm this essential insight.

A novel is most itself when it refuses to submit to the reduction of a pre-existing formal concept. It must possess within a dynamic orientation to the moment of its writing or be denied its own essence. In the name of what extraneous value would that denial of the novel's essence be allowed? If use diminishes value rather than enhancing it then "Pacific End" should first consult its future readership before the first word is ever written. Worse still, market research should ascertain first whether any book will be purchased along an index of probability from this commercial point of view. The contents are irrelevant if the book as an object is simply sold even if the book is never read or even opened as long as a sale has been concluded. The book as object becomes irrelevant of course as book just as a house unlived in is no longer a really a house and a country that turns people away is no longer really a country and our planet, should it become lifeless, will be no longer really the earth.

My father and I seldom argue over unimportant details you see; we always go to the center of things where our real opposition resides. If faith in God for instance is a static affirmation (his position) then it becomes mere supererogation to go on to explore that initial set of relations by tracing their relevance to our every daily action (my position).

"Why don't you go to communion?" my father asked me one day. I answered him, "Because I am still engaged in the process of defining what it is to be in communion." So it is natural in a similar fashion for a novelist to ask what a novel is in the very process of writing one.

In this approach I am part of a very old novelistic tradition from Herman Melville's allegorical memoirs to Henry Miller's fanciful self-portrayals to Jack Kerouac's efforts to turn his own life into poetic prose. Only a pedant denies another the right to call what a writer is doing a novel. The task of self-evaluation is the artist's responsibility. Who is more commendably exacting than the writer in his efforts to extend his formal resources by elaborating new modes to explore content? Is there ever content without form as a condition precedent? The content of the novel springs into being as the form is filled just as the form announces itself only as it takes shape.

Perhaps what we see emerges to be seen just in advance of our observations – divine creation seen as an ongoing event rather than a primordial one. The instrument is attuned to our ears for music to exist, the pear made sweet just before we bite into it. The novel is mere words until we discover what it seeks to convey. The senses discriminate outline from background by virtue of our intending. This inversion of our usual notions of cause and effect has much to recommend it, an anti-Newtonian correction to our assumed epistemology.

If we have immortal souls then why do we so readily allow physical reality to contain us and reduce us to itself? It is said that many saints were able to be present in two locations simultaneously. Did physical time stop in one location while the first act was performed in one place and then allowed to resume its course afterwards or was synchronicity simply irrelevant to the subjective experience of the saint who no longer even noticed that his existence had been bifurcated in order to exercise two different actions simultaneously? Perhaps reality is like so many grains of sand ready to accept the form of the child's pail. If reality itself is thus malleable then why may not the novelist devise a similar fluidity to embrace his artificial world? My father insists that to read a novel is to read about what never really happened. I answer him by saying that novels contain what happens all the time; the best of novels possess a universal relevance as proven by recognition on the part of the reader.

Of course my father raised us to adapt our perceptions to what was acceptable to him so that I was long in the habit of consulting precedents even before being trained to think like a lawyer. Like many parents my father presumes a reversionary interest on his children's lives. Disagreement is automatically construed to be an act of disrespect, a variance from the moral equivalent of Greenwich Mean Time. Only on occasion is it possible to for him to adopt an open and interrogative stance and grant that his own convictions are not universally applicable; but then to be honest I am just like him in this trait. Only my abiding curiosity prevents didacticism from hardening into a static state impervious to reformation. The wisest people learn to curtail premature judgments it seems to me and writers are not always the wisest people no matter what we believe ourselves to be.

✳✳✳

On quite another topic it is hot in the valley so I am secretly glad to be still on the coast writing "Pacific End." I am rendered harmless by virtue of my absence. The family cabin in the mountains just like Kafka's Castle exists in its unique inaccessibility and there is for me only the ever-changing sea for companionship. I prefer peace in life and a pacific end? Just at this moment there is no talk of raging against the dying light but rather a peaceful acquiescence to the demands that I absent myself from felicity for awhile by relinquishing my desire for deeper communion with those I love. It is as though I possess an innate facility to eclipse other minds, an ability that I carry like a gun about with me under an assumed second amendment guarantee, a sort of mind militia. Robert Frost questioned the wisdom of erecting walls between neighbors but they seem to be necessary in my case.

This puzzles me. I see thoughts as in most cases lacking in the quality of mental surfactants that can so readily be presumed to diminish others. I consider us all to be in a cooperative position as regards consciousness. Blind continuity becomes staccato patterns. I applaud individual sallies of assertion and view them as permissible because it is in the common interest to extend the various fields that surround us by stretching the enveloping fabric supplied by words and concepts. It is all about novelty and what can be more novel than a novel?

So again I come back to poor tortured Herman Melville who with each new novel further alienated his audience simply by virtue of being original in his thought. No doubt with each new effort he must have thought that he had finally arrived at the universal significance that his own style, an echo of sacred scripture, implied. In this hope he was always disappointed. Melville was more than a mere teller of tales, which no doubt he could have done quite well. He was engaged in plumbing unknown depths by casting the moral plumb-line ever deeper to reach the deep sediments on the ocean floor – and I alone am returned to tell thee! Is this not what the novelist always does when he is most what he intends? To press, press onward to the end even if that unique end is ill-defined and perhaps indefinable;

this is the novelist's task.

Everything is permitted to him in this pursuit, even to end his novel with a didactic historical theory as in "War and Peace" by Tolstoy. The only real unities for the novelist are those, not of time and place, but of sincerity and creativity. The point of view of the novel-writer is as wide as what he seeks to convey. In this he is like a mural painter. Each panel adds new significance to the whole. Even the story element is subservient to his widest conceptions of relevance. The latitude of the novelist is as wide as the world that he seeks to contain. This is why the novel will never be dead; it is always in process of being born like life itself!

***

Everywhere there are chance intersections of experience, strangers emerging out of their unique and unrecorded dramas to be translated to the page without my knowing the beginning or the end of their stories, why the smiles, why the tears. The most complete novel would be one about to be dispersed as its narrative-line followed a new set of characters met at each intersection; therefore the complete novel will never be written. We assemble our life stories like a collection of what were once called snap-shots, crude reproductions taken by cheap lenses and recorded on film to be dropped off at a drug-store to be developed. As memory technology has expanded so has the available data-stream with the result that a new form for the novel might seek to replicate the continuity of an image-set as recorded by the passing witness of eye and ear. Like adhesive tape with two sides the author would record both the event and the impression made upon him in marched simultaneity. The author's unique sensitivity would be the point of stability in the ongoing narrative. But why should the writer be the presumed center rather than his subjects? Does not complete omniscience demand multiple points of view?

As an example, the conversations going on next to me include these statements while their context is unknown to me, "My sister makes her noodles from scratch." "I just returned from Colorado; I liked it better than Utah." Will my subjects submit to cross-examination to fill in the gaps and explain their motivations? Then there are all the faces that I encounter each day, each with a story. My hearing is so easily confused now in a crowded room – sounds pile on sounds so that I can write amidst noise without distraction. But oh how I would wish for a sound prism to separate the conversations for later review when at leisure I could trace the hint of the stories present to their source and imagine their probable outcomes. Like Andy Warhol's film "Chelsea Girls" I would record everything without comment trusting to an implicit form to emerge out of the supposed innate logic of events. I would be like the Barbara Walters of all existence compiling cogent interviews with everyone I meet. But who is newsworthy and why and who in this vast mix and conglomeration would deem themselves worthy to be recalled by an indefinite posterity of readers? The alchemists were wrong to seek gold. The true magic elixir is the universal solvent that would bleach out and then retain the stains of experience as they happen to be later distilled into a set of essences displayed in a dark apothecary of the soul to be compounded by novelists on demand. "Ah you would have sorrow? Here is an essence gathered from a young lady of Hyeres who stood on the cliffs above Monaco gazing out to sea."

***

I have been reading lately of the fire-bombing of Dresden at the end of the Great War against Fascism. The British, jaded by the losses at Coventry and desiring revenge, had adopted a strategy of area bombing by night. Red or green marker flares would guide great streams of planes dropping incendiary bombs and fire would do the rest. There appeared to be no thought that after the war something valuable would forever have been destroyed. Victory carried all before it like a raging fire. Every war is a common loss but then that realization requires the leisure of restored civilization to affirm. The decision to wage a war means daring to lose everything of value in pursuit of some presumed greater good – but is this ever possible? What can be a greater goal than to preserve simply what has been created of grace and beauty with such effort and sacrifice? War is the ultimate triumph of the particular interest as waged against the universal good and as such always deficient. But then hesitation is fatal once armed conflicts begin - tears can blur a bomb-sight and reflection can cause the pilot to bank his plane too late. So Dresden burned on February 13th – 14th 1945. A few months later the war in Europe

But what has this fact to do with present history as recorded in "Pacific End?" Is it merely the irony that no less pacific end exists than war? Each side refuses to acquiesce, yet both suffer losses that are only deemed tolerable because victory is said to justify any sacrifice. It takes poetry to mourn the dead adequately because poetry unlike the novel is more constrained by limits, more concentrated, each word matters. What is said cannot be qualified by a further chapter containing a dramatic reversal or revaluation. Therefore the novelist is culpable in a way that a poet is not for forgetting anything of overriding importance to the whole.

But what is this elusive whole? In writing a novel the process of decision must consult something but if not a plan then what shall be consulted? Perhaps we consult a sense of innate verity that slumbers within us. "It must have been this way." Then suddenly the unique sensibility of the novelist is again front-and-center as Virginia Woolf realized – perception is always the key, just ask Mrs. Dalloway! I will teach you how to see what I write by writing!

In this way the author recreates what has always been since Lady Murasaki wrote "The Tale of Genji" but by speaking of a day in Dublin in "Ulysses" or a long and restless night as in "Finnegans Wake." The writer of the novel cannot rest until he can write finis to his task and then promptly, if he is inclined to novelty, begin his next book while the beleaguered publisher remains asking his incessant – but what is it all about? The writer must be the defense attorney in an endless lawsuit between publisher and writer – one a businessman and the other an artist. The artist says, "Look to the thing itself." The publisher says, "But will it sell ... this thing that you have rendered up to me? Why must I be the one to subsidize your next masterpiece and take your word for it that it is?"

The novelist of course answers, "Because you have been chosen."

Or perhaps the writer is in search of his own nirvana. I look out the window at the Pacific Ocean past the old street lights that give this area of town its air of fashionable nostalgia. I gaze past cedar-constructed Victoriana and I think, "I am not too cold or too hot and I have Balzac's aid to creation in endless cups of coffee at my side, so what is lacking to me or to that process in which I am engaged?" I know that when this favorable environment is not present as when a tide recedes its former state will seem inexplicable and all manner of strange detritus lie upon the now wave-bereft expanse. Crash – whisper – renewal of expectation – crash – whisper – renewal … the sea … the sea! But then the sea is always new to all but the most jaded of people. Even on that day when August was most asserting itself and an air mass born far out at sea drawn from the tropics came down upon the coast. As the afternoon advanced the sea took on that glare that seems to bleach all things bare before it. I sought refuge in the old melodies and coffee of Nye Beach. To even think of autumn that day was to think of returning to a way of life that was already dissolving not simply from memory but from that actuality that impels us to resurrect our lives out of habit and to venture forth each day. I had spent the summer trying to establish again the ability to leave things behind, to reach beyond them to rediscover old habits and capacities. We carry within us a repertoire of our former selves, many of which have perished, not through fulfillment but from long neglect. They carry with them our former cherished projects and imagined landscapes of desire. I hoped to find in them the life that I had not yet dared to live before it was too late.

✷✷✷

The monotone of the sea provided the still basal rhythm of time, not time as remembered, but as an irreplaceable dimension and resource for anything to happen at all. Time not of pointless regrets but time as it is in the mornings on the coast when the day will never know the later harsh glare of afternoon. How wonderful if death is only a short night of the body before dawn! Lately, as I observe the aged, I can see more clearly how the piled memories can so oppress the spirit that some sort of eclipse of consciousness is essential if only to prevent the ache produced by the desire to remedy all of the irremediable mistakes we have made. The soul must be provided with a healing of the wounded integuments of its own abilities. The wonder is not that we perish at last but that as weary as we often appear that we have survived this long.

Yet what is a mere sixty or seventy year allotment when the span that they provide is laid against the measure provided by history? The span of our influence is so short that it is only the constant influx of the young among us that prevents everything from dissolving into a stagnant quagmire of what has already been. The novel as a world within worlds must similarly be self-renewing if it is to partake of life and fulfill its promise as an art-form. This inner impulse is what drives the author to create even while he is confined to what he has already concluded about life. Yet his text must be permeable to the demands of current experience so that nothing is missed.

Proust understood this effort to preserve the richness of what had already been, but he recalled the past with such completeness that it was as though it was still occurring and yet to be encountered once again but with the eyes of all of the experience he had collectively assimilated during all the days previous to the actual composition of his text. The result of this process is not static but rather a preserved encounter between the reader and the writer. Its very anonymity is a prerequisite for the novel's scrupulous honesty even though clothed in the sordid garb of fiction. I say sordid because words and phrases are blunted by familiar usage by those who are not novelists.

Perhaps this was why Henry James sought to create exact definition in narrative by a refinement that seems affected, whereas what was really involved was the desperation to achieve a meaning beyond meaning, to stretch perception into forms adequate to the subject matter that he was trying to grasp. To evolve new capacities for new visions is the order of the day for one who would pursue novelty in the novel. The novelist seeks to exhaust his own resources as a final proof of his artistic integrity, the trust that he bears.

Or does he flatter himself? Who has appointed the novelist to be the arbiter of all of human experience? Self-anointed he proceeds as though only as a writer does anyone really live. The rest of humanity is content to simply encounter the days or the nights and perhaps recall certain things fondly over a fireside and to relinquish life's sorrows with good grace. No novelist worthy of the name aspires to anything less than immortality – this is why much that passes as fiction is not really a novel but a memoir in disguise. The form must be constantly recreated just as science never ceases in its pursuit of truth.

But what is the truth to a novelist? Every discipline has some principle of verification once the problem or question presented is adequately defined. The novelist however dealing as he must in human truths spends most of his efforts not on finding answers but in defining the questions or even the possibility of questions. To be didactic is considered to be an error, at least in the sense of good manners to the reader. We expect a certain level of objectivity from the novelist. His characters must be allowed to unfold according to their own inner dynamics rather than being led about by a rope. The author must, no matter how omniscient he may be, stay concealed behind the curtain of his narrative, unless his narrative is in the first person and even then he must not overstep the bounds of his assumed characterization. The character is not meant to be co-extensive with the novelist even if the novel is seemingly overtly autobiographical. We demand artifice if not artificiality in our authors or else where is the art in the composition?

Of course the naturalists such as Emile Zola claim to proceed as if prior to composition or while writing they had subjected their own assertions to some type of scientific inquiry and filtered out their own prejudices. The naturalist refuses to gratify a reader's false hopes that affairs will turn out better than they should. A cold stoicism and a preference for sordid subject matter characterize this school of novelistic theory. Of course we must take the author's word for it that his own jaded views have not biased his presentation every bit as much as those of the lover of romance. A romantic temperament though is not inconsistent with tragedy; lack of realism does not diminish the horror in the works of Hawthorne and Kafka; these worlds are grimmer than those of Zola, Dreiser, or Norris ever thought of being. For the novelist form not only precedes subject; it is itself the most essential element of the novel's expressive force. The novelist like the poet portrays a world by verbal means and that world is his own. I will go so far as to say that in encountering the novelist at work the human community develops to new levels its cognitive and emotional capacities. But perhaps this is mere vanity – to treat the novelist as though he or she is like the founder of a new religion rather than being just yesterday's idea of an entertainer, a Chaplin or a Jolson.

Thoughts such as these obsess the writers of novels as they go about doing what they do. We are formed by what others have done before us every bit as much as scientists are. Even if we only wrote for each other as poets so often do, we require some external framework provided by critical theory to guide our faltering steps. All of this leaves out the world of course with its vast and unending tutelage. Novelists are meant to look outward at the non-interpreted stream of events to provide them with nutrients and raw material for later digestion and assimilation into form. I say assimilation because the text of a novel is not mere transcription. Once the novel exists it must be interpreted largely by applying standards that are not only organic to it as an art form but unique to each individual work. This is the principle of integrity that good artistic works must manifest: a unique display of order, evidence of selection, and non-randomness – anything else is not a novel but a mere stream of data.

***

Such were my thoughts as I pursued the phantom goal of "Pacific End" across the late summer days of the year 2016. I knew that a return was inevitable to the life that I had placed on hold when she left. I would leave the coast soon with the hope and dread that I had not forgotten (did I ever possess it) how to start again from, not scratch, but at least from a new set of presuppositions. The advantage of a new place is that it might be possible to appear radically different there than one has been: more beautiful, competent, or expressive, or so at least I told myself. This ongoing narrative of our lives is so apt to be commandeered by scripts, not our own but ones practiced and grooved into our days and nights. We pull loose only with the greatest difficulty. We carry our cages about with us. New origins demand new seed which we cannot always provide. This realization led me to desire to step aside from the usual authorial attitude and to take dictation from events themselves as they unfolded from chance meetings, to depend not merely on the kindness of strangers but upon their largess in simply existing as a background to my own solitary consciousness.

Does our own skin really separate us from others or are we all part of a larger organism not merely mystically speaking but in actual fact? The human molecular consciousness had begun to feel to me as unnatural. Why imagine that the light that illumined events had only a single source in the beam of my own focal attention? I was unconsciously seeking a verbal equivalent of the panorama presented by the many types of cross-hatching of individual intentions. I was seeking a correlation co-efficient to the stream of events only small facets of which were clearly presented to my conscious view. Who were all of these people? Why did I suddenly feel that they were not strangers to me at all? A few words were adequate to enter into relation with them. It was as though the ocean's presence as the background of my days and the vastness of the mountains where I had sought to reconnect with my father provided a new point of relation to all that I observed so that we sailed together on the frail barque of earth, a common crew. Or was this conviction merely evidence of my loneliness, my sense that I would remain always exiled as so many novelists are simply by virtue of our choice of profession? This need to manifest an inner world is not universally shared or the bookshelves would be even more overburdened than they already are with contenders for the rarified attention of readers in a digital age. Perhaps having said so much I should already begin to wind this whole thing up and make a gentle end of what has been from its incipiency a foolish project. For one thing I am drinking too much coffee. It has occurred to me as well that I am somewhat deficient in that delicate balance between dialogue, narration, and commentary out of which every novel is made.

"Talk for me! Tell me your secrets! Curious readers want to know!"

But the sea mist came in close today and the water ended at the beach just down the street just as my own penetration of necessity stopped at the doors of the perceptions of other people just as unique as I am and not existing in a human equivalent of a colloidal suspension or solution to be abstracted at will by me. People exist primarily in social units and not as individuals, I began to conclude. Social bonds are often cemented by a dog or children. Isolation began more than ever before to seem unnatural to me and I began to understand the omnipresent habit of texting in the youth of today – the need for virtually constant connectivity. Perhaps I and many like me have been generationally deprived: "What are you talking about for so long on the phone? Don't you have some studying to do?" Or as my father so often puts it, "My father very seldom saw his own family." Isolation exalted as the supreme virtue! As she who must not be named put it, "Don't contact me again." I had grown accustomed through the years to these periodic dismissals, a favored mode of communication that had been repeated so often (and always obeyed by me) that it could function as a screen-saver scrolling out magnificently in many-colored fonts.

Why must those whom I love be at such variance with my own deepest convictions? Or does that very hunger that besets novelists awaken resistance in those who feel the universal desire for inquiry that we manifest?

"You who would embrace all things might crush me if I allowed you too close to that small secretive core of pain that is my life – partial, inarticulate, and unknown even to me."

My mentors Thomas Mann, Herman Broch, Robert Musil, and Herman Hesse – those pioneers of the inexpressible - they would understand. Is it merely accidental that my favorite writers are all German or is it true that ancestral diseases of the soul may exist? Perhaps it is this desire to probe the inexpressible that is present from Kant to Nietzsche that I share. In any case I desire to be a practitioner of what may be called "the philosophical novel" as being more congenial to my own ways of thinking and the issues that I have most wanted to explore. This explains the unique tone and message of "Pacific End."

***

The ocean is a natural place to be philosophical and to gather old stained editions of the classics at bargain prices, later to stack them on the rocks off of the tidal nook at Yachats where my father once bought property back in the nineties. It was a time when my excitement about the coast for a short time became his enthusiasm. It was nice to know that my passion for the sea could so enhance his life, because it had always been his interests that had fired my own. He used to pore over pictures taken along the old historic beach trail and make plans to build a house there. But more it was always primarily a matter of playing the real-estate buying game: to subdivide and sell at a profit; then the part that remains you get for free. Each of the years when our phantom dwelling existed only in the mind was just that many lost memories and who can place a price on happy memories? Meanwhile each year brought new commitments and the family dispersed like oil dropped into water. It makes rainbows at first and then resolves itself into a uniform stain, one indistinguishable from the water of which it is a part.

I often make the mistake of too much retrospection, I see now. The family of our youth is already passing into new families each to be formed as we meet and have children of our own. My generation was not taught the arts of swift adaptation and the rejection of cant. We had always been told that as Americans we were supremely lucky and that we were living on the very summit of human progress. Doubting was not simply unpatriotic; it was an act of temerity verging on the absurd. There would always be plenty of room to dream and time to realize those dreams in word and action – until suddenly there wasn't.

No one told us of the backward eddies that could lead the stream of our lives into brackish backwaters, reed-choked and stagnant. It takes a willingness to make mistakes in order to test reality and we had been taught that America never retraces its steps but charges forward always to new triumphs, America as the self-anointed vanguard of the human race. So it was that we sold the property in Yachats to an expansive new development made up of people who knew that in a human life too much delay is fatal.

Dreams have the shortest shelf-life of all. It takes remarkable daring to live while the blood is free and leaping in our arteries and our veins though blue are still almost invisible below the still taut skin of youth just as it takes repeated disappointments to know the full price exacted by desire denied. But these are thoughts for a misty day, one when the far horizon shrinks and only the near salt-wrack of torn-up kelp litters the shore.

The previous night I had spent hours at a place called Circe's on the old bay-front watching the dancers. It is one of those buildings with high ceilings and old timber just waiting for that infusion of new money that turns the actual into the phony-picturesque. It takes a little seediness for anything to be real, some thirty-year-old furniture and some old fish-packing plants to season the night with the wet stench of fish and diesel. Sidewalks should be cracked and old calendars should still hang above antiquated cash-registers. There are too few of these places remaining in America today but now and then you can still find them along the coast of Oregon where people still struggle to get through the long winters by relying on each other.

I knew at once that I had found a place congenial to my task of review and recognition, the inventory proper to a sixth decade of life. The light-show of many shapes and colors, the old songs from the golden eighties mixed with new ones, the late-night infusion of tall blond girls and their escorts to season the regulars; all of these fascinated me. To see people happy in the moment, content to be young and vital but not encased in pointless dramas is always a pleasure. Permission to simply be: what greater gift can be given us by those who were both our protectors and the source of our later doubts? To quench expressed delight because it is inconvenient ... how many of our neuroses stem from this source? This realization alone forces us to travel the old roads looking for what might have been, preparing to meet or to find a pacific end. There it was that phrase again that has haunted me since I opened the old biography of Thomas Wolfe and read of the book that he did not live to write: "To make an end, to rust unburnished, not to shine in use" from Tennyson's poem, "Ulysses" or with Robert Frost to lament the end of a love or a season. Poets do not relish terminations, nor do novelists. The price of pacification is the acceptance of fate, of the unalterable past or at least to forgive our own follies and sins. Pope Francis has proclaimed this year as a Jubilee of Divine Mercy, so to show a little mercy to me today may not be amiss.

∗∗∗

I have yet to resolve on the required period that must supervene before a current observation may be legitimately granted the patina of reminiscence. We generally assume that time gives perspective to events rather than simply recalling their eroded skeletons. The novelist may be granted some latitude in this regard because the writer knows that he must write now even in the midst of the confusion of living or risk being cut off from the flow of words that sustains him. To delay is to risk losing that novelty of expression that is his only claim to a readership because if what he writes has already been said then of what use is repetition? Risk is of the essence of the game and game it is for who will maintain that any novel is essential in a print-glutted world? The sheer weight of written matter is oppressive and now that vast quantities of data may be indefinitely retained on disks and drives the oppressive factor is becoming exponential. For those who still think in terms of the tactile embrace that comes with holding a book the novel can still be grasped in the intimate way that formerly was inseparable from the book-reading experience. By creating a world existing between covers the novelist seeks that dignity that was formerly made tactile by holding a book rather than a storage device that can recall any amount of data on demand. For the first time convenience of access can alter an art form in its very essence by changing the framing media by which it is preserved and transmitted. Perhaps objects must impose various external costs and inconveniences of access if they are to be properly valued. A novel according to this mode of thought should have a coffee-stained cover and wrinkled pages as testimony to its former encounters with a reader. The freedom to mar its face by underlining and by tears, though the writer will not benefit directly, will in some spiritual way alter the nature of the reading experience. The novel is sentient in some mysterious way that only the novelist can grasp as he reaches outwards into other minds that in the act of the author's writing of the novel remained only a distant encounter. By reflecting back upon itself even while engaged in reflecting upon the world of its possibilities the novel becomes a self-existing and self-realizing human enterprise and by doing so ensures its ultimate value and chances of survival.

Turning from the novel to the one who writes it we encounter that act of faith that narrators can both disclose and veil a select realm of experience in the novel. Perhaps we do not so much read a novel then as an object but rather encounter the dance of the seven veils of the novelist. If so then the persona becomes the focus of interest and it is the authentic voice of the author that the critic pursues and not his projected images. Taken to an extreme this approach to the novel proposes that the author merely endorses his works from a detached position like a trademarked perfume or designer of a pair of jeans.

However profitable this approach may be for criticism the impression from the immediate reader's point of view must be that the writer has not suffered enough as penance for this duplicity. It is insufficient to simply say by so-and-so in a long chain of similar works. To write books and to profit as a result involves a certain betrayal of trust. We expect the novelist to suffer for his art. Novels must be written one-at-a-time and be experienced for that very reason as self-contained, discrete, and even insular. A sentiment analogous to the phrase "until death us do us part" freezes the relation between novelist and his creation so that divorce or repudiation or any lack of sincerity by the author is seen as a betrayal. We view novelists as glamorous figures so that to read their biographies is a tantalizing glimpse behind the scenes. Like other celebrities we wonder where they lived when they wrote such and such a novel. We seek out influences in their life-circumstances. We assign characters to their real-life models, always forgetting that the true writer of novels thinks in a synthetic fashion that moulds and merges whatever pre-existing material may be at hand. So much depends upon the tonal quality of prose. Facts never appear divorced of the context that is the true gift of the novelist – to shade and to portray. Manner and expression is everything. Nothing is true except within that world that the novelist has made his own in the act of writing. This is why the novel is analogous to a symphony and why as a musician the novelist must be so regarded. This is more though than a critical stance, it is a pre-requisite to appreciating the unique experience that a novel affords.

***

I wrote the passage above while located a short-distance away from where the sea pursued its usual activity and a smell of disinfectant arose from the floor of the coffee-house where I had been forming these thoughts. I was plunged from the worlds of reminiscence and from theory back into actuality, the place where the novel is said to reside, and I wondered how best to write "Pacific End."

I found a similar indisposition regarding my travels. As the summer waned I discovered that I was having trouble finding a way to return, to go home again. The definition of home is as variable as that of defining the parameters of the novel. Is boredom and imprisonment the price that security exacts in both? To experiment with new expectations and forms is to risk estrangement from readers accustomed to more usual narrative voices. This very condition of estrangement has become the subject of the post-modern novel.

These ideas can be traced back to the novels of Andre Gide and even to Knut Hamsun's novel, "Mysteries." Their effect upon the blurring of identity in the protagonist – the question of whether it is even possible to define a point of view in a character, one lacks a stable sense of self, is where the post-modern novel begins. If the novel is deprived of the assurance derived from its prescriptive or at the very least its indicative character, then the reader is plunged into a world without metrics for progress or poles for orientation. In such a world one truly cannot go home again. History likewise as an orderly sequence comes to a screeching halt and the parameters of discourse shrink into the domain of isolated perceptions. The novelist then can only speak of what is happening now. A traditional sense of plot requires not simply orderly succession but evolution towards a morally consistent point of view or at least a credible conclusion. The post-modern novel is one without stable plot or character – can it be long before such novels are even lacking in outward events thus resembling lyrical poetry? Events in novels and in life share the integrity of perception. But what if perceptions are broken into fragments, mere sensations unconnected with the will to either pursue them or to moderate them in some way? Can such an invertebrate existence still be seen as human? To live in an age of diminished faith is to lose not merely expectations but aspirations as well.

This is the world as portrayed in T.S. Eliot's "Four Quartets," a world beyond wastelands because even the detritus of ruins retain a human character. Decomposition as an act is perfected when the original character of the decomposing object has been lost and only physical elements remain. From this point of view the final goal of physics, to unite all forces into one is profoundly decadent. Life in contrast thrives on ornamentation and elaboration into new forms, to maximize ideas by embodying them in a definite but limited form.

Complexity plus limitation: there we have the form for a truly living literature, one that does not aspire to finality but to the provisional while still believing in the significance of the act of writing. Faith is a prerequisite not merely for salvation then but for life itself. To act is to be plunged into time from the glorious stasis of the merely provisional. That which visual art freezes into graphic or sculptural form the verbal art of the novelist sets free again by the act of verbal description. Here again the novelist is akin to the musician because any successive variation is tone or rhythm suggests music in some form.

***

But to return to my bald statement of the problem in real life: I did not know how to go home for fear that what I had left had already been reduced into the static perceptions of my habitual way of regarding things there and that the changes that I had encountered this summer would alternately make it either impossible to find the self that I had left there or worse still that returning I would be encased into a set of expectations that were no longer attainable. The fear that I felt then was that home would either be entirely familiar to me or so altered as to have put to death forever what I had known and could never hope to find again.

To glimpse the variety of life in all of its fullness was to sense the inadequacy of any verbal formula to contain it. Perhaps the filter of our prejudices is essential after all if only to keep from running after each potential candidate for our affections. Universal love must remain abstract or it will lead to madness as it attempts to attach itself to every passing drama as an intrusive extra to the cast. The sheer language of flesh is such that its every configuration when beauty is present compels first arrested attention and then a desire to in some measure incorporate its majesty in a phrase. Perhaps erotomania as it was once called is more widespread than we imagine and only curtailed by that sense of blessed estrangement of which the moderns so often complain. Take this away and we would fall into each other's arms with an alacrity that would bring all everyday traffic to a standstill. Perhaps the ravages of age are serviceable in the same way that insulation is to a wire, to prevent the constant short-circuiting of the elemental currents of human affection. If so then our nastiness to each other similarly keeps us from yielding to importunate desires that might override any partial allegiances to mere ideology or to mundane loyalties.

The human race desires unity, of that there can be no doubt. This very universality of our affections is embodied in the body in a way that only Walt Whitman appeared to grasp. The stale mantra of the sixties, "Make love not war," was for all of its banality the statement of this most fundamental of all observations. It is as though our bodies rebel at severance or as if as Schopenhauer observed our bodies are pressed forward towards the realization of new life by the vast future throng of the not-yet-conceived human race. The very pressure that rushes the old into death is not their own obsolescence but the current of life itself demanding renewal by pushing aside those who can no longer contribute offspring. Against this tide the novelist like a rock in a stream seeks to erect something permanent to contain the flow as it passes or to at least to deflect the water as it rushes by. The novel provides a net, a web to capture events as they rush by, quickly, all too quickly.

***

The dull regionalism present in the novels of Thomas Hardy represents the antithesis of this movement towards universal affinity. Hardy is the representative of pointless disappointment. "This is evil," he seems to say, "That even when we seek in one person to sum up the whole so that in our union all others will be known as well, we fail." The sin of idolatry is that by isolating God into a discrete image we distort God's triune nature. Only God so infuses the Trinity with divine unity of substance that no such reduction is possible. We as contingent creatures cannot achieve that perfect union that in seek in to find in mutual self-regard – to do so would stifle charity by our vain aspiration to be like God knowing good and evil. Instead we have been shattered into a degree of multiplicity that frustrates our desire to reassemble Eden from its fragments, the same now trodden into the mire of history.

The novelist desires to make peace out of the welter of events and finds that he can only record them. He too is a victim of history. In all of his exalted pride the truly novel work escapes him and he finds that what he seeks to do has already been done before. His reach exceeds his grasp. So in despair he returns to the word itself and becomes convoluted in his own text as though he would weave a robe of many colors or alternately he lays his pen aside and refuses to write as he pursues more experience. Each new meeting may revise his views. Each new form creates a new force to contain his would-be expression. It was this realization that began to provide me with a clue to what would be a pacific end ... to realize that I had at least defined the problem in writing "Pacific End."

***

It was the same problem as that raised by the manner in which the sun races across the sky and the water turns from the gold of morning to the hard silver sheen of late-afternoon so that the human gaze can barely tolerate it. It was then that I would seek out some place to write of what I had observed in the course of the day, knowing all the while that the summer days could not last –

that like the artist in Thomas Mann's, "Death in Venice," I should soon have to realize the limitations of what can be captured and enjoyed because the truly beautiful must remain inaccessible, refined into idea and image.

To remain always in a state of possibility, to be a man without established qualities as Robert Musil sought to express it, this is the quintessential task of the artist if he would be true to his subject, the world of the21st century. He must even forget that he is writing, composing, or painting. He must forget the pen or brush in his hands. He must leave the piano keys untouched by actual music for fear that mere sound will be inadequate to express the idea or to embody the image, that Plato-like he exists in a world of shadows. To be a contemporary artist is lose one's self, to die in homage to a beauty or a truth that exists somewhere else in that realm where eternity alone is present and this world possesses not even the fragile logic of a dream.

✳✳✳

It is the sheer harshness of reality on the Pacific Coast as represented by wave upon rock that reduces thought and expression to stray and wary electrical stimuli between cells in a brain that resembles nothing so much as a timid mollusk in its shell. The drive to externalize thought into form whether it be through architecture or by writing novels is one and the same impulse – to seize eternity by the tail before the inevitable forces of dispersal take hold and the cellular mass that has defined us seizes and then ceases and fades away into the dark immobility and silence that is death. So overwhelming though is the sense of being alive here and so insistent is the sheer act of perception, particularly when it takes the form of light leaping from a jade or azure sea, that death is an unimaginable concept. The disproportion is simply too great between a present ability to see and a future inevitable fate of not-seeing.

Can the mere dimension of time make such a difference in our status before the physical world? Is death a consequence of location at a particular point in time when it we might have stood in abeyance? Just as the ruins of Dresden could not be reassembled in space on the day after the bombing, so a dead body cannot recover what it was in that distant era of our youth before the erosion caused by the succession of dividing cells falls into place and the body perishes? It is this realization that drives the fluid through the flower and causes the leaves to unfold to grasp the sun even as the novelist grasps at words and the fleeting images that precede thought to record them forever in the evanescent medium of the printed word.

To any text there must be a point of entry, at least so my architect friend has advised me. Even a spider web must be anchored at three or more places to resist the wind that would otherwise collapse even a two-dimensional web. How many points of reference then must the novelist provide to the reader in all fairness? Must the author emerge from hiding even if the author is deliberately and by design enacting a verbal version of the strip-tease show of former days when sex could be enhanced by the magic of partial revelation in space and by the inevitable delay of promises deferred?

"Nothing so destroys interest as total availability of gratification in sex or in literature," I tell him. The tension of poetry for instance is supplied by its ambiguities, by its indefinite references, by the way that words reach toward meaning and fail to encompass a subject. Perfect perspective and total accuracy belie the shading of form into background in painting.

Things must remain things and our thoughts about them remain personal and tangential just as the light on the waves must be both absorbed by the water and still glance off of them to reveal the fullness that even our short visual spectrum demands of light. I try and tell him that I am seeking a new density to expression in the novel by a statement that reveals what it is doing even as it proceeds to do so in what must be a mere preliminary sketch of the not-yet-existing-novel that will become "Pacific End."

Does anything really exist prior to our perception of it and if it does how will we ever know? The thoughts of Hume and Kant regarding the thing-in-itself have yet to be translated adequately into the theory of the novel. To push the limits of prior expression is to be novel in a world that takes pride above all else in what might be called a practical banality: "I have no time to read novels." Novels like the brief tenure of fashion-shows or like chalk-drawings on the pavement may soon exist to be washed away by rain at the end of the day. We currently live in the age of the continuous event stream and the novelist must recognize this if he is to achieve verisimilitude. He must criticize what he does even as he does it.

I try and explain this to my architect friend over the poor connection of a cell-phone line. We end by my assuring him that he has provided the next day's subject matter for my novel.

✳✳✳

The gulls are surfing the September winds today and the mists of the last days have cleared away. I keep putting off my departure – a few days more of summer, just a few, etched like a dentist's tool into slate, scratch, scratch, scratch. Who will I meet today wandering along the beach amongst the sea-wrack and detritus thrown up by the sea? Each night the sand is piled higher and familiar rocks are buried so that I must seek new places on the beach to rest my head when I pull my hat over my eyes to sleep. To lie among the rubble of my past lives by this vast insentient mother who possesses time in such abundance that she can afford to allow species to perish while she rolls over once again slowly in her eternal sleep. There is time for the whales to evolve on land and then return to the sea, time for their nostrils to migrate to the top of their heads, for their hands to become flippers, for their mouths to become sieves.

Time – time – time ... the waves beating all through the night while I sleep... Then to return to daylight as though the world was newly created while I slept like a present for a child wrapped by a solicitous parent and left waiting by the child's bed to be discovered when it wakes. All of this sense of expectancy I would compress into my book so that when the time came to end it I would know that I had fulfilled Thomas Wolfe's dream, not in the way that he would have written it, but as he might have done if he had lived long enough to doubt that what he was doing even mattered in a world that has lost its abiding myths, those former guideposts to the human mind if it would remain human.

The novelist desires above all else to remain human. The novelist possesses one job that cannot be outsourced or reduced to robotic motion-study. The fight against compression and reductionism is the battle of our age. We each desire to stand out from the mass. "This set of traits and preferences and events is me! Oh and I have opinions too so I Twitter. I am part of the flow, a molecule maybe, but still part of the river of these fleeting days, of Walter Pater's "frost and sun;" so do we each effectively declaim as we send our texts and voices out into the all-encompassing ether.

***

And the sands gather, blown along the September strand, already summer lies buried and I must return to home while still wondering if it exists with any semblance to what I left behind to gather material for a novel in May. My title like a refrain or like the slow and incessant beat of the sea follows me everywhere I go. The year 2016 begins to dissolve into history just as 1916 did when the great powers were at war and a generation was dying in the trenches. Will we soon have a wall along the border to Mexico and elect our first billionaire President or will a woman hold office and her husband explore a new gender-role to a President? History is no doubt present in this year, at least in America.

It is a good time to write as I am doing here because something is definitely ending and I am after all on the ocean seeking in its depths and behavior for some vital impulse to drive a narrative that refuses to have any other subject than its own composition. Perhaps it is an elegy to an age that I am writing or to the significance of writing at all. Poor novelists, lost ones of a dying art-form, ever reaching towards a synthesis – to tell life like it really is. They say that novelists are self-involved and vain. The novelist has infinite options and none at all because who reads serious novels anymore? We are the Max von Stroheim's of the age creating works of art for those little people out there in the dark, hoping that they are still there just being quiet or just waiting for someone who understands them in their hitherto uncelebrated lives: silent, isolated, and afraid.

***

Nature has seen to it that peach-blossom pulchritude is not a rarity. From their pouty lips to their elevated brows and waving lashes, from willow-bough bodies to voluptuous curves each and all have pranced and paced past me this summer without diminishing the low-grade fever of sorrow that her absence has entailed. The only comfort for me now is that I refused her nothing, bowed to her convictions, confirmed her need to write a saga that must include abandonment as its central theme, and allowed her to say once again that her life of perennial suspicion and mistrust was justified.

✶✶✶

There were consolations though in the summer days. As the days passed experience began to pile upon experience for me and insight, that most elusive of qualities, came to me like the endless trains of sea waves breaking on Cyclops Head. I began to hear stories and to observe people with the attention that only a sense of personal exile can make possible. It began to occur to me that, surprising as this sounds, I was not the only lonely person in the world. All around me were people living out their own individual dramas and losses, many with coping skills and talents far less than my own. Youth and beauty were no guarantee of happiness and age was no indicator that the springs of the life-force were drying up.

There seemed to be subtle and invisible silken strands that united the people that fell about me like snowflakes or like the sea-spume trapped in Boiler Bay. The edgy borders of city life began to dissolve, past and future tenses flowed together just as the fresh and salt waters mingle at Alsea Bay down by Waldport. Connections multiplied and mingled until all things began to join and waver; as various eddies of experience form. Did that happen to me or do I merely recall a vivid story as I walk among the blowing sands wondering, "Shall I stay or shall I go?"

✶✶✶

Thomas Wolfe was always obsessed by the themes of wandering and return. Exile from a beloved homeland is perhaps the oldest font of myth. We drive the young forth to strange lands whether prodigal sons or wayward daughters. Both alike may wake up wondering if the husks of dry experience have been worth their wandering. To prematurely exile the young while they still carry about with them all of the myths and fairy tales that are the legacy of what the prior generation wishes to believe is an act of cruelty. The powers of resistance are too weak. A single chance meeting may dislodge the course of a young life. For me it was a chance comment of my father's as we ate at Art Louie's Chinese Restaurant one winter night with my family.

"Do you know that priest over there?"

I looked over casually and said, "You know, I think that is Father T----."

And from that single incident came later endless meetings and college-classes and two years among the Jesuits as a novice followed by the great emptiness that ensues when a vocation is partially pursued or prematurely ended. Timing is everything. I both entered and left the novitiate too early, leaving something of myself perennially behind. We leave traces of ourselves in every relationship, traces that cannot be purged by any mere willful act of later reparation.

✷✷✷

"Do not contact me again! This time I mean it."

But she who cannot be named had already begun leaving me when we first walked out together that spring and summer ten years ago; leaving is her métier. She has polished and refined betrayal like a Roman spear; she the empress on the throne of Caligula gazing down at the contenders in the forum, the woeful gladiators who would prove to her their devotion to the spectacle and the glory of her private empire of regret. To confirm or to deny is unnecessary at this point because the theme once realized merely repeats itself. New material is gathered to reflect an old story. Myth works because it repeats itself carried along by its own weight of meaning like a glacier pushing through a valley.

So I turned from my own pain to the anguish of Thomas Wolfe's last days on his back day after day in Seattle waiting for his lungs to clear so that he could return to New York and his new editor, Ed Aswell. The accusations of formless autobiography had wounded him with the critical accusations that his works were as much due to the editorial skills of Max Perkins as to his own mountain-hewed native genius. But he was tired now, dead-tired and he had an unnamed hunch, so he wrote to Max that something had spoken to him in the night, the very night that was gathering thicker around him every day. He might die; he the great gargantuan author sifting all experience like a baleen whale was failing. So they shipped him back to Johns Hopkins where they diagnosed inoperable tubercular lesions of the brain. No trip to a magic mountain ala Hans Castorp for him; no Germanic transcendence into the wisdom of an era as embodied in the Great War of 1914-1918.

Thomas Wolfe never lived to see what the Nazi menace would inflict. He saw it coming though. He felt it with that unique sensitivity that was his. His theme was more than simply his endless hunger to somehow taste all of human experience and to reduce it to print. Had he lived would he have known an old age in a cork-lined room like Proust? Record! Record! Let nothing escape! Like all authors he waged his undying war with time. There is for such as us no way to a pacific end.

***

In Dover before I left Europe for home, oh so many years ago now, I was reading the letters of Dylan Thomas and a biography of Virginia Woolf. Already "Pacific End" was foreshadowed. But I had so little experience then and what I had was so limited by categories not of my making. Obligations ensued when I returned to America; a life happened. Suddenly I found myself awake at sixty-four with a certainty or perhaps a hunch that like Thomas Wolfe the seasons of my life were well advanced like the advent of evenings in Newport that summer when the sun reaches a degree of declivity that informs the beachcomber that only a spare hour remains of daylight. The sea changes color from blinding silver to a dark teal and the color migrates from the waves to the sky where a symphony of orange and gold or red and amber vie for supremacy along the horizon. People gather then melded together in one common regard of sea and sky, the wind rises as if in regret, and the Yaquina lighthouse sends its eternal warning far out to sea. The wind that accompanies sunset blows toward it where it stands on its advanced position at the end of the great finger of land that separates two great sweeping beaches. I began to write my novel as though by its own repetitions so akin to the rhythm of wave and tide I could catch something of the summer that was dissolving about me even as I wrote into the September days.

I now only dared to make commitments to a future that extended no further than the day. My life divided itself involuntarily into discrete segments – no theme or plan or continuity existed beyond the mere need to assemble incidents that would otherwise join the huge cacophony of similar incidents accumulated over some sixty years of recorded thought encoded somewhere in my particular brain. I tried to turn the searchlight of self-regard outwards toward the novel form itself and to the never-ceasing welter of "material" that a novelist might seek to turn into his particular production. I dreamed of a mural-like novel that would tell a story from discordant elements united only by the canvass upon which they were recorded. My goal was not to distort through conformity to any pre-existing idea. Could there be such a thing I wondered as organic form emerging by itself from chance events, just so many throws of the dice on a green-felt board? Why should all of this incident and motivation remain unrecorded? How does a writer return to the thing itself with minimal modification? How to escape the personal until it sinks like the lemon-yellow sun illumining the sea? I desired to be like that after-glow that keeps darkness at bay by the soft pink reminiscence that still glows along the knife-edge of the horizon while the sun proceeds towards China?

***

Many critics believe that the novelist should explore character in depth or portray a society or idea in all of its many dimensions rather than to merely explore impressions. Traditionally the novelist is allowed scope to achieve these goals and in this scope his production differs from that of the writers of novellas or short stories. These latter achieve their effects by intensity and concentration while the novelist is granted a wider canvass so as to attain completion of ideas or conceptions. The upper limit is not specified but novels as short as Flaubert's "November" are rare while Tolstoy's, "War and Peace" are treading the upper limits of the form.

Beyond these limits great latitude is granted the author to explore or to exploit depending upon the reader's patience. But what if character itself is an illusion? What if we recreate ourselves daily to match our habits and environments? Might it not be possible to choose a new life by main force? Why are we bound to this set script that we have been living?

Nicholas II of Russia tried to live up to his wife's idea of what a Tsar should be and provoked a revolution as a result. He would have been happier as a gardener on one of his estates.

"They must fear you," she said. "They are like children; they need a strong Tsar. I will be behind you. I adore you. Our friend, Father Gregory blesses you."

How could such a pathetic little domestic drama lead to the deaths of millions after the Tsar and all of his family were killed? Character is a fulcrum if placed in such a central position by fate. Does "Pacific End" have characters in this sense – perhaps this father who appears now and again out of the shadows or perhaps she who cannot be named?

***

My father talks now of moving to Maui; "You only live once," he says, always in pursuit of a moving frontier. To end life on an island with an ocean on all sides would be one way to hold invaders at bay. "I am a loner" he says, "I value my solitude." Perhaps he married too soon.

"Somewhere there is an unlived life here," the novelist says to himself, "Else why this need to maintain separation with such vigilance?"

The omniscient author desires connection beyond all else – to penetrate all secrets and to leave a record while she who cannot be named desires most to be everything to someone; to be a mermaid and to cut-off the diver's air supply. She must breathe for him or he will drown. To leave her is to die. Her lover must be perfect in all respects except in this one regard; he must not be able to live without her.

Of course such massive dependency is itself a flaw and would thus probably result in his being cast off fathoms deep to sink down into the shadowy abyss of the darkest canyons beneath the waves. She who cannot be named is not aware of this paradox in her character. She sees herself as abandoned and nurses her anger and pain as she prowls about like a shark for her ideal lover. "I want everything or I want nothing;" this is the eternal dialectic of her actions; is asking everything from just one little person not really the humblest of demands to make upon life? Her dream is to wind her lover up in a web of total knowledge and control and then to brood over the struggling form saying with satisfaction over and over, "There now, there now."

In just such forms is character revealed; the rest is mere incident, one more example of the pattern. Surely the novel should seek to escape this very intensity to break "the surly bonds of earth" whatever that means. We shoot frail bodies into space in inadequate contraptions and then try and impose meaning after the fact. The art of public relations always demands a good story.

✳✳✳

So in September 2016 with the Dow industrial average at over 18,000 we wait for the November narrative to begin – Trump or Hillary. Doesn't she have a last name or is using the name Clinton a reminder, "Been there, done that." What is the state of the union in 2016?

Give the Russians back their forty million dead and who can say where they would be? As for the Chinese, a loss of forty million dead between 1959 and 1961 was a mere drop in the bucket – a little glitch in Chairman Mao's long march toward the perfect Asian state - people used as humus for the soil to enrich the land.

And history rolls on like the sea, remorseless, patient, silencing all human cries. 2016 may be summed up as a tawdry little Presidential drama to delay the great American re-booting from industrial Empire to central information node for the world economy. The new American hero is a trader in derivatives with several off-shore accounts – the rest of us are merely cattle gorging at a feed trough on corn that has been genetically engineered. "Don't forget to vote; make your voice heard!"

***

How many drafts will there be of "Pacific End" I wonder? Its tone already implies that I am looking back upon what I am currently living. Are these slips of construction or do the present, the past, and the future interpenetrate each other? Will it be only for editorial convenience if I fudge this issue and leave some of the scaffolding in place to remind the reader that novels are constructed; they do not emerge as whole cloth printed and woven with a set design? After all I have cunningly deflected criticism by using the qualification that these are only notes for a novel and not the novel itself. A dry run and a dress-rehearsal are allowed in other forms of narration, so why not afford an equal courtesy to the bewildered novelist caught between rival versions of existence?

The novelist must feel her way to truth. This may mean imagining how things might have been if everything had just worked out. It may mean looking backward to see where a fork was inadvertently taken that changed the entire prospects that once beckoned so alluringly. It may mean lamenting things years after the fact or belatedly seeing that there was a cause beyond our own lives that we could not resist because we could never have perceived it. Our actual life may appear like a ghost image on a screen where no one can say which is real and which are just duplications of possible lives that have remained unlived.

The deeper truths cannot be reduced to statements and are thus beyond even language to express. Our words have evolved to match the level of our experience; metaphor and symbol draw connections where exposition fails. This is why poetry does not fail because its meanings are elusive and why poetry resists paraphrase or even translation.

The novel maintains a greater margin for error because no

individual element is critical to the whole. A poem may be attacked and critiqued at any point but a novel can at best be apprehended as a complex whole. It is like a castle on a hill that may be stormed but never totally defeated by incomprehension or ill-will. In it the author may wrap herself up secure behind ambiguities and partial exploration of themes, or at least so I tell myself.

Containment and scope are always in opposition and the author must choose which of these to favor. In the case of "Pacific End" I choose (or chose depending upon which draft we are talking about) to allow myself considerable latitude and even to veer back and forth between extremes. I have a definite penchant to pursue a crippled dialectic as my path to truth. I see things in opposition and then seek ways that they may reveal subtle connections or reveal hidden contradictions.

Incidentally this is the reason that I fell so deeply in love with she who cannot be named, precisely because she was both light and dark, comprehensible and hopelessly contradictory by turns, reliable in her affection and possessed of an astringent quality when her shattered edges would predominate, so that in the end no portrait of her would ever be possible because her form was elusive and perhaps as unknown to her as I was unknown to myself. We were linked by the sheer multiplicity of our pieces like twin mirrors shattered – which of these fragments once contained the image of you and which one the image of me? Could these questions be sorted out in "Pacific End?"

Does the author write herself into existence so that the act of writing is like eating – cease and you die? Are all novels essays, attempts to reach the elusive novel-source or the ur-novel that must remain unwritten in the same way that space must exist between two objects for either of them to exist? Was this finally why the two of us parted, because if we had stayed together one or the other of us would have emerged as both and the other have ceased to exist? The shadow of disillusion pursued us both and each felt that to lose the other was to die.

Instead, we went our separate ways and one of us started writing...

***

My general advice to novelists is: if you are short on character then be long on plot – pack your tale with incidents. But what if what is happening has always happened and will again like the sea climbing up the bluff at Cyclops Head while I lie in the sand in a little den made of rocks and a driftwood log?

The sand is so warm today that I have decided to put off my return journey once again – to push summer deeper into September, knowing all the while that I cannot freeze time. The rock that stood six feet above the beach in May is now at almost sand-level, the result of wind and tide. The pool beneath the Lorelei Rock is no longer eight feet deep; it is just a puddle now and the waves keep coming. The light has a steeper slant on the cape. My summer of forgetting is almost over.

***

I sip my coffee and look down on the grey sea softly coming in beyond the cedar shacks at Nye Beach. Pandora is playing "The House of the Rising Sun," and I remember the summer of '67 and plunging into the cool waters of the lake or waterskiing behind the tiny pontoon watercraft with the old Johnson engine. I dragged my little brother up to San Juan Island for company that same year. We ran out of food and money and I drove the family station wagon home from Anacortes at 90 miles an hour so we could get some food and could resume that interrupted summer on the lake and play tag under the docks.

How's that for incident? Not enough? Then try this on: by this summer's end I had learned how to appreciate the poems of Robert Lowell, his lonely struggle to turn madness and regret into words. By mid-September of 2016 I knew suddenly that I had remained too long that my summer lay about me like a shattered mirror. The sea turned dark one day and the people became strangers to me once again. Even the familiar became estranged as they bore witness to the futility of the dam that I had tried to erect to save summer and to recapture what had been lost.

***

"The neighbors think that you have been taking advantage. Camping on unimproved property is against county regulations."

"But I sought permission. I have hidden nothing. Besides we have paid taxes for over twenty years on property that was only occasionally used. When did we deny access to anyone here when we were gone – no walls, no fences, just an open understanding? When did we exhaust our remedies or assert the full spectrum of our rights of ownership rather than provide open access?"

"That changes nothing; you are taking advantage now."Goodwill has a short shelf-life. The reign of limits in America is supreme. Donald Trump even promises to build us a wall to keep the Mexicans out of the lands that were formerly part of Mexico.

So I looked about for another point of access to the sea. I passed the homeless in Newport who sit all day in the bus shelter outside city hall. One carried a sign asking for an act of random kindness, a man with the face of the forlorn Jesus whose successors live in the woods all over America, even eight years after the recovery from the Great Recession of 2008.

But I was busy looking for an understanding with the powers that be – to a find a place where I could remain by right and not take advantage or break any rules, so I drove past.

"The state offices are up a hill off Highway 20," I was told.

I took the road indicated and suddenly there was a mausoleum and crematorium before me followed by a graveyard of all those who would no longer take advantage of anyone having paid for their two square yards of dirt. I thought immediately of that line by T.S. Eliot, "I had not thought death had undone so many." Suddenly these monuments seemed obscene to me and the afternoon although sunny had the chill possessed of all irretrievable events, of all indisputable facts, wherever no hope of appeal exists. "Surrender your hopes all you who enter here!"

The graves were planted thick with a pure facticity as though potent with one last assertion, "Read my stone and learn who I was and when I was here and perhaps a tiny message besides." I thought how better it would be to simply let the vast collectivity of the sea give up its dead when the final trumpet sounds rather than to occupy these separate plots.

"Build us a wall, Donald Trump, to keep the dead at bay!" I am speaking of these dead who reign supreme on the moral high ground above Newport, taking advantage of no one, having paid their just dues at last to life's inscrutable purposes and the demands of everyone staking out their various borders not the least of which is time itself.

I had turned too early so I retraced my steps back to that level plain where assertion and argument still matter. I found the office and clarified my status. I found a way to remain a few final days to complete my spiritual re-birth so that I could retrace my steps home, not in defeat, but as someone who completes a task, achieves "closure." I wanted to feel that part of me would always remain a part of the property I had loved so dearly and the vain hopes that I had once entertained of its possibilities.

✷✷✷

I was "pulled over" later that night. I had come to a stop sign at the highway. I stopped and signaled for a right-hand turn and was promptly pulled over and bathed in blue light.

"I am pulling you over for failure to signal a turn."

"But I did signal. I always do."

"In Oregon you must signal for one-hundred feet before making a turn."

"I didn't make up my mind until I came to the stop sign which direction I would take."

"I don't make the laws. I need your driver's license, registration, and proof of insurance."

Waiting…

"I am not going to cite you tonight but where are you going after this?"

"Anywhere but here; I don't want to be taking advantage of your community and I'll signal earlier next time."

He taught me a valuable lesson: in America everyone wants to know how long you plan to stay.

"Our check-out time is 11:00 A.M. Enjoy your stay."

Of course no novelist knows just how long it will take him to finish his task and for one who is attempting to write "Pacific End," that strange book of gathered impressions, it is harder still to signal 100 feet before making any turn.

***

If only the world would stay in focus for me long enough for the photographic image to set. A setting in print is as frozen and absolute as an exposure of film once the book is published. For this reason many novelists are reluctant to submit a final manuscript to their publishers. Others, unsure of what they think on certain key issues in the novel may adopt a posture of studied ambiguity. It is not unusual for authors to harbor pet ideas and even to manifest certain paranoid tendencies. After all, even to assume that the private world of literary creation is worth an audience's patient perusal is evidence of at least a minor degree of megalomania.

"The novel meanders; it lacks focus," my agent, if I relied on one, would no doubt say to me. "Just what is it you are trying to say? Take that police incident: stuff like that happens every day and every bum is looking for an act of random kindness so he can get drunk or high. You can't make a novel out of raw data just looking for a pattern. Things simply happen; there is no underlying pattern to events. Get a thicker skin; this is America after all. All you Obama-care wusses need to grow up. Everybody wants a free-ride, to take advantage, to get to America illegally and take what we have worked to create."

And killed for, I might add. The highway into Newport is dedicated to all those killed in Iraq and Afghanistan – no part of America is without its memorial to our militarism.

My Dad again, "I was watching O'Reilly last night. Hillary fainted. How can a lady that faints be Commander in Chief? She'll have to meet all these generals every day! I think I'll sell my house and move to Maui. Not too many people live there."

Islands need no walls, not a Mexican in sight; but then I don't watch O'Reilly. But if he's a Catholic and has no trouble going to communion, then he must be a saint, my Dad believes. Conservative commentators get big salaries for telling outraged Americans about who is out there taking advantage of them. They earn their keep. O'Reilly is not out there asking for an act of random kindness; it's all covered in his contract with Fox News.

***

In the old days they used to interview novelists like Gore Vidal or Norman Mailer because people thought novelists had something important to say. Now we watch comedians who show us how ridiculous and stupid the other guy is and lady-journalists talk and show off their legs between commercials for drugs that can sustain erections in elderly men. I think: if any guy still has an erection after four hours then check; maybe he is lying there dead with a big rigor mortis smile on his face.

I think again of the monuments on the hill, the stone pillars pushing upwards to a silent blue sky while three miles distant the waves are pounding onto the land and leaving the day's detritus to be gathered by the visitors from Utah, Alabama, and Idaho who know enough to go home when its time to do so and not go native as I have done this summer.

A Question: Where do you belong? Answer: Anywhere but here. (After all, the bus stop outside City Hall is already filled).

But then I think, of the man in Syria on the evening news who was crying because his entire life had just washed away in an instant by the death of his wife. This makes me think of she who cannot be named and I realize that I love her still.

***

I have just heard that we won't be staging my play this fall. Maybe that's part of my reluctance to head home. Novels are such a lonely pursuit. The novelist never sees his audience unless he does a reading for an honorarium at a college or university or does a book-signing.

"There now, do any of you have any questions? Yes..."

"Where do you get your ideas from when you write?"

I think about Tennessee Williams who never stopped traveling but whose plays suddenly stopped being relevant although they still sought explain our loneliness. He could afford to pay his way from place to place but his words began to make his audiences yawn – death of a playwright.

That word, "Wright" makes me think of my dead roommate. Disbar a real lawyer like he was and you might as well kill him. Courts all over the country are making sure that nobody takes unfair advantage; nobody dependent upon the random kindness of strangers, like Jesus looking for Veronica or Simon of Cyrene to help Him on the way to Golgotha, whether outside of Jerusalem or outside Newport on a hill.

***

"It's moved since yesterday," says a man who purchased lingerie yesterday for a woman measuring 36 D. The woman at the counter moves to help him and I turn away from the mirror. He sounds like he comes from England, confident and sure of himself. Maybe he drives a Jaguar and the object of his largess is seated primly in her seat waiting for him to surprise her with today's addition to her stock of lacy finery. "It's a rainy day on the coast, oh what to do?"

***

Incident piled on incident – all chance meetings, no pattern – Journey sings "the wheel in the sky keeps on turning" – God watching his people – and the waves are beating in off Yaquina Lighthouse that is sending its vain beam out into the foggy day – not to beckon but to warn ships away from a premature landfall.

"Stay away, this is America – DO NOT GIVE TO ME your huddled masses yearning to breathe free!" And all those who are already here look out into the vacant parking lot and sigh with relief, one less stranger.

Yet still I hover like the fog out beyond the breakwater, if they but knew. Novelists, like the novel form itself, are so hard to finally dispose of. There is always something more to say … even when the horizon reaches no further than one hundred yards and the

Yaquina Lighthouse cannot be seen. It is time to depart. Timing and location, they say, are everything. If I return this winter will Circes remain as I have known it; will it be as hard then for me to return to the sea as it is now for me to go home knowing as I do that she will not be waiting for me?

Last night a rap song warned it's listeners at karaoke that the artist was a guy from Compton who kills people. I sang from Boy George: "Do you really want to hurt me." The answer of course is, "No, we just want you to signal for a hundred feet and then turn and go."

Everything has been flooding in upon me all summer with newness if not with a grace. Now the ebb tide has set in. My compass heading is still reading north. I thought of the dead people up on the hill above Newport with their short messages, those that will never leave there now. Here were more stories now for me to tell her, even if she who cannot be named isn't listening anymore to my tales. I had only wanted to give her good holding ground by showing her that the world in which I had been raised possessed its own sense of security, at least as remembered by me. She had loved the music and movies of other eras not her own and by doing so appeared to me as timeless and ever my contemporary in whatever was the latest enthusiasm that we both shared. I was as apt to look over at her as she was to seek her lead from me.

But she had been escalating the stakes daily in whatever game we were both playing, escalating them way beyond what I could cover and stay in the game. So I just went away after her accusations seemed to be spinning everyday into ever newer forms, each more extreme than the last had been. I thought if I allowed the sediment to settle a little I would be able to see through the clear liquid in the little globe that held our two figures dancing. The echo came again, "You knew this would happen; you chose it!" Ten years should have shown her that I hadn't done so. Why is it the case that pain bonds us closer to another than the simple exchange of mutual consideration? I hadn't abandoned her and never would have; I had only just swum up to the surface for a quick breath of air before retuning to the deep sea where she lay entangled and inert.

The summer was gone now and I knew how vain it was to prolong the best moments, as pointless as it was to hope that I could induce autumn to suspend its stealthy advance. I knew now that it is always a mistake to think that we can freeze our life's seasons or embalm our perceptions or hope to preserve them beyond the passive impress of memory.

Part Two

Things Disperse

And suddenly I was home again. I had attempted, what Thomas Wolfe had assured us was impossible: You can't go home again. What he realized was just what Heraclitus had proclaimed so long ago, that one cannot step into the same river twice, that nothing remains stable, and that absence invites the forces of dissolution to redouble their efforts to erase, not simply our memories, but the very substances that we imagined were impregnable to time.

Things collapse, just as the twin-towers of the World Trade Center had in 2003, or the stock market in 2007 before the long recessional economy began – bailouts to re-establish speculative opportunities for the same renegades of yesterday who had savaged our economic structures to skim a profit. Like termites in the wood of the body politic they have bequeathed us the America of 2016.

The election was closer now and the debate season neared – fiddling before the conflagration. More police shootings had occurred and racial outrage seemed to be growing everyday. North Carolina had more to worry about than passing bathroom bills as crowds gathered in Charlotte to protest another killing. Of course the real message was not that black lives didn't matter but that too many black people lived in at-risk neighborhoods and police lived daily on a hair-trigger alert from day to day in order to survive. In a society suspicious of immigration and entitlements the old unhealed sores of yesterday still festered.

I came home to the early rain squalls that proclaimed the end of summer and I saw my life fully and saw it whole as one filled with leaf-mold and dust. The soil beneath the maples awaited another season's cascade of red and yellow leaves that having feasted on the sun must now pay the strict exactions of the year. There is a toll levied on every generation, for one a war, for another a depression, for another a plague – to live long enough may be witness all of these. When I returned I felt that Americans were not so much alienated and divided as simply bored. The slow hum of the Internet had hypnotized us, dulled our senses; it had sent us into a coma that was still beset by restless dreams, dreams too buried and sullen to emerge into even the iron-clad oblivion of coma.

✶✶✶

I was still engaged in writing "Pacific End," but with this difference: the form was changing under a new impact derived from a setting that should have been familiar to me, but was not. In even a few short months things had shifted so that everything was just that little bit off center.

It is not the sea-swell that creates vertigo but the subtle shift in the expectation of the inner-ear that must register and interpret what is occurring in the tiny inner-sea of the cochlea. In the same manner great events may leave us unmoved while a slight variation may breed that sense of inner uncertainty that causes us to doubt or to lose faith.

It was strange to exist again in proximity to she who cannot be named. Normally I would let her know that I had returned; but who was I and had I really returned? I had moved between two points separated by three hundred miles; that was all. Could sixty short days work so great a change or was our silence only the fitting monument to the past ten years when one or the other of us was always walking away or refusing to answer – the thrust and counter-thrust of our unceasing effort to either find each other or to escape.

✶✶✶

Within a week of my return I was reading the poems of Anna Akmatova, she who new how to celebrate all of the nuances of an empty room. The radiations of words radiate outwards and overlap so that a reader if properly attuned can share not simply the voice of the other but become so impregnated with that voice that the reader becomes the author for a time. In this sense all of literature is but a single extended discourse.

The novel is characterized by the longitudinal development of a theme, character, or idea; whereas a poem may shade into the universal and a short-story may be confined to a single occurrence, the novel must embrace change and a transit between two-states of being. Even Joyce's "Ulysses," confined to a single day, still shows progress: the father finds a son and a wife learns to realize that her husband is in fact the truest love of her life.

Infidelity often reveals the true worth of a marriage – woman owes her first allegiance to her own idea of perfection though it can never be met. The only true epic is the one that recognizes and accepts that things fall short and that the Tower of Babel will never be finished. Is that what novelists are doing? Babbling? Or is a novel a discrete and insular edifice raised against the waters like a frail sandcastle erected bravely before the onrushing tide?

A novel is in many ways the ultimate in the presumption of individual assertion. It says, "Life is like this."

The novel aspires towards the comprehensive statement no matter how regional in setting or short in actual length it may be. What can be shorter than a universal formula? After all Einstein summed up mass and energy in a single equation; can the illustrious novelist be expected to do less?

***

But I was engaged in writing "Pacific End," a novel the very title of which proclaimed its project of being a summation, one with its end always in view, just as the ocean was never out of ear-shot during much of its early composition. But it is in the word "pacific" that all my trouble begins: Who ever "goes gently into that good night," Dylan Thomas or no Dylan Thomas? We resist because simply to live is to resist. I wish I could say this to she who cannot be named, but she is not listening this autumn.

"Good luck finding someone who will listen to your stories and care to count every detail of them."

This is good advice for every aspiring novelist to consider: what if nobody cares what you say? Only in a world where the tide is always setting in towards shore can one guarantee that someone will be walking along the beach to see what has been deposited among the flotsam and jetsam there.

There is a random quality to all creation if it is to be honest, random like love is because we do not choose to love. Love is suddenly all around us and the other becomes special, chosen out of thousands of likely candidates, inundating every crevice of our souls until no ultimatum or recrimination can touch it or diminish its substance and permanence.

Absence is the price exacted in order to forget, but when the tide recedes the bare rocks of a lost regard are again revealed.

***

So I came home as she who cannot be names foresaw to an emptiness born of the rotating year. The tide was ebbing now and she had counted on this, forgetting perhaps that neither of us had ever dreaded October. We were always among those who prefer the minor keys. But these personal reflections were only a backdrop to the writing of "Pacific End," which had its own formal challenges.

The novelist must seek to hide the personal element in his creation if his message is to be universal. Even when he says "I" it must be understood that this is a device of narration and not a true confession. True intimacy demands deflection – indirect lighting, or as my father says, "Novels are about what never happened." All choices foreclose the infinity of other rejected choices. We trace like a comet a single trajectory across an indifferent sky.

It is said that a neutrino can pass through the entire earth as if it were a cloud without colliding with any particle of matter. Everything is more permeable than we suspect and at the same time more concentrated. The devotion of a lifetime may be forgotten in a moment and a chance encounter may persist in memory for years. It is this fact that upsets the search for closure and summation in the novel; it may be impossible to select the essential facts and to differentiate them from mere background and setting.

The novel finally is only itself for better or for worse. But life demands continuity, so where was I to look for a pacific end to whatever we had shared? I began these reflections at the ocean in a town that proclaimed its newness even in view of its vulnerable location, one subject to whatever the vast ocean might throw up on its shores. The light on Yaquina Point warns mariners to stay away, to avoid contact with what will not yield. Some loves are so specific and the maze of communication so convoluted to reach the solitary heart that no real entry is ever permitted. It is said that aloha means both hello and goodbye; that was what every encounter with she who cannot be named was like. "Farewell weary traveler ... oh and when can I see you again?" We look for the lighthouse only to stay clear having discovered it at last – that is how love sometimes is; at least it was like that for us.

So I came about on the tiller and ran before the wind, back out to sea until her light was no longer discernable to both beckon and repel.

✶✶✶

I suppose that I am writing "Pacific End" to explain things to myself and in order to begin to recover the easy trim of a vessel used to sailing before the wind. Form often demands division; so from things coming together I turned to focus on things that were coming apart by the inevitable force of diffusion that blends and dissipates.

Literature seldom breeds an easy consensus. The consciousness among author, critic, and readers is the inevitable triad of all literature; one expresses, one interprets and evaluates, and the rest simply make what sense they can of what has been written to reduce everything to a clear statement without shades or contradictions. I came home to find out where the country was headed. The best anodyne for personal pain is to lose oneself in history, the great reminder of our personal insignificance.

✶✶✶

The Pacific Ocean was named "pacific" because its full dimensions exceeded the imagination of those who thought that they had discovered it. Maybe all ends are like that as well – we can't imagine what lies beyond the furthest point that we can see. The perspective on the horizon limits all observation and reduces everything to a single line traced half-way up to what might have been either land, water, or the lower border of sky. The observer shrinks back into himself and says, "This is how it seems to me even from that furthest expansion of vision that the ocean alone affords to the human eye. Beyond this I can see nothing."

It has been said that there are no tracks in the sea. The navigator steers by the stars. No trace or signpost tells the sailor when to come about onto a new course. There are currents which are nothing less than rivers in the ocean and these show some regularity but when combined with wind and tide they vacillate and meander with the times and seasons. This betrays the notorious fickleness and changeableness of these vast waters so that the ocean has been accused of treachery when it is merely manifesting its own responses to those vast forces that act upon it. The ocean is in this sense the ultimate symbol of passivity. A physicist would have no problem with imagining it as a fluid-filled basin, whereas to a poet it is alive and possessed of personality, of moods, of abiding temperament and volition.

From such conceptions the idea of providence arises. Perhaps the best proof of the divinity of Christ to his followers was that even the seas obeyed him. What can this mean but that chance can be overridden by conscious choice combined with power? The question that remains unanswered is, why the natural order is allowed to operate for the most part unhindered by God. Is this a gesture of respect by the deity for the created world or simply a sign that we are adequate to take a position towards intransigent existence? The odds seem stacked against us but our insignificance is belied by human progress and those moments of moral triumph when we emerge above the surging waters and find our searching feet grasping sand as we come ashore. We gather the shattered timbers and torn canvas and make a shelter against the night and the wild beasts and begin to reconnoiter our present location. We may be rescued by another ship appearing one day on the horizon, but in the meantime we do what we must to survive. We gather wood for signal fires and wait for whatever comes. We cannot know how long we will be deprived of familiar company, spending our days gazing outward at the unvarying aspect of water and sky.

✳✳✳

The real problem is memory. We are more likely to lament the loss of past happiness than to rejoice that change has also at times benefited us by removing oppressors. How must the survivors of Auschwitz have rejoiced to awake and see that their guards had abandoned them in the night on the frozen plain of Silesia, without even valuing them enough to waste a final bullet to rend their meager flesh? Desperate as their situation was, for the first time in years they were free.

The post-war philosophers took uncertainty as their starting point – all is change; the most that we could do was to take a position towards the unaccountability of events. We chart a course from where we are, not from where we once were. To recall past grievances too intensely is only to preserve them.

Nothing made this more evident to me than the pictures of the Nazi work camp at Mauthausen. It was once a stone-quarry and the prisoners were forced to carry huge blocks of limestone up a hill called the Himmelstrasse because so many had died from the effort or were beaten to death on the way to the top. I imagined that so great an evil must leave the land blighted for generations thereafter, but the ground where the prisoners assembled for inspection is today a lush green meadow. Flowers appear everywhere and the bitter stone steps are like the lovingly laid paths of a park.

Is this a mockery of the suffering that went on there or a vindication for it? All is erased or modulated with time. The tide rises and falls and all is cleared away for those who have no need to forget because they have no memories of what once occurred here. The number of the dead dwarfs the numbers of the living, but the living ones own the present hour. The slow gristmill of history reduces all things to ashes. We build upon the ruins of what was once grand and new. The emperor is trampled in his robes and another wears his crown.

***

The novel form admits interludes. We depend upon them to break the thread of incident. What use is mere duration without periodic assessment? Have we moved any distance from our initial point of departure? As I write I hear two people, each of whom has lost a spouse, talking at an adjoining table, not dreaming that a novelist is scanning their words for the universal meaning of their unique tragedies. They are seeking to reconnect to the life-force that once sustained them and that they have been nurturing since alone. Suffering is a bond between them; another has been here too. The conversation has rotated past commiseration to the present moment. Hope is re-ignited and they laugh from time to time. They have both endured; there are still grounds to hope for a future. They are not alone.

***

Not all divisions are as amicably healed. There are racially motivated riots going on in Charlotte, North Carolina over another police shooting. It will no doubt be a focus of the Presidential Debates that begin Monday. Trump is looking for traction and Hillary is counting on his ability to alienate vast sectors of the voting public every time he opens his mouth. Jill Stein of the Green Party will of course not be present. Who cares about the planet anyway? The big questions are who will make the best Commander-in-Chief and who will get to nominate the next justices to the Supreme Court. America is at one of those rare points of seeking a new definition of its fundamental sense of itself. We elect symbols not people. Who Trump and Clinton really are is immaterial beyond what they share in common – an ability to manipulate systems and to thereby attain wealth. The rest of the vast American body politic will watch them posture and fence with each other and ask themselves if their backyard fences are high enough to keep the neighbors out.

***

This year is racing by and a vast gap exists that constitutes the happenings in the life of she who cannot be named and mine.

A great ice-shelf has broken away from the glacier and begun to drift away into the night. She is celebrated in anonymity here in "Pacific End" and in that sense is a character in this novel without characters, one with only a mere succession of references and speculations, life itself granted a recording medium and given a provisional voice.

The novelist steps aside and lets events dictate content. Does a pattern emerge as in Thornton Wilder's play, "Our Town?" (I recall the shadow of the funeral home on the hill by the sea and its implacable threat).

I noticed elderly people more this summer than ever before. They seem obsessed by the selective reaping of their associates and the way that chance operates to thin their ranks by illness and accident. It is the sort of conversation that seems stilted and unnecessary to younger people. "Why waste today in lamentation?"

This year of 2016 has seemed a year bereft of the comfortably middle-aged. Everyone has been either very young or very old. These appeared to me as two adjacent species, one sleek and lean and immortal and the other maimed in various ways, grateful simply to endure long enough to have reached their present age. These latter seem to be improbable representatives of their era. These fill the Casino that plays songs by Rickie Nelson and Frankie Avalon about young love while the various trolls huddle over screens with flashing lights and dream of the prospect of unearned wealth after their long lives of labor.

Every cemetery I have encountered this year along the roads I have traveled has had the word "rest" somewhere I its title. None have seemed to remark that a rest is a respite not a permanent condition. Why not simply say, "If you didn't like living, then this is the place for you."

How about names like Termination Acres, The Slopes to Oblivion, or Happy Lawns of Extinction? As you drive out a friendly motto could be displayed, "Y'all come back now, hear!"

✱✱✱

A motto is gradually emerging in "Pacific End:" - Stay busy as long as you can and don't think too much."

Time is defeated by sustained activity and by forgetting. It is our loyalties to what has passed that defeat us. What is the reward for fidelity to a lost era? The ocean is fresh every day though it is the mother of all sepulchers. Children run swiftly though the waves on their tiny legs. What is it to them if various pockets of regret are embodied in the aged man who shuffles along the shore lost in meditation or the woman being helped my her daughter down the path to the beach?

But why am I so irritated by old people lately? Do I resent the aged because I see my future self in them? The novelist never wishes to imagine that his own works might become antiquated or made ridiculous by being accurately tuned only to the time when they were written.

To strip away the circumstantial is the only solution, the only promise of attaining lasting significance.

✱✱✱

The conversation going on next to me today is all about failed operations. How do doctors face this everyday? Aren't they tempted to say, "Where do all of these human wrecks come from? I can do nothing with this; give me some young flesh, not these cadavers from my first year in medical school!" Novelists may not be so different from doctors in this regard. Finally you've said everything that anyone cares to hear.

But to be impatient with the human condition is itself a sign of age. Maybe we forget too much after all and in doing so we become self-centered as the light on the stage diminishes to a spotlight's circumference. Youth has the capacity for adaptability and constant surprise. To have known all things is to lose the easy capacity for startled delight. It may be to passively submit to a pacific end out of sheer boredom.

Old age should be a season of sacrifice, to make a return for everything that has ever come our way – the net result should record neither a loss or a profit but simply an equal exchange of time for dispersal of all that we have ever been so that the purveyors of the bone-yards will only inherit white ash, bleached and dry with our efforts.

***

Sympathy is the great force that restores and re-unites persons. In novels we find that someone has already been where we now are. This is why dramas bring an audience together in pity and in terror. We cannot return to give succor to those who have perished; we can only bear witness.

By February 14, 1945 most of Dresden was only a memory for its inhabitants and it was time to begin clearing away the rubble and burying the dead. To see it then as the flames expired was to know the difference between a mere possibility on a drawing board in a British flight-planning room and an accomplished fact. Once done it could not be undone, only scanned for meaning. "Was it all justified, by what calculus, by whose scale of values?"

If things fall apart or drift apart or are ripped apart, how shall we be made whole? It is said that the novel as an art-form represents character development as plotted against time. Even in the social novel where individual character is subsumed into the mass it might be expected, if we adopt this view of the novel, that some movement would declare itself in that enveloping medium in which the individual swims like some passive fish in an aquarium bumping into the walls that constrain him under the fishy delusion that a flat surface with its opacity merely indicates that the watery distance is infinite.

In just such a fashion humans imagine that granted sufficient duration that they will exceed their current limits and the intricate webs of circumstance that enmesh them. We return to those dark pools where familiar experience persuades us to linger imagining that our lives have any prospect of meeting there that combination of predictability and freedom that our own limited capacities can sustain. The result is that over time the novelist begins to see people en mass and not as possessing a unique fate. He then turns away from development and betrays his own art-form by freezing actions in transit as the painter does.

The temptation is to see people without empathy or with contempt, to adopt a stance of glacial indifference. What are these forms that cross my vision each day and break the line of reflection into fragments with their sudden needs and their crossing agendas? Why record these and not allow them to just melt away and yield up that empty space, the same that now exists between she who cannot be named and me?

Was this not the single most clearly evident issue between us: that no effort of either party could fill that unique set of demands that was entertained by the other to make the narrative complete? Even in areas where intimacy and insight combined with motivation might be assumed to reach their highest form, in love, community of interest fails to unite; where then shall we look for an equivalent patience from mere strangers? For this reason lawyers speak of "the arm's-length transaction," one where self-interest is presumed and where due-diligence will reveal any failure to inform or potential fraud in the conveyance or agreement.

Perhaps only hermits can speak of exercising unqualified love. Even the communities of Cenobites though may hold resentments to their brethren in the monastery. But here there is at least the existence of some prior acquaintance that provides a basis for human feelings whether positive or negative; but what shall we make of the murder of a stranger or of acts of terrorism where individuals are affected intimately, perhaps in the very continuance of their lives, by acts that are directed to a class perceived as an obstacle?

Isn't abandonment when it strikes to the soul a private act of terrorism?

∗∗∗

To be a novelist demands objectivity; life does not. The novelist alone may strike without warning because he alone cares enough to record or even to imagine the course of non-existent conflicts by making them believable as embodied in portrayed characters.

For the rest of humankind, to leap too swiftly into empathy is to ignore what may be the most unexplored of questions: how can masses of people be drawn together and poised against another mass of people so that for a time the individual forgets his own agenda and even his own life in the vast inconvenience that such mass movements would otherwise be presumed to entail? What explains this naïve belief in the great and transcendent goals of human action?

A sufficient degree of laziness might be proposed as the universal solution to these self-inflicted disasters of humankind. It takes a crowd after all to make a war or a revolution. Generalization is the mother of all atrocities. To withhold our consent to mass-movements is thought to be either madness or a conscious focus for the resentment of the masses by calling into question the bond that unites them. To refuse to join in is forbidden and usually severely punished. One cannot be a conscientious objector to life.

***

The extreme degree of perception exercised by the novelist may finally lead him to adopt the most dismal but perhaps the truest of all generalizations about the life course: that we have a point of origin, endure for a time, and after a period of diminishing resources perish. The underside of empathy is disgust.

A careful observation for instance of the average person of either sex after the age of fifty is to be struck with wonder that anyone could ever have managed to complete the sexual act with one of these wizened creatures. The earth groans beneath the sheer multitude of human beings that currently exist. Procreation is finally not a tribute to beauty but to the universal efficacy of friction between two moist surfaces. After a certain age the protruding abdomens of one or both partners would appear to preclude all genital contact absent some extraordinary acrobatic ability.

Women for the most part become virtually indistinguishable from their spouses and it requires a degree of imagination equivalent to Kierkegaard's leap of faith to see them as the maidens that they once were. It is precisely at such times that the tendency to generalize may rear its ugly head and the wisdom of the Islamic mind in mandating the veil for female flesh should be approved, for practical reasons even by the infidel. What is sacrificed in the case of young women is recompensed by the blessed eclipse of what she will become during the long and lingering years of her long superannuated existence after the springs of nature are no longer nourished with the freshets of spring.

***

That nature gilds youth with charm is understandable, but is seminal fluid so precious that it must be conserved for the fertile ones, seeing that a woman past ovulation is not pointlessly inundated when she regrets her transformation and desires to retain the semblance of her fertile self? Or is a woman's transformation from maiden to crone a sign that wisdom is best housed in sterner vessels and that woman reaches her summit as a human being precisely when her generic functions of conception and birth are past?

It is the static nature of human life as a background for all actions that finally impresses the novelist as it does the essayist. Once all tolls are paid along the highway of life one approaches the final destination at last like the salmon with their pale and bloated bodies littering the streams in autumn. Where is the sense of development in this prospect; where is the novel to find a subject if this is the inevitable end of life? Against this grim realization how is a pacific end possible? Is it not more likely that the novelist like others will regret and deplore the fatuity and vanity of all his efforts? Why not simply spare the reader the effort of the encounter? Or are novels only for young people who alone possess the residual strength to nurture life's varied illusions?

***

I must confess to having entertained notions such as these when I had returned from the sea to face the quagmire of the inland cities and became caught up with the historical consciousness of this year, the one when I wrote "Pacific End." I felt the heaviness of America's thwarted hopes as the two titans prepared to debate each other for the governance of the world's oldest democracy. I saw the aged faces reflected in the flashing lights of the slot-machines as Americans sought to augment the tiny pool of wealth that a lifetime of effort had allowed them to corral. Would their residual funds be enough to see them to the grave?

I had seen what waited for them above the hill on the coast and all across America? Were the dead in View Nam the lucky ones? Was this the brave new world that my generation had boasted that we alone had discovered? Or was it simply that the form of the novel that I was writing demanded the counterpoint of disillusion to balance the optimism born from gazing out in wonder at the summer sea?

When in doubt how best to proceed with the novel the wise novelist poses a new set of questions to add dramatic tension to what otherwise would be too conclusive and self-assured. After all, not since the 17th century, at the very dawn of the novel's form, had moist writers dared to sound the human condition with the true rigor of salutary disillusionment. These times appeared to me to demand a reinstatement of the specific virtue of the sharp-word, timely uttered. Where else could we seek for a true estimate of our collective situation in 2016? Was it not the primary business of the novelist to challenge the reader's preconceptions and comfortable assumptions? Or did I write "Pacific End" merely to please myself and not to gratify the desires of what might be the non-existent reader, or at least the rare wanderer into the forbidden zones of this much- celebrated but dying art-form? Why not flourish the sword before falling upon it?

***

To linger upon terminations is morbid though so I decided to continue what was less a novel than a diatribe. After all, I was engaged in seeking reconciliation in this year of Divine Mercy. Petition not accusation is the proper form for one seeking mercy. Who is the novelist that he should hold human life in contempt or judge those who are too busy living to ever write a novel?

Ever since the Book of Job it has been the province of the demonic to disparage human beings and to unmask human pretentions? Is the enterprise of the novelist then to tell the truth as he supposes it to be or to simply use the occasion to vent his spleen and slay what remains of innocence? Who is to say that the partial enterprise, the cherished project, the unique and particular love even if misdirected, should be set at naught as life's established purpose?

Perhaps the novelist should encourage the reader at all costs and get ready for what possibilities may still remain at half-time to use a homely American football metaphor. So it was that I returned at last to compassion and to the life-affirming quest in opposition to the ever-vigilant microbes of unsatisfactory human relations that threaten to ripen if they are cultivated into a systemic despair.

A saturnine view of life would ill become me as a novelist for the simple reason that we expect our novelists to maintain a more than usually acute human sympathy. The novelist must be judicious but tolerant. The reason for this is that novels fall into various types based upon the likely motivation of the reader. The light novel should amuse and entertain, the social novel should trace trends to their subtle causes, and the experimental novel should elevate the reader's sensibilities by probing the nature of perception and expression.

But what of the novel that questions life itself by seeking an underlying structure for human experience, poised as we are today at the very edge of extinction? It amazes me that even in the ruins of cultural certainty that people manifest such stoic equanimity in the face of questions of life and death significance. Is it merely that we are too busy to take much note of the lights flickering into darkness around us?

I think often of the dignity of John Millington Synge's short play "Riders to the Sea," which manages to retain all of the dignity of Sophocles or Aeschylus and then compare this with the vulgar euphemisms about rest and peace, with no assurance rendered that a resurrection will ever take place, to make these terms real. Comfort is seems has been our undoing. We must look to the ghettos to feel the knife-edge of terror or squalor. In suburbia all is whispers and good form. Try and imagine the former practice of keening at a wake if you doubt me. Sorrow let alone anguish are considered to be bad form; they might even produce laughter. As good Americans we should be above such vulgar displays as real human emotion. After all we have learned to live comfortably for over sixty years with the possibility of immanent nuclear extinction, so why make a fuss over just one more death?

***

It has been the American playwrights that have garnered the most honors on the world's literary stage. We are a nation of talkers. It is more natural for us to read "Mourning Becomes Electra" than to read a novel by Henry James, although few Americans now actually read either. We cannot be considered a literate society in any traditional sense immersed as we are in various ephemeral phenomena the description of which requires few words.

This was the background of "Pacific End" as it took shape in my mind during that summer of 2016. Caught between various sunsets I questioned what I was doing as a writer or even why I would ever care to raise questions that could later be embodied in a complete novel format. Why use words when actual objects can be engineered by a three-dimensional printer? Forget copyrights, patent and trademark is the thing! If what a writer produces doesn't go viral but merely trickles slowly through the neurons of a few devoted and discerning readers was it worth the effort of composition in the first place? If it can't be made cheaper in China do we really need it in America?

***

But I still kept writing anyway, driven by that imperative to understand, if only for myself, what was happening around me. I needed to reach a position towards my life before it extended any further into the blasé ether of the 21st century.

I had already graduated beyond most novel forms. I wondered how to extend the form, to embrace new questions, to start where Kafka's "The Castle" leads, where Robert Musil's "The Man without Qualities" was headed, where Herman Broch arrived with his "The Death of Virgil," our modern version of Dante.

I called these novels "terminal works" because they represented a sort of last will and testament of some of the most creative minds of the last century. Other works could be listed in this category:

The Years by Virginia Woolf; The Magic Mountain by Thomas

Mann; Finnegans Wake by James Joyce; The Sleepwalkers by Herman Broch; The Glass-bead Game by Herman Hesse; In Search of Time Lost by Marcel Proust; Jean-Christophe by Romaine Rolland; and the Strangers and Brothers series by C.P. Snow

What they all have in common is a monumental effort at a comprehensive statement: this is human life. Detail in time and place does not detract from the universal tonal modulation in these novels but anchor it. A fully realized regionalism may even be a prerequisite to attaining universal significance as is true of William Faulkner.

Of course the main point is that even to maintain that an essential human dilemma exists is automatically to take an essentialist position in a post-existential world. In a world of multiple and temporary discourses nothing is considered to be final. A list of qualifications and presumptions would be tedious though and any source of permanent authority would be considered to be an act of usurpation. Nothing is grounded beyond its market value or its ability to elicit free consent. Complete privatization finally equals solipsism.

This may mean that the ultimate goal of the future novel is to terminate in itself as a purely self-referential act – step inside and never escape for you have entered the literary equivalent of hell. To know hell at all is already to have made an irrevocable choice for it.

The idea of a constitutive choice makes no sense in our current frame of references where any position can be either infinitely qualified or abandoned at will. Our forebears thought differently. Pity and terror in tragedy are reflected in King Lear's repetition of the words, "Never, never, never" – his daughter is irrevocably dead. When there is no God there is neither condemnation nor mercy but only meaningless succession. If the novel is dead today; it is not alone. Philosophy dies first and literature follows - the rest is mere sound and fury. To realize this fully is to return to pity and terror for the whole human race.

To even perceive this problem was perhaps the reason for me to write "Pacific End." Those professions that encounter human dilemmas on a daily basis know that acts of quiet heroism are commonplace though uncelebrated. It is these stories that expose the lie of human insignificance; but absent art millions of people can simply vanish and history will heal the wound within a generation. In this sense human tissue becomes as irrelevant as single cells within a human body; it is the function of organs that matters. Even fame buys only a few paragraphs of news-print for the obituary and perhaps five short minutes on the evening news. It takes an extraordinary atrocity to bestow adequate mystery to mundane occurrences so that they will be recalled a month hence. Reduce the facts to fiction however and a bid at immortality may still be made.

One wonders how many Emma Bovary's lived in France and how many a Heathcliff and a Cathy may have pursued a doomed romance beyond the Yorkshire moors. Then there are the squalid everyman characters of Emile Zola or Upton Sinclair whose role in the novel is to be indistinguishable from their type. These also attain a heightened significance by being enshrined in novels.

But what of the rest of us who live and die unnoticed and more obscure than poor Hardy's Jude ever thought of being? Where should we look as we approach our own version of Anna Livia Plurabelle's descent, when as the river Liffey she bids farewell to life? Should novelists work on commission for those who absent their verbal ministrations will soon be dispersed like so many milkweed fibers blowing on the wind?

"Please make my life matter; it hurt too much for no one to ever know what it all cost me!" is the cry of every man and woman who has ever lived.

I think back on the cemetery in Newport, poised like a towering wave about to submerge us all, and of the silent witnesses of the stones mounting their eternal vigil there. How inadequate is even stone for the tasks that we assign them while frail and insubstantial symbols on paper may still endure through the passing of ages?

✲✲✲

Publishers today like to say, "The key to book sales is steep discounts. Push print into reader's hands by offering them one sweet deal."

Now there's a business plan for you!

Publishers feel the pain of the bookstore-owner who has yet to add an espresso-bar or sandwich shop to attract readers to her over-freighted bookshelves. Books are slow movers after all. They may languish on a shelf for years waiting for an ideal reader to show up.

***

Meanwhile every grocery outlet boasts a few familiar names whose novels sound something like this...

"Joanie Greenweather {great name} clutched her purse to her well-proportioned bosom as she turned the corner into the darkness of an evil-smelling alley. Was the man in the raincoat still following her? Perhaps she had been foolish to run. After all, this was Istanbul not Iraq and though she was a woman, she was not helpless. She had been assigned in the states to the consulate service and had a working knowledge of Turkish and Arabic. She was an American, so why was she running when she might have stood her ground and asked the bearded stranger why he had been following her?"

And end at last after some 280 pages of action and romance something like this:

"As she boarded the express train she knew that she was leaving Istanbul never to return. She thought how foolish she had been a mere six months ago, how uncertain and afraid, seeing menace where as time was to reveal, she found love. At least she had found passion as well. She thought of the nights with, no she would not say his name, even to herself. To her now he was only a dark form turning off the bedside lamp. She would feel him slip in beside her as the strange oriental street noises drifted up to them from the street below in the Arab quarter. He was gentle but insistent as he demanded what she alone could give him, or so he had always told her. Had she been naïve to believe his protestations when she knew that he had ties to the heroin trade? But then we all have our faults. She was no longer a pert college girl at the sorority house in Connecticut. Those days seemed as remote now as the America to

which she was returning with only the tattoo of the twin hearts to bear witness to those endless nights of love.

A tear trickled down her cheek and she reached into her purse for a tissue and found instead – a letter. She opened it hurriedly. Yes it was from him! It read: Cara Mia, I cannot live without you. I have cut all ties with the brotherhood. We shall meet in Paris. Dare I hope for this? I have wronged you cruelly, but I cannot face the future without you. I shall wait for you each night on the steps at Sacre Coeur and pray that you will forgive me. Come to me my beloved and we shall...

But she could read no more, for she knew that she had already accepted his invitation to love and to life and even as she clasped the letter to her heart she knew that no matter what the future might bring that they would never again be parted."

***

Publishers urge us to flatter the passions because who wants to think anymore? Who cares about a magic mountain or a man without qualities? All mountains are magic and few men possess any real qualities. Only women are still reading novels anyway. Write something about a vampire cult at some little coastal town or about some guy who needs women to feel pain for him to feel love – women will understand and read novels such as this in little furtive bits at their coffee breaks. Besides, once it's off the shelf you're half-way home as an author. It is the quick turnover that matters: Think flow of product! Think re-orders! Think books on the pretzel isle! Now go back and write me a book!

***

October had come all too swiftly and with it had come the rains of autumn. I still tried to hang onto summer for awhile, at least until the bookselling convention where authors, publishers, and bookstore proprietors mingle. Flashy covers on crisply printed pages beckon. Familiar imprints share space with specialty publishers. I pick up a book with an intriguing cover of a melancholy blond in a simple black dress only to learn the day later that she died at the age of thirty-six by her own hand.

The title had intrigued me. It spoke of being prisoners of our own flesh; of beauty as a curse – Why can't you see my thoughts instead of my cleavage? Prostitution provides the perfect base in experience for a novel discourse with the eventual suicide as the ultimate act of summation and assimilation of writer and text – my body is my art and my death is my wordless statement.

"The booksellers are all going broke so we must shift our expectation of royalties forward like the young woman in the book who must have known about payments indefinitely deferred – writing as prostitution. Still she was the recipient of literary honors in Canada and in France. The publishers gambled: if she can only survive her present season in the hell of disillusionment until wisdom arrives she will become a valuable property.

As authors we hand out bookmarks and collect cards in a basket. Publicists and editors mingle in the crowd and outside the leaves are already blowing around the courtyard where I used to walk in November nights so many years ago when I still lived in the city. Where have those ghosts gone? Many are dead now from AIDS; but then they were beautiful. They wore long backless evening-gowns and lip-synched to 80's songs while the red and purple lights shown down on bourbon cocktails and white tablecloths and the haze of cigarette smoke filtered like fog through the vast rooms.

This cattle market is what dreams consist of when reduced to print. The silent volumes plead, "Read me! Read me!" Only the university presses are more reserved as befits catering to a specialty readership. "If you can't afford it you are unworthy to read it." No free samples here; scholarship needs no gimmicks.

The smaller publishers leave tiny candy-bars about to lead the groping fingers like mice to pick up the books. Desire is so easily transferred between adjacent senses – novels as candy for the mind. I will eat Chinese food later and then drive home in the dark. Still, the old town didn't look too bad. Every street is thronged with memories for me. I have been to so many places within a twenty mile radius over a course of forty years. There is the house that my roommate bought a few years before he died – wonder who owns it now?

Ghosts blow like the dead leaves along the gutters on Hilltop and my memories with them. I eat chow-mein while the darkness falls and when my fortune cookie opens there is nothing there. Is this the message that I can expect no guidance now and must chart my own course without her?

"Be empowered," the universe speaks to me; "Dare to chart your own course to a pacific end."

No Dead Sea Scrolls are here to bolster or to undermine faith; we must dare to publish and perish. A conversation from the afternoon returns to me, "I paid for an editor. It was so helpful to have multiple trial readers to hone and to polish my text. I read once that Dostoyevsky wrote under pressure and couldn't afford an editor and that's why his characters have this frenzied and feverish way of talking and just go on and on. I learned not to waste verbiage; paper is expensive."

"What could be worse than writing like Dostoyevsky?" I think to myself. "I'll have to get an editor then," I replied humbly.

Regarding this question of editors, they say that Thomas Wolfe lay on his back at Providence Hospital for weeks before being transferred to a sanitarium on Lake Washington. He thought of his mother's boarding house and about his father carving stone angels and the brother who had died too young. Was the author dying now? Would he live to write "Pacific End?" Was it time to write Max Perkins and tell him how much it had always mattered to have his skill and understanding as an editor, to turn the volcanic gush of his words into novels?

I think about the dead woman writer. Did her editor say, "You sound too much like a prostitute?" Or did he say, "Why not take a chance and say just what you want to say and in your own manner? Surely there is something to be said for authenticity and for felicitous accidents of expression. Are only poets entitled to be difficult and obscure?"

***

When I came home I saw here also the same homeless people with their cardboard signs and downcast or evaluating eyes. I wondered how many of these were on heroin. One thing the war in Afghanistan has given us is cheaper heroin – thanks Dick Cheney. "Can you spare a dime for a cup of coffee" has now a request for a fiver that is enough for a fix.

This was what I came home to when summer ended. The Olympics were over and I had left the beaches of May behind. The waves still beat on Cyclops Head and karaoke went on at Circes but I was home again and looking for a way to reconnect to that me that I had been when the year began. I had begun to wonder if events have no real succession. What if things just happen until suddenly they don't anymore? What supplies the thread of narrative that makes a story? People come into our lives and then flicker out again like the candles that burn before the statue of the Blessed Virgin Mary.

You are like family to me." And then, "I ask only this of you, that you do not contact me again." Between those two statements it usually requires years, not a mere seven days.

The nights restlessly passed and the leaves changed to a hectic red before being ripped from their branches and set adrift on the winds. A different boat was in my old slip at the marina but I did not go down to look. I cancelled an appointment for a blood-screening until I could see if the infection in a molar was gone. I didn't want to go anywhere now or hear any more stories about things breaking down or dying. I didn't want a wall along the border with Mexico. I didn't want anything … or maybe just one thing and I had ten years to prove that it was impossible to ever find it or keep it. There was everybody else and then there used to be us and now there was everybody still and just me. I didn't have a monopoly on suffering though; no one ever does. What I did have was what artists have in abundance, the desire to do more than to simply experience without translating experience into form. This means that for the writer experience is reflected back from some medium and in this way it can grow in intensity like the echo of a pistol shot in a closed room or a wave recoiling from a headland to meet an oncoming wave.

***

Novel writing can be a dangerous profession. By the time a

manuscript is finished it has already drained the author and then the sharks begin to gather to take their little pieces of the trailing flesh attracted by the blood in the water. We definitely don't do it for the money. We would do better to just knock on a door of a hotel room and say, "Hi, I'm your escort for tonight." Don't tell that to publishers though; they like to think that they are doing us a favor when they open the hotel room door to let us walk past them smelling of Obsession and wearing a dress that comes off easily. It is important to look just good enough to be a plausible date. Never say directly what is going down. Appearance is everything – we novelists thrive on illusion, just like other people.

People read for the most part to confirm what they already think is true. In this respect a novel serves the same function as liturgy which must always follow and not precede conversion. In the same way an election is over before it happens, confirming what the polls have already predicted. The only tension is the result of a calculation about just how lazy your opposition may be on election night. "Why vote if I already know which way my state will go?"

For that matter why write novels that few people will ever read? But why be a pessimist? My great aunt said, "Life isn't so bad, if you don't weaken." Perhaps she was on to something; she lived to over one hundred. Maybe we write novels so people don't weaken. Pity and terror purged can save a life. "Say it; don't do it!"

✳✳✳

I have tried to explain here what I mean by things falling apart, the emptiness that I experience as a disaster rather than as liberation. We exist in a web of relations to persons and things. Only those who are losing their memory can imagine what it is to be returned after a lifetime to the immediacy of perception that is that of a child with no discriminating tools to say this is like this and unlike this. For those whose web of association is coming apart things just are; there is no longer any way to predict what people will do or what will happen. Maybe this was why the French woman-novelist just referred to embraced death, because a conscious death is at least an orientation if only one to non-being. Simply reverse the directional signal of life by suicide and you know where you are going; but then that very "you" has entered a realm that may entail even greater anomie. If so then there is no escape even in suicide, we must confront ourselves and this world that suspends us over the arbitrary actions of others who are similarly situated to ourselves. The circle of mockery is unending; round and round we go and encounter the same faces in the crowd eating popcorn and laughing.

***

Dostoyevsky wrote of this state of mind in his "Notes from Underground." Hedda Gabler heard the inner laughter as she closed the door before the shot rang out in Ibsen's play. In this manner we encounter our experience in fictional form because the authors have been there. So in "Pacific End" I probed what had been my experience in 2016 when I returned from the sea to find out if anything was worth salvaging from "the shipwreck of my life's esteems" to quote the poet, John Clare.

Perhaps we begin to forget out of sheer exhaustion of the brain-cells. We are overloaded with incongruous circumstances after sixty years. We would like to narrow down our loyalties and beliefs to a hard inner core to which we could tether the frail craft that sustains us. What if even our friends never really knew us? What if we never really knew ourselves?

We turn to God for affirmation because He is said to care. Maybe that is why people love their dogs: only their terrestrial love is immune from the need for a firm rock of identity; as long as we smell the same then all is well.

We play our favorite songs because they recall to us our lives. Where is a universal reminder as effective as Proust's French pastry? We look in a mirror and say, "Who is that? Did I ever live?"

Is this not the ultimate horror of age?

***

I thought of Guy de Maupassant and his short story, "The Horla," this autumn. He wrote it when he was going mad. I was beginning to realize that all that held me together had been our brief communications so that the constant waiting for word from she who cannot be named had become over time all that I was.

From what direction would the next accusation come?

"I must know everything or I want to know nothing."

Maybe the wounds went deeper than I had thought they did when I had I ceased to be omnipotent, "I will only feel what I allow myself to feel."

Had my tentative coming together by the sea only been a prelude to my loss of a center around which to group sensations so that no we meant no I as well? Had this been what I had long feared, the thing that always brought me back to her? What if the brushfires of incomprehension and estrangement were to spread? How to plant new growth in thin soil when winter was approaching?

I suddenly realized that I was my associations, a brief configuration of impressions rather than an executive directorate. It is the ego that is the illusion. Perhaps "Pacific End" was writing itself. How crazy do you have to be before you are crazy? Maybe the poet Robert Lowell could have told me.

I had been reading about him all summer, but he was dead as was the French novelist who came to the conclusion that unless she was being used, she didn't exist. The scale had tipped too far to return. Beauty wasn't enough to escape betrayal and shame, nor was her mere facility with words. Novelists it appears often run greater risks than just remaining unpublished. Where is the universal editor of experience?

"Forget the words, forget the writing - You are out a little too close to the edge, time to come back to where commonplace things anchor those who would never think of writing a novel."

***

But then living on the edge is sometimes the only way to gain a perspective on the times that we are living through. Otherwise the author is reduced to serving one of the many banal institutions that surround us and appropriate us to serve their own uses at not our own mythic visions. Travel and expatriation, that great resource for novelists in the past who desired to escape regionalism, do not carry the same weight and promise that they once did. The result is that novelists today tend to develop their own unique use of language much as poets have always done, to sift experience and give it back transformed to the reader.

Technique trumps substance in a world that is saturated by discourses. It would be naïve to assume, as Montaigne once did, that mere honesty regarding the everyday could advance our knowledge of human nature, naïve because we no longer believe that there is only one human nature. Instead, we signal to one another from within our private worlds conditioned by a past that no one else shares. We bid for the same sympathy that we expect from our therapists, forgetting that the therapist is paid to listen whereas the reader of our effusions is not. He or she must come to us bidden only by an intriguing title, a bright dust jacket, or the recommendation of a friend.

Language itself is db being deconstructed into its sign value – what weight does a word possess in the immediate context of the surrounding words? Drama and short stories may still seek refuge in heightened incident, but the novel must create a world, instill belief, create sustained sympathy, and maintain faith in the reader that the world of the novel is as the novelist suggests it is.

"Come to me and dwell within this place," says the novelist, "a place that only I can create for you, though I cannot modulate your mode of entry or the quality of your attention."

The novelist unlike the film-maker does not exist as part of a team with a unique ability to control the expectations of the audience by bracketing the time expended upon his production so as to attain his effects in the most complete manner. The novelist cannot select out of the pool of potential readers those who are able to respond to his own unique manner of presentation wherein there reposes whatever residual appeal the novel as an art form possesses.

The result all too often is disappointment all round. Why gamble away precious time on so risky a venture? Why add to the sheer biomass of paper committed to this specific use or worse still see months or years of labor quietly consigned to some file that can contain gigabytes of information? Would Thomas Wolfe have devoted the fire and hunger of his youth to such an enterprise as the contemporary novel? Would it not have been better to stand on the western edge of the continent and cast rocks into the sea?

***

The result of this trend is that we do not look to words to contain experience but to images. Even flesh becomes the ultimate hologram. "Are you really there?" we ask objects in the evanescent ether that surrounds us. How do we regain the thing as it is in itself?

But if we ever manage to do so will we not feel oppressive the heavy weight and texture of substance when we have so long been weaned away from things to images? We will not be able to bear it when our sovereign will is subordinated to an accomplished fact that has been burned into time and can no longer be deleted; the habit of doing things over or amending the decisions of the day run aground on the shores of the irremediable.

"Give me back my life; spare me these memories that grind my thoughts to dust."

The key is given too late to bestow freedom. If Kafka was still writing he would pray that his character would even be granted a trial; instead a general reprieve has been granted to us: "We do not find your crime of sufficient magnitude to be remanded for trial." The maximum of human insecurity is attained when it takes an act of terrorism to even be noticed.

Paranoia is always the refuge for the insignificant – if only someone cared enough to steal your mail. "They are reading my thoughts and following me," the paranoid says. "How fortunate for you," says his therapist, "I can't even get my colleagues to read my submitted articles and I go home alone at night to greet a cat and a blank screen on my computer."

***

The election was growing closer every day as the leaves fell away from the trees and I watched the year dying around me. It was time to rebuild our nuclear arsenal and to elect someone with the leadership potential to damn well use it if necessary. The expectation of conflict is the most salient characteristic of our time.

I was reading a history of the first 2000 years of the Christian dispensation. I had a tooth that needed work and I couldn't find a way out of my stagnation. Beyond that I just had the usual dull misunderstandings and the continued silence of she who cannot be named. I didn't know what was happening down on the coast. Everything had no doubt fallen back into the residual place that events occupy when we are not there to observe them.

Of course what I termed "stagnation" was really my inability to write the text of events according to my own desires. I could not alter world events even when they seemed most opposed to an order of justice and right order. I heard of events that had emerged at home during my absence, of deaths and of illnesses that showed how that sense of the transient and the contingent represented in shell and tide was not merely symbolic of our common fate but a literal setting into type of the text spelled out by driftwood and the castoff residue of each cycle of changes by the sea. I saw that no immunity had been granted me by the summer days and that I was part of the alterations that would not await any permission that I would care to grant if they decided to take me out.

A novelist comes over time to imagine that words can alter reality: "I will not have it so!" I could not restore what had vanished in two months or had changed beyond what might have been imagined in a night's dark dreaming. Where was the hand that decreed such things? What critical distance could restore the comfortable sense that my will could achieve its effects simply by willing them? Perhaps I could not connect again because the sense of correspondences had bred within me a false sense that I could float on the vast currents of air like the gulls riding the updrafts, plunging only when I willed into the purple waters below the cape. Each day would recreate the summer dawn and nightfall would end with the same harvest of the sun drawing down into the distant regions of Cathay but all the while the tides were drawing down the summer days into the inaccessible regions of the past where the driftwood of my days lay already dried and bone-white.

I should have known that for all of the faces we meet each day there is only one face that we come to realize was essential when it is lost. We may not share that choice of faces but the prospect of loss is always there – if I turn away, when I turn back will you be gone with no way to return to the beginning? Shatter the vessel and it is dust. But this is so inadequate a response to the living eye, the gentle smile, the gesture of welcome at a greeting or the tear at parting. Who could ever will a final severance among those who love before it is ineluctably ordained by time and season?

✷✷✷

And yet for all of these losses, willed and unwilled, there are compensations, much as the meetings this summer restored my faith that the words uttered in solitude might resonate in others. We desire to overhear the dark soliloquy that we each speak in order to sustain that dim altar-flame that must be kept burning within for us to face the day and to make it through the long night vigils when we wake at four o'clock and begin for the thousandth time to review our lives.

"Is she who cannot be named awake in her citadel of silence and aware that I am thinking of her? Why is her hand paralyzed when so often before she would awaken me and let me heal myself by being in that moment what she needed me to be?"

Novelists are in many ways the silent and unseen ministers of the world. If so I have done my internship in recent years. But can we ever stop learning, absorbing from the ambiance that surrounds us? But that ambiance is changed by our own coloration projected like the colored flash of lights at Circes to either illumine or shadow objects with our own emotional coloration.

I have never been more aware of this so that since coming home everything that had been familiar lay bleached and dead beneath an ash-grey light, like the florescent lights at border crossings or midnight filling stations. Engagement was lacking...

There was the word, "engagement." I saw and felt how much we depend upon the overlap of other lives in order to define our own. Isolation is required for reflection, but without an image in the mirror there is only the dim silver-sheen of mercury behind glass, flat, empty, and without depth. Since I had come home it was like this each day, like the rainbow sheen of oil on water with neither substance penetrating the other, opposed ions pushing away from each other in order to sustain and extend their unique identities over time.

The novelist makes a mistake in seeking to be embodied rather than dwelling outside of the frame of reference of humanity to record in the cold light like a painting by Vermeer his impressions, fleeting wisps of objective relations with a power to convince relying on precision of usage as opposed to sympathy or trust; but the novelist's personal habits of perception are always pervasive within his work, not just in choice of words but in that overall grasp of significance that tells him what to include or what to omit. How much better to eschew written words for brief expressive gestures as in the room that surrounds me as I write these words –my great gamble on the relevance of the immediate circumstance to contain meaning.

There at a table across the room are four young people in the artificial elegance of a fall dance, probably homecoming, with precisely coded gestures and smiles tried on for effect, subject matter in their conversations eclipsed by the insouciance of flesh. But then without more evidence all of this is supposition, seen from outside even if chiseled into imperishable prose. How much less accurate are predictions as to the course that their young lives will follow when the swinging door closes behind them, and they enter the October night.

They will never be seen again to amend this swift portraiture imposed upon them by a glance across a crowded room. As a result of this essential limitation the novelist weaves all too often what are really various self-portraits projected out of the welter of his own unlived possibilities drawn from within his own unique schemes of reference. The rest is imagination that most fertile of unreliable sources. Those who listen most to life's events never take time to record them. Our literature consists then of the reflections of our solitaries, those who project their unique imaginations into the partial data provided by those who dare to encounter life unmediated by discourses in the naked crucible of events.

These are for the most part the very readers who must decide whether to believe the novelist or not. He seems in his projected consciousness to know them although they have never met. To know one event is to know all similar stories by quarrying out of the bedrock of human nature the emotions that as in music play a familiar melody on vastly differing instruments.

It is said that women have a predilection for novels. Anyone who has observed the gregariousness of women will not be surprised by this assertion. No set of circumstances is sufficiently unique or even trivial that it will not seem to draw forth exclamations of delight from any group of women friends as they encounter each other and proceed to dissect the minutiae of the everyday events that have occurred since they last met. The exchange of little gifts and mementoes is a commonplace among them and the slightest new adornment or alteration in each other's appearance will be noted and in most cases pronounced as a vast improvement. It is this commonality of consciousness that sustains them through their various trials. Women weave the vast tapestry of home and hearth that sustains the human race. Theirs is the miracle of birth and to their final ministry is the body consigned as it is prepared for its eternal rest. If they have not often been ordained as priests it is because their ministry to life and death has always been so pervasive that the act of ordination would have been superfluous.

***

My sense of life that autumn of 2016 seemed to have altered overnight. I had purchased a spurious sense of immortality from the sheer habit of living combined with the universal and sweeping perspective that students of history acquire. I had begun to assume that it was my right to connect all of the partial chains into one vast synthesis ergo I must survive to do it. Since my studies would never be complete and since I had delayed certain common life-tasks such as forming a family time would be extended in my case so that the vast preliminaries being completed I could finally live an individual life: one of love, of service, and one that would allow me to resume my travels eventually, the ones that had been interrupted so many years ago when I was first reading Thomas

Wolfe's novel, "The Web and the Rock," as I did the grand tour of the continent. I recall that the spine of the book was broken but the cover was pleasing and I had already developed that physical bond with the volume so that once having begun that particular copy I must do it justice by reading it to the end. This habit of forming fortuitous bonds and unaccountable loyalties has grown upon me through the years so that I usually felt that I was pursuing a foreordained course through the course of my life. This inner sense had spared me the self-doubt that might have led me to change my ways at the proper season and to articulate one version of the ever elusive text of a life rather than to defer the most important decisions to another day.

How do most people make commitments? I have made few and those that I have made were led by a circuitous route to disappointment and betrayal. I suspect that other novelists have encountered a similar set of difficulties. Breadth of vision causes the particular loyalties to diminish. The mere existence of issues of point of view makes everything relative. A statement is no sooner made than the instinct of dissolution leads the scrupulous author to qualify what he has just said. This tendency is amply demonstrated in the writings of Henry James and of Samuel Beckett. It is present also in me.

My sense of disconnection this fall might be traced to a sudden awareness that time was not merely passing but had passed to that extent that I could no longer deny the imposition of a milestone upon me with all of its spurious benefits of seniority – or to put this in a phrase less elliptical and evasive, I now qualified as a senior member of society. I had entered that season when actuaries sharpen their pens and note the climbing probabilities of various systemic failures of precisely those systems upon the uncomplaining performance of which I calculated, allotted funds, and dismissed any need to turn aside from various insalubrious foods and deleterious practices.

To say that I imagined myself in possession of eternal youth would sound foolish and presumptuous if it were not for the fact that I had been abetted in my denial for years by my own demands and desires and the scrupulous avoidance of ordinary responsibilities so that I could pursue my own extraordinary calling to understand all things and in short to be a novelist. I was meant to occupy the privileged position of clarity and freedom that flies like a hawk above the mundane needs and cares of others. I had begun lately to suspect that this position of which I was only one claimant was not sustainable indefinitely. I had already had private revelations of a sort several years ago when she who cannot be named still occupied that place reserved for her alone. That summer I wrote a short story about a dead hawk that I may as well include here for what weight of evidence it will bear that I aspired to master the form of the short story or sketch as practiced by the Russian masters Turgenev and Chekov before thinking of writing, "Pacific End."

***

The sound of its passing was harsh and sudden as though it was the house that had suffered the injury and not the bird. In fact it was not until later in the afternoon that the family had discovered its tiny body of golden feathers and gently closed eyes on the beauty bark outside the study window. The wings were not spread but lay folded gently about the stiff straight and almost weightless body of the hawk when the eldest son picked it up to take it away and bury it. So light in fact was the bird that it seemed to be more of an idea of speed and clarity, at one with the air that had so recently contained it, than a physical being at all.

Such a lovely creature should not be buried he thought. It should be perched as though about to take flight once again. So it was that he had sought out a tree stump and gently placed the bird there as though upon an altar on a bed of soft pine needles. The sun had broken through the dry branches then and touched the brown and gold of the collar feathers and the tiny head with its symmetrical features and its firm beak noble and dignified. What fate had drawn it to the study windows when acres of open woods might have drawn it just as well? It was just one of those inexplicable concatenations of chance, not dissimilar in its way from the traffic accidents that occasionally took the lives of motorists on the highway outside the closed community, with its bike trails, its cozy lodge, and its view of the Sisters Mountains where he was visiting.

When he looked back upon the incident it seemed emblematic of the course of that summer. But then each summer was emblematic for him, an effort to grab at time, to finally set all in order before the winter would return again to claim him and to isolate him on the boat where he lived in the Northwest. He seemed to have been looking for a breakthrough for years. Maybe like the bird which must have seen for a moment in the gleaming study window a path into the silver darkness enclosed within the cool house with its polished wood surfaces its shining granite counters and its immaculate furnishings, a passage to another world. But the breakthrough always seemed to elude him, though on arrival he seemed to glimpse it at times. It was always a seven hour drive from his home so that his arrival over the pass onto the high plateau always seemed like a triumph of speed and endurance. He had come up this year by what he called the back way from out on the plains south of The Dalles where the road dipped ever and again into hidden canyons. There would be a river at the bottom of these and fishermen casting their lines into still pools as his car or motorcycle, depending on his choice that year, would climb the steep ascent to the prairie lands high above. The sun would shine into his eyes as he turned westward and savored the thought that he would soon see his family once again. Maybe a text message would come to him from home and he would carry it as a silent talisman of victory that he had successfully reached the mountains again and would sleep that night in the shelter of the surrounding buttes and that she would be thinking of him there.

The wind would come up in the evenings in the mountains of summer and shake the trees and the air would be clean and resinous and his spirit would grow clear and clean like the air and things would be as he thought they should always be. There was promise again in life as there had been in his better hours throughout his life. He had beaten his doubts and fears down once again, so that the speed of his body and the vast expanse of the pastures and the distant prospect of the volcanic peaks of the Cascades promised vigor and peace. All of this was contained in the experience of arrival each year. He could imagine again a life where he would always be arriving somewhere but never staying because he knew that to stay would be to hear stories of death or of illness or corruption and penury. Then the triumph would begin to resemble what he had sought to leave behind him, the heaviness of time and the constrictions of the great snake that seemed to be winding its coils about everything that he knew. So that when the hawk had met its death in that one shattering instant he knew that the snake was responsible and was hidden back there somewhere along the road that he had traveled and that it was pursuing him still, even here in this lovely mountain refuge.

He wondered if it would always be like this in life with friends dropping away, selectively defeated by life, so that to hide their disappointment and shame they became first selectively inaccessible and then simply absent so that the ghosts of their youth like the blowing sand-wreaths at dusk was all that now remained of them - all of the old promises forgotten, all the vows to resist the ever-present forces of decay and age. They lived now in whatever remained of the young fellows they had once been, but it was a life now lost to him who alone had tried to keep the faith.

It was all so typical and that was the problem. The charter of the fellowship had as its first canon, "We shall not age." As he looked back upon the years he saw that he had kept the torch alight in a high wind ready for the hand-off in life's relay race. It had not been enough to go on alone because to do so would violate the second canon, "We shall not abandon each other or the dream." But they had done so and the proof was that he was sitting alone over a steaming bowl of white chowder gazing out at the fog shrouded beach at Lincoln City that they had all once known so well in past summers when they were all there together.

He had arrived the previous day from the mountains where he had spent the last three weeks in the shadows of the high cold peaks and now he was by the sea again, the well-remembered, beloved, and yet desolate sea. Through the years he had come to love it for its very desolation, as though its cold ocean heart alone could ever know his pain. He felt that he was a member of the last of a generation of disappointed writers who had grown to maturity after the shattering caused by the war in south-east Asia. That had been the time when America had shown its might by killing villagers and burning their homes an addiction that had grown so great that now America was wreaking its usual destruction by using drones guided by young men in air-conditioned rooms in the deserts of Nevada and Utah to attack helpless wedding parties in distant lands.

No one was shocked anymore by American atrocities, only by their publicity when certain leaks occurred, leaks that no ordinary citizens had a right to know anymore than they had a right to a life unmediated by the silent economic powers that coiled about their lives. None of this was to be the plan for his life. As his nausea had grown through the years at the course that history was taking he longed for an escape that was becoming more impossible with each year. If travel agencies still existed he could picture a big mural-like poster with the caption: "Visit the Seychelles before you have to dive down and swim underwater to find them!"

June that year had brought humidity and unrelenting rain so that when July came he was in a hurry to be off. He had done so thinking that this was the year when he could push through and find again that electric excitement that he had once counted as a possession, the conviction he would never lose so that he could afford to read books like "Tender is the Night" by F. Scott Fitzgerald knowing that what had been irreparable tragedies in other writers' lives would only be for him a source of a sweet and gentle melancholy and hence be experienced as beautiful. But now it was all too close, too real. He was not immune to life after all and words were finally good for little more than to portray the affectation of despair.

The night was coming down on the coast now and the figures of the families on the sand were coming in, silhouetted against the dying sun, yellow as it had been at Pescadero years before when he had written his poem about the horses stampeding before the ocean wind at dusk at Big Sur. He had sold the poem in the Carmel bookshops, as though he had been the new Robinson Jeffers and not just a lonely young man from Detroit trying to escape the industrial winters there in pursuit of a dream of California that was already lost. A few years later California cities like Modesto, Fresno and Bakersfield were more like Detroit than they were cities of the golden west. It began to occur to him that he has been born into a generation that was doomed to witness the decline and fall of a former order of civilization so that he turned now to the Chinese poets of the Tang Dynasty as alone able to speak with a voice that mirrored his own sense of disillusion and desperation. These alone knew what it was like to sit at a mountain pass beneath a fir tree and to lament.

The last wave of patrons was ebbing away into the night and with them the noise and the passing bowls of chowder and fish. He got up to pay his bill and entered the chill evening to drive over to the lodge where a fire awaited him in the great gas fireplace upstairs. He would sit there as he had so often sat before gazing into the flames and looking at the rafters of the high ceiling and out of the windows into the surrounding evergreen trees. There would be time tomorrow to walk the beach on the Siletz peninsula and try once again to put it all together into a form that would allow him to return home in a few days and seek her out to tell her of his travels and gaze upon her once again.

She had never accompanied him on these journeys of his to the mountains and the sea, but it was still as though she was always at his side wherever he was, so that what he viewed was always in reference somehow to her. As the years had passed he remembered places where he had been when one of her sweet messages from home had arrived and what she had said then. So it was that she had been with him after all, the connection never broken, the seamless web of his thoughts of her was woven about all that he had experienced, so that nothing could be said to exist until it had been filtered first by his thoughts of her.

She had seemed to hover above the quiet bay at Yachats where he had once stood gazing at the sun as it burned into the evening haze when he had heard from her. The saw-tooth shapes of the rocks guarding the private bay still held the impress of the memories of the past when he used to come to camp on the adjacent land that his family had once owned. Yachats was home to him then. There was a gate on the highway and it was possible to drive down the steep bank and enter there and to stroll through the deep woods to the bay. The lot was narrow but deep and threaded by a little invisible stream in the center. His father had always intended to sell the back section so that the part fronting the ocean would be theirs for free. The years had passed though and the little cottage to be placed there had never been built. Each year he had traveled down to Yachats he had seen visions of his sister's children running on the beach or exploring the rock crevasses where the starfish lurked and the sea anemones spread their flower-like tentacles. But these visions had never known fruition and the quiet woods, the wildflowers with the lazy bees, and the tall grasses never knew any feet but his own.

Then had come his mother's last illness and the land was sold. A new addition of beach houses was built just to the south and his family's land became a mere buffer-zone to the realized hopes of others. He seldom went that far south in the years that followed because to do so was to feel again the sorrow of dissolution and to know that others had built upon what his own family had discovered. There are families who possess a genius for the partial gesture, a genius for diffusion. Perhaps his own family was like the tide that seemed to advance with a great display of froth and foam only to subside fruitlessly, to draw back, and finally to merge with the great anonymous tidal flow of humanity, sans history, sans property, and finally sans memory. Such families have no sense of permanence or tradition but inhabit only the great carnival of spectacle that is New York, Hollywood, and Las Vegas. Whatever existence they possess is mediated by central broadcasting and I-pods. Their greatest failing seemed to him to be that they were so easily impressed by our national propaganda. They were like clay molded beneath the sculpting hand of the vast commercial engines guided by men who held the vast unwashed American electorate in contempt.

His own love was reserved for the mythic stones that he had once called "the citadel." They formed a low castle-like ruin just south of their private bay and when he had been younger his own flesh had seemed as pure and clean and immortal as its lines. His love for the rocks and the tides was as changeless and adhesive as the stern grip that kept the colonies of mussels intact through the long winter gales. His feet knew the sand beach where his father and he had once swam together just north of their steep and hidden inlet. Private: that was the key! Private meant reserved, set-off, special, just as he wished life itself to be. He wished to be a collector and not himself part of a collection, catalogued in some government file kept somewhere in cyberspace.

He had always known that it is great love and familiarity enhanced over years that makes land become part of one's very soul. He was one born to hold and to keep, to nurture and to cultivate, not to simply view, eat, and leave as though life itself was simply a plasticized motor inn by the side of one of America's endless lonely freeways.

It was for this same reason that he loved the girl. He recalled how she had once emerged out of the night like a phantom by the windows of his boat to beckon him to come with her on one of her nameless adventures. They had gone to the old graveyard in Seabeck, a graveyard so old and abandoned that the stones had been invaded by the creeping underbrush. The night had been warm and a gentle misty rain was falling from the evergreen tops of the trees above them. She had been like a ghost presiding there as a tutelary spirit over the grounds that seemed to be hers alone, hers to open to him the vanished tales of the lost lives that surrounded them there. Who else he had thought could so revere the lost and impermanent dead? It was for this reason that he had called her flesh of my flesh and blood of my blood. A sentiment too visceral to be heard without seeming droll was for him the actual truth, a truth that had for years bridged any partial estrangement of their lives. She had walked the same path as he had and known the anguish and the pain of a nameless legacy of sorrow; he knew that whatever he spoke to her would always resonate within her and be like the sea itself bearing witness to this unity of tide and stars that was his refuge on the coast.

As he gazed into the flames after he had settled in for the night he thought of her in the distant north. The night had settled in and the distant lights of Lincoln City could just be glimpsed over the waters of Siletz Bay. The dream of Yachats was now no more, but the family land at Otter Rock still remained and it was there that he would spend the next few days trying to decide if the hawk that had just died on his recent visit to the mountains was an emblem of his own visions or only a bird, lost and confused by space and sunlight, attacking its own image in the glass.

During the course of the last year he had entered into a strange disposition, a desire to suspend all partial plans and to leave behind the very definition of himself, to approach the world again without placing it first against the template of his desires for order and for form. Instead he was looking for a freshness and objectivity bearing no wake of nostalgia or prior memory. This attitude seemed to him to be one with the vast indifference of the sea, the self-same sea that grinds down all things into one uniform strand stretching out before him, its sands blown about by vagrant winds and piled over the larger rocks in the cove.

Even the land itself at Otter Rock was pressing downwards into the sea to return again as anyone could observe by gazing at the strata of the sandstone cliffs. He had adjusted to the fact that the lot would remain unbuildable by local zoning standards and would provide instead no more than a private park or refuge someday. He had planned upon cutting paths through the abundant verdure to ascertain the slope and water flows beneath the undergrowth. He would build a sort of Zen temple there by the sea to which he could resort in the various seasons of life that remained to him.

His life had escaped the plans of his youth. He had once imagined a comprehensiveness of conception beyond any one human capacity to ever achieve in a single life, as though his one brain could siphon out the plankton of all previous thought and reach some vast conclusion. Instead he was entering his sixth decade with little beyond one vast manuscript that had embodied his appeal to the cosmos, to redeem the lost hours of primal experience that might have been his. He measured his losses by the furthest zenith of his hopes rather than by what he had in fact achieved. If he was unfair in this, he was unlikely to abandon the sheer thrill of what he had once vainly imagined to be possible. Life would soon be measured out to him in teaspoons and the horizon would be shrunken to a few footsteps ahead in the fog of uncertainty. It was for this reason that the dead hawk had seemed the perfect metaphor to one too weary to seek a better one for his present state of mind and heart. Before falling asleep that night he thought of it again and of how the snow would come soon to cover it in the dark night of winter.

The next day dawned fresh and clean and he drove up to Depoe

Bay and watched as the fishing and whale-watching boats headed out toward the distant harbor marker. Some of the heaviness of the preceding day had passed with the night and he was in a better frame of mind to access his prospects upon returning home to Puget Sound. The tidal surges that day were slow and majestic and he watched the breakers send their spray into the air when they hit the concrete breakwater below the bridge over the highway. The north point was sharp and clear and he recalled how one year he had walked the lava cliffs there and looked north to Boiler Bay and south to the elbow that opens to Whale Cove.

His footsteps had been light and sure on the steep lava cliffs and the surge of joy had been in his heart then. He shook his head at the thought now. This was a day to avoid all comparisons with prior years if he was to find a clear standard of assessment for the present hour. If he was to be asked what form that assessment might take he would have answered that he was looking for a sense of stasis, a point analogous to those two points on the earth which connected might determine the location of the axis around which the earth must spin daily.

There was a time when he had imagined that a great secret was pulsing in his very blood, but then his youth was proclaimed at that time in every pore of his skin and the pulse that beat within his arteries had years of untrammeled and unburdened time ahead in which to search for that sense of stasis that had haunted him even then. What had then seemed to be an inevitable legacy that he would realize through a gentle effort now had grown to be a desperate search for the one clear idea that would unite all happenings into one great whole.

Why it should have been incumbent upon him to reach this vast and pointless synthesis had never been clear to him, only that he must reach it in order to complete and justify his life. The result was that he felt that life was daily escaping from him. Where was the wife and child, where the vast enterprises that would succeed him, where "the high piled books in charactry holding like rich garners the full-ripened grain?" He needed a witness, a record, some remnant that would remain when he was gone and there was none, at least none adequate to the vast and vain ambitions he had entertained in his youth. That was his problem and it was one whose solution so far had eluded him.

Lately it had dawned upon him that nothing would ever have been adequate to achieve such an extraordinary completeness, so perhaps it was better after all that nothing was precisely what had been achieved – from the vantage point of infinity all amounts, no matter how large, appear equal. The poems of the Chinese poets seemed to realize this in the universality and simplicity of their descriptions. For this reason these poems were less the product of individual history and were rather representative of the human experience per se. Is this what he had had in mind?

No, because what he had craved was not merely to write of the universal but in his own proper being to have lived and been all other lives – this was his own madness and the explanation for his failure to achieve what was inherently impossible even in its incipiency. For this reason he had never dared to be his own one, single, and limited self. To not have been a self, not to take a stand, not to make irrevocable commitments had been his nature to the present day and were the source of his great emptiness as he stood gazing at the infinite distance of the sea in the sunlight.

He desired above all to create a world that seemed worthy of the trust that it takes simply to live each day. In the absence of such a world each day seemed to be so encased in the possibility of disaster that no sensible action could be taken to avoid it. The sheer number of factors impinging upon every choice made decisions either reckless or irrelevant and probably both. Only the sea retained its own vast simplicity so that to merge with or even to bear witness to it was reassuring and a comfort him.

The sense of dissolution that would often beset him in the presence of others was here reduced to its elementals before which strangely he felt himself adequate and able to cope. Some vast kinship seemed to unite him to the sea and from that union he would have something to bring back to the girl whose own thoughts had so merged with his own that as the years had passed she was always present to him, a presence conveyed most often by that inaccessibility in which she kept herself, one that matched his own.

He understood her because her experience seemed to mirror his own in a way that was completely unique. The linkage that existed between them was more than a mere bond. It was something essential and rooted in his very being as though they were twin poles rotating about a central axis, as certain and defined as the earth itself that pulsed beneath them. Each was a creature of the night, those silent hours of obscurity and safety when the absence of light veiled and softened all contours, and when in the comparative safety of solitary repose they could find a peace denied to them by day, each sequestered in a separate place from the other, and yet for all of that present to each other if only in the echoing chambers of thought and stilled desire.

Lately he had come to imagine a new beginning to his life and to court amnesia because the sheer volume of his memories, like his vast and mostly unread library, seemed to lack any center. The desire to reinvent his life from scratch seemed the shorter course rather than attempting to solve the several equations that had consumed his recent years. It was easier to simply allow everything to rest where it lay like so much driftwood cast up by the last winter's storms. He was living in a world that simply was and that was all that could be said of it. People acted as they did because they acted so – nothing more could be said, no general solution seemed possible, and even if he was able to reach one it seemed pointless to try and communicate it, even to those whom he had loved.

Once again the Chinese poets had come to his aid. Their poems were simple recordings of particular instances. Each object appeared in its uniqueness and particularity and needed no other significance than simply to be itself: a leaf falling from a tree on a mountain side, the sound of a rivulet falling from a cliff to a pool below, two friends drinking wine in a garden. Such images seemed proof to the passing of dynasties and the marauding hordes of vast armies could not dislodge them. Instead these images, each tied to a separate and discrete fact, could be assembled into short poems of undoubted perfection. What they lacked in continuity of discourse was replaced by that convincing witness that embodies the truth of things in singularities.

It was the difficulty that he had in seeing his own life as part of a larger whole that most oppressed him. This abiding sense *of impermanency was made only more piercing by the regular progression of the waves down upon the great cyclopean headland just off the beach of the land that his family had owned for twenty years. Each wave had come to symbolize a generation and five waves became a century. An hour of observation exceeded a millennium then until he was thrown backwards into unfathomable abysses of past years or forward into a future so far beyond his imaginings that he seemed in his little prison of the present to have ceased to exist.*

To add to this global and temporal vertigo he began for the first time to admit that a familial reunion was unlikely to occur after so many years of diffusion. So far beyond any sense of commonality they had each grown with the years that the world that was still so alive within him was for them like a dim memory of a past existence. The land itself which had once seemed to him so permanent was flowing into the sea with a stern inevitability. Great forces were crushing the layers of sediment and clay into one chaos of various levels that could not be healed. Even the land then was less to be viewed as a solid mass than as a transient event of opposing forces that were ripping it asunder.

What did it matter then if it was sold if it could no longer bear a hope that someday the common heirs would see in it what he had always seen there? Would not the yearly taxation figure mock ownership with the futility of land that had no real utility because no home could ever be built upon it? Its every association would thereafter be only a painful reanimation the failed hopes of his youth. Better to spring free and use his final years to embody new memories on a foreign soil than to recall the vanity of all that he had hoped for here.

They were an unsentimental lot, all of them. "I have put it in my will," his father had said to his children. "I don't want any mourning or funeral. After a year you may silently inter my ashes next to your mother's ashes." Even the subjective response of mourning was to remain under his control as though to outlive him was an impertinence that had best not be dignified by being noticed openly. Better to reduce everything to cash before he died, to wash property of all prior associations by merging it into the holdings of richer men who could afford to retain it. This general scorched-earth policy would prevent anyone from really succeeding to an identifiable inheritance that might imply some strange superiority in the very fact of their survival. In just such symbolic ways do we manifest our underlying fears; our possessions alone testify to who we are.

The great headlands and the shifting sands had always represented for him some permanent evidence that his family existed as more than the transient gypsies they had really always been. Now it began to fade, even before its sale was consummated, as though a misty curtain of sea-fog was moving in to veil its former majesty from his view. In twenty-five years would it really matter anyway? Everything would be in other hands then. To lose it all – that alone was immortality to those who lacked all such loyalties, who were already ghosts in life long before their death.

When he returned home it was to the knowledge that he had long been deluded by vanities in his quest for continuity. It had been a mistake to imagine that a viable past could be constructed by main effort or that he could place people like marbles on a tilted table and have them keep their assigned places. His life's narrative had for him only the value of a testimony to his vast foolishness. A past of such chaos and pain would always be a past best forgotten anyway. The present, even more painful, was a testimony of rebellion long overdue. Walls and secret receptacles of trust and of desire had broken through and all lay crumbled like the sands before the advancing tide.

Only a complete break would be sufficient to restore what little sanity still remained within him. He therefore decided to foreshorten his perspective until he could only see the next hours ahead. He surrendered any goals beyond what could bring him safely down to the boat and to sleep, the boat that fronted on the silent lights of Liberty Bay where he could forget the vanity of all aspirations. He knew now that there was no breaking out of the cycle of time. He left each and all to go their own way. He wouldn't climb the pass next year to see if the bones of the hawk were where he had placed them with such reverence. Predators would have no doubt taken them all away. The long cold snows of winter would *have reduced the brave bright feathers to a shapeless mass which the spring winds would blow away.*

Everything was breaking up but not like an icy sea but rather like a landmass cascading downwards to be reduced to particles. That was what it all was, just awkward and unrelated pieces that resisted assembly according to any wider pattern or design. The data would still insist upon pouring in though, raw and pointless. Things would move about like puppets on a string blown about by a vagrant wind. It was will that was the problem – to will anything rather than simply to let change occur as it would do anyway in any case.

He recalled all of the past vanities of his life, from California where the raw-boned brown grass cliffs jutted into the sea, of Montana highways twisting before him, each mile bringing him closer to an anticipated end of recognition and welcome. Each incarnation of happiness had made the former seem to belong to another person and to another life. Was he the plaything after all of the same delusions as the rest of the human race? Perhaps his vaunted individuality had been the cruelest illusion of all.

He had been really only a conduit between the dead and the future unborn and of no further significance than any linkage ever is, one readily mended should it ever be broken. The soaring hawk-like spirit was as inconsequential as the empty sky. Only one phrase seemed adequate to his present need now: "Be still and know that I am God..." These words became his new guide. To them he surrendered and took the first steps out of darkness into light. But the soaring hawk was dead.

***

The story had ended there and I didn't alter its confession. Similarly, I had returned to my life in the north where all of its formerly essential elements seemed to have been withdrawn and dispersed into unknown channels leaving the tidelands now open and bare. The easiest way to attain a happy life seems to be to spend it for the most part with people who are simply good company but whom you do not love from the very depths of your being as I had she who cannot be named. These latter ones are the ones who leave the storm-wrack and shattered timbers behind them when they leave. Walking the beach months and even years later it is not unusual to find some lingering bit piece of wreckage and for a moment the pain returns undiminished by time and by later loves.

I had spent the summer of 2006 letting go and had returned to see what if anything remained of my past life to salvage. Maybe it was all her now and I would never be able to hope to rediscover what I had been before ever meeting her or did she merely arise to confirm what I already was in my innermost heart, a hidden illness of my spirit made manifest at last through her ministrations? When the story about the hawk was finished I put it away in a drawer knowing that I had already moved past it and the times that had spawned it. I was already past talking of soaring hawks.

I wanted to write a novel now in the same voice, something more cohesive and extensive, not just another mood piece such as F. Scott Fitzgerald's short story, "Winter Dreams," a story that I had once so admired and wished someday to imitate. Every writer wants to get beyond this first stage of life when raw feelings supply the text for our lives rather than the careful and refined reflections of maturity leading to an inevitable conclusion. I didn't know what Thomas Wolfe would have written had he lived to write his own version of "Pacific End." Dying early has its price. The like of this sometimes just doesn't happen and Virgil's last feverish days must remain unimagined. Hans Castorp never visits Davos and a gap on a library bookshelf must be filled by other volumes...

And all the while the great and patient sea works its inevitable changes and the land and all who inhabit it fall away into the sands that receive them and then become in turn the sand.

Part Three

Transformations

At the end of the film "Casablanca" Humphrey Bogart tells the French police-inspector played by Claude Rains dryly that he could use a trip. What is a trip but a geographical term for the transformation that we hope a change of scene will provide? Some of us desire more when we speak of transformations. To escape the limitations imposed by the body requires redemption and even then we will not, according to Christian orthodox teaching, be rid of this anchor into specificity; our bodies will rise on the last day. We will not have the advantages bestowed by nirvana dissolving into the vast cosmic soup – no longer even a separate noodle, let alone a chunky piece of chicken. Even people without faith need something beyond the present scene of trial and travail to bring them comfort. For these some sort of transformation is coveted. Riches, beauty, fame, union with a beloved, or for some of us a gender migration across the great divide symbolized by matching sets of genitalia. The goal is to be more than what we were.

In contrast to this view of transformation the mystics like St. John of the Cross advise a scrupulous weeding of the garden of our self-regard. "To get to a place that you know not, you must go by a way that you know not." This pressing aside of distractions and impediments goes by the name of the Dark Night of the Soul. As we age our bodies begin to mock our former estate so that what in our youth must have seemed a great sacrifice becomes with age just one more cleansing of the many-roomed mansion of the soul.

***

As if my body knew that the best way to cancel one source

of pain is to substitute another source of pain I returned from Oregon with that reminder of our mortality, a toothache. I was told after I returned that if I had the abscessed tooth in my lower jaw extracted I was likely to lose the opposing tooth in my upper jaw as well sooner or later because it would not be sustained by continued contact to drive it deeper into its own socket where it had long securely rested. Abrasion is essential in other words if we are to retain our accustomed relations to things. Chew or be rendered toothless! How do we differ then from rodents who labor under a similar dental imperative?

Rats and people have always lived together and neither trusts the other species. The greatest communal extinction in human history, unless we decide to wage atomic war, was the Black Death from Bubonic Plague in the 14th century. Today a dead rat was lying upon the ground when I went to the storage unit to seek out my copies of "Cousin Bette" by Balzac and "Barchester Towers" by Trollope. Was the rat's presence symbolic of something important or merely accidental? Did it realize and take comfort in its final moments in the thought that a mere rat might be memorialized by a higher species in a novel, which if not as significant as the one by Camus entitled, "The Plague," might still at least recall the power that in vast numbers its own rat species could still inflict severe damage upon proud humanity? Even a rat must covet some degree of individual recognition.

This particular rat was victimized and met its premature death because I do not desire that my cherished library should be gnawed and digested or transformed into nesting materials for rodents. It is sufficient that like this present submission should be gnawed by publisher and critics, both of whom owe their existences an ethic of elimination, the first to see that various novels shall not be printed and distributed prevails. Published works are soon neglected and abandoned through unfavorable reviews or reduced to nesting material for their own reputation should the critic ever approve of the work laid before him. The aspiring novelist as neither rat nor critic merely records such transformative effects as his own talents afford him. In this he is sustained by a confidence, one that is fortunately rare, that his own sensibility is worth preserving and examining in the few leisure moments that life bestows upon the frantic masses of the 21st century to read what he has written. No cycle of Waverly Novels by Sir Walter Scott for this age, no Strangers and Brothers Series by C.P. Snow, and no Proustian extravaganza in seven volumes or the endless correspondence of Clarissa Harlow as supplied by Richardson need apply.

Terseness is of the essence. "Just what are you trying to say – to assert that life is like this and why should we take your word for anything? Novels are seldom the pathway to material success and riches. "Who are you anyway? Yeah? I never heard of you."

"You've heard of Thomas Wolfe, haven't you?"

"Sure, he wrote "The Right Stuff" and "Bonfire of the Vanities" and his wife Virginia wrote, "Mrs. Dalloway."

Oh well, one wolf is like any other and who's afraid of any of them?

{Awkward transition} Speaking of Lon Chaney, the poor fellow was an alcoholic. He was like any other father-haunted man. Legends are hard to live up to. I will know that I am rich when I can afford to order anything on a menu without feeling improvident. The really rich can order the best thing on the menu and send it back as improperly cooked and not get charged for it. Jack Kerouac and his crowd were happy with a plate of hash across from a bus station in Denver and George Gissing in Victorian England didn't do much better until he wrote "The Private Papers of Henry Rycroft" and was granted a quiet cottage at last.

Charles Dickens did pretty well but made the mistake of doing public readings from his works and tired himself out and Tolstoy fled his estate to escape his wife and died at a country rail station. All in all novelists aren't a very happy crowd. If I had realized this earlier I would have fled the classics section of various bookstores and sought out the business section instead. When has being adjectively deprived been a bar to even running for the Presidency?

Just ask Donald Trump. Who cares anyway if Strether and Waymarsh, the provincial ambassadors, can get Chad to return to America? See if that trivia answer will buy you as much as a subway token.

***

More changes …What? The annual lutefisk dinner is cancelled after one hundred and three years? What is the election compared to this outrage? There it is again – CHANGE, unasked for CHANGE.

I go up to the little Bohemian café and pull up a chair at the patio to do my October reading. The leaves are at their height of predicable alteration as opposed to CHANGE. The water in the quiet bay below is barely ruffled and the sun is surprisingly warm so that I regret my choice of a sweater however appropriate that choice was in the chill of morning. I sink into the deep sentimentalism of Ann Radcliffe's, "The Mysteries of Udolpho," a book I had begun in a dentist's office years ago when I had my one and only cavity filled in my twenties. Now some forty years later I have yet to read it to its conclusion, just one of the many novels that I have admired but have had to put aside under pressure of the avalanche of later candidates for my attention. Now existing as I do under the impression that by finishing even one of these long deferred tasks I can make concrete what has heretofore been merely a flirtation, dipping into a paragraph here and there, I think that I can transform possibility into permanence.

Too much of my life has been like this, storing up experiences for a more appropriate time when all of my faculties might focus on them and perhaps find in this specific book a worthy place to dwell, for that is what novels aspire to: the creation of a world sufficient to bear our weight when we turn aside from the trivia of moving from place to place about the innumerable supernumerary tasks by which we sustain life and secure a brief habitation while dodging various diagnoses.

I went to the doctor today and they drew blood to track various proteins and ions and lipids and be sure the resultant mix is the ideal one to sustain life without the addition of various drugs whose side-effects are usually far worse than whatever is being treated. Too much of life is precisely like this: we vote democratic in order to keep the greedy and heartless Republicans at bay.

Would it be too much to be able to simply vote the issues and then let the politicians come forward to execute our collective will?

Instead we must selectively weigh and parse personalities and hope that at least some of what we desire will materialize in the next four years. No change where we desire change but when it comes to lutefisk swimming in butter and lefsa with sugar and cinnamon and great steaming potatoes served by sweet and cheery Lutheran lasses suddenly there is only a long and empty afternoon followed by the bleak advent of winter without fortification and the security that I have eaten enough lutefisk to ward off viruses, molds, yeasts, and even the forces of ISIS.

Instead I am asked to bow to necessity, to compromise, to lift my eyes from my Gothic novel and to encounter reality. Today the book's accidental content is provided by a young man who is studying to be a nurse whereas he was once paid $80,000 a year to make microchips that are now being made in China. The people there live in vast prison-like compounds without fear of unemployment because they cannot even escape to entertain other offers, a refinement of the issuance of the company scrip that was used by the 19th century American coal-mine owners to control their workers. Nursing at least cannot be readily outsourced because the job is tied to the body of the patient. He has figured it out.

I think, "It's too late for me to pursue an alternate career path. I am like one of those species of birds that Darwin found in the Galapagos Islands that have evolved into a dead-end direction, one perfectly adapted to a narrow range of foods with a narrow beak or one perfect for prying open an indigenous shellfish that has since died off because of a new virus."

The birds just stand there on one leg and look sadly at the sunset, too late to evolve a new set of characteristics or adaptations for the changing conditions. Similarly, I dream of the lost world of Gothic Novels like the one I am reading, one where the novel of sensibility might not be viewed as simply absurd and abjured for fear that any such refined sensibilities will lessen any residual survival instincts that I may possess. Better to see things with the bottom-line sterility of the young but dead French-Canadian woman writer that I have mentioned who combined in her novels the self as victim and villain in one long exegesis of suicide. The logic of the era that we live encased within is reductive to precisely this end. It takes a desire to become anachronistic to avoid the plague of texts and tweets that surround us daily.

"Why didn't you read my e-mail?" my publisher asks me.

I answer, "Because I am not wired for instant response to the impersonal web of flashing data points that so impresses you."

"I wish I could live like you," he says.

"And I wish that I didn't doubt the wisdom of the present collective confidence in a computer modulated world."

I think later, "I wonder if it is still possible to step aside from the temptation of instant availability and create a certain Walden Three?"

No lutefisk this year.

✳✳✳

I read in "USA Today" that young voters are thinking of voting for third-party candidates as I usually do. This is reassuring to me. Maybe they will reclaim the country. I look down at my phone and see that my Dad has just called me. Things are going well for him and I think how grateful I am that he us strong, healthy, and still motivated. I realize how deeply rooted by own body is in the soil of his life and how that permanence sustains me. I know that he is one of the great and stable stars that I use to navigate these stormy seas of change. It is strange to me that she who cannot be named was another one of these points of reference and that much of my sense that things are coming apart now can be traced to her absence this October.

I tell my position in many ways like those very bats that I fear so much by sending various signals out into the dark and reading the echoes when they return to me. What is most terrible is the thought that I might personally experience now what is our position collectively when we send out various space-probes. They send data back for a time, but then suddenly somewhere on the outer fringes of the solar system just before drifting off into endless darkness they fall silent and with exhausted batteries drift away unnoticed and without meaningful coordinates into the ever growing expanse of endless space-time.

***

It is the repetition of common events that gives us our location. These tell us who we are. As I have written these words night has fallen outside and the bright autumn day has been subsumed into darkness. It is now too late to reclaim anything left undone today: to give more blood, to surrender to various hijackers of our time and consciousness, to adjust to sensible demands. Events leave brief memory traces in the handful of individuals that I have encountered today. The specifics will soon merge into the dull uniform fabric of habit and ritual so that years hence or perhaps next week I will not recall what I did or said because neither was of sufficient magnitude to lift it above the surrounding waters of the ever-rising sea, one that is not due to global warming but to my own global cooling, the still ongoing influx of events that can no longer be contained within the narrowing circumference of the amphitheater of my skull. Something must be sacrificed. The membrane that separates me from others grows thinner with time. I am less likely today to guard my dignity long since sacrificed because it is not reinforced and made actual by a corresponding property interest. I am falling like the leaves drifting in the vagrant currents of this autumn day. I lack that firm sense of direction that is provided by an overwhelming aspiration.

Is it you or me sitting in the chair while you are getting your hair cleansed prior to having it dyed? Who is that couple at the table across the room? Is it I who write these words or some fragment of me? Does the medium draw forth my words like the phlebotomist who drew my blood to read its message, one inscrutable to me who only feel the brief sting and look at the test-tubes with their yellow stoppers?

As I get older will I ask that someone retain my DNA to clone me and give me another chance at life? Engineer me to a razor's edge; bring back all the suicides who have been condemned to a purgatory of later regret. Splice in new organs to buy me time. Centrifuge my personality to separate out the essential parts from mere plasma. Bring back those that I have loved and lost.

Remind me that even this boring day, imperfect and too short as it is, might someday be of such value that I would embrace it again and ask that it never be forgotten; because after all it was enough and if I had not been spoiled by time it would have been seen as capable of revealing to me all of the secrets of my inner being. Once locate any position in space-time and no matter in what direction you move the universe will bend around you and nothing will be lost. Trusting the conservancy of events is the pathway to a universal peace.

✳✳✳

I wonder if she is brooding tonight gazing out into the darkness, still angry at me for who knows what? As our thoughts cross each other unseen in our silence does she wonder why I would be willing to concede anything to her, even my disappearance and silence, out of love and because she asks it of me, demands that it should be so?

The door opens and two men come in from the chill and I know it is time to go if I want some dinner. I am already breaking my new rule of never eating after eight at night. I can feel tiredness playing around the edges of my consciousness. I will sleep well tonight in the chill.

✳✳✳

No one experiences fortuitous events as un-designed; there is always the underlying sense of a tight causality, that one is being punished for something or that some personal oversight has been involved even in the unforeseeable. We think, "This whole thing could have been prevented by a combination of foresight and determination." The problem of course is one of relative positioning. The task is to remain just beyond the range of adverse forces while sufficiently close that good fortune is not eluded as a result of one's excessive caution. Even then though there is the problem of events or conditions that arise in secret corners or those that suddenly encounter a medium that nourishes them from tiny seeds into adverse and monstrous growths. Even routine is no guarantee that complete safety has been secured. In fact a habit of recklessness can breed not only tolerance of adversity but may instill resourcefulness and those skills that are submerged by too long habituation to a stable world.

All happenings are in one sense the result of whatever inscrutable first cause set things into motion. We know only the distant repercussions of that primal affirmation of created being, that there should be something rather than nothing. To will anything is to will all subsequent events that flow however indirectly from that act. The slightest intervening variable can break whole cycles of events whereas to produce them with regularity and certainty always involves mere probability.

A novel then if it is to deserve the credibility that it invites from the reader must mirror this very incertitude and contingency of outward events. Yet few authors actually adhere to this basic rule. Instead of awakening pity and terror predictable novels entertain us by indulging our wishes and soothing our desires with the expectation of eventual fulfillment. To portray life as it really is would entail the possibility that the careful evolution of a plot of some four hundred pages might be upset in the final few paragraphs by some trivial event.

Art must please and entertain or the artist risks forfeiting the goodwill of the very persons who financially underwrite his projects. The avid publisher scans the bottom line quarter by quarter and the bookseller sandwiched between various retail establishments takes note of which items of his stock are not moving. Authors are encouraged to act as sales-agents for their own work: to make personal appearances, to smile and sign books, to appear on media discussions, and to create a buzz to advance the familiarity of their names. Each of these techniques of course implies that the book cannot stand on its own square feet as the creation that the author has projected, one that exists now beyond his singular biological self. Authors often feel that their work often exceeds its source.

"Where did that insight originate? Is this the work of my hand or of some possessing spirit?" The author may feel is lean and impoverished except when he is writing.

***

But we were speaking of the impact of fortuitous events such as the remnants of Typhoon Songda that has turned its force away from the usual path these storms follow to make landfall in Asia and in this case it will affect the northwest coast over the course of the next week.

Today the sun was bright with that autumnal perfection and stillness that I imagined would go a long way towards healing my recent discontents, those bred of tales of misfortunes to friends and to the families of friends. Sorrowful happenings had been more than the low hum of adverse forces waged in distant lands; they were closer to home. I could feel misfortune interjecting its force into the outer circles where I was accustomed to feeling if anything a vague envy that others had made better choices than I had made. They had trusted life to give them some measure of their expectations rather than anticipating various arbitrary events or disproportioned responses. To be confirmed in my own dark expectations of events did not encourage me to adopt a more sanguine course in the future. I am habitually more likely to nourish a gentle melancholy than to indulge in any expectation that I might be surprised by unanticipated good fortune or find an unsought love. I am accustomed to making an ardent effort to prepare myself for various actuarial-calculus infused events that might rear their ugly heads in the ensuing years. So it was that I asked for a talisman to ward off what suddenly seemed to be all around me and could find it only in the act of writing "Pacific End" with its humble aspiration to be notes on the form that novels might take rather than being itself a novel, although in the actual writing I have thrown out hints that I and a few others might be characters in a drama that now and again comes to the surface like the outlines of objects when they are seen through an obscuring blanket of fog. The voice of an indefinite narrator and an uncertain or absent plot modifies the expectations of normal experience with its presumed clear edges and established values. Why speak of chains of causality when so many events are strangled before they assume even an inchoate form. Truth in expression is best maintained by a sustained relation between conflicting elements just as life is sustained by the pulse beats between stillness. Prolong the pulse and the result is fibrillation; prolong the stillness and you get cardiac arrest; both in balance are the condition for sustaining life.

The expectation of continuity is our most cherished illusion. We expect to attain at least a marginal sense of closure and time for review before the end. We think that it is never too late to begin the pursuit of a long deferred recovery from our habitual deleterious choices. At any moment we think that our poverty and obscurity will be interrupted by good fortune as we purchase our lottery tickets or sit before the flashing lights of various slot-machines. Our boss or spouse may suddenly shift from abuse and ridicule to appreciation and praise. Our long martyrdom in obscurity may finally be honored by recognition. In this sanguine spirit Thomas Wolfe, who had already exhausted expressions of loneliness and woe hoped to discover that his journey to America's west could be redemptive in a way that mere geographical transposition seldom is.

In a similar manner I thought that I might find in various faces and stray scraps of conversation this year a truth greater than either Thomas Wolfe or I had ever glimpsed. In Nevada when the mines brought up only poor grade ore that does not justify the costs of milling, the mine itself was said to be in borrasca.

Novelists often find themselves in a similar state, one where any assertion is immediately countermanded by an opposing thought or conviction. Words begin to lag and grow heavy and the writer thinks of summing things up quickly or skipping steps in his exposition. Shorter books are cheaper after all to print and this makes publishers smile. If you run dry as an author, others are waiting to take up the baton that you have dropped. On the other hand a valuable literary property should be mined for all that it may contain, even if it leaves the author wrung dry and inside out after several books.

It is not uncommon for playwrights to end their careers by writing plays that close after the first few weeks. Novelists who do not know when to gracefully bow out end with their novels remaindered a year after publication. Only after they die are various lost manuscripts or uncompleted works brought forth like revenants from the grave to delight literary ghouls or as evidence that the author was still in possession of some of his former talent although he was sadly and mistakenly neglected in his final years.

There is always the hope that a discerning critic will spark a revival, but as the years pass this event becomes less probable. At last a lifetime of work merges into that vast sea of unprotected work, the public domain. Even classical writers are demoted from leather bindings to occasional paperback editions of the classics, books much honored and little read.

If this seems a grim assessment of an aspiring author's prospects it should be recalled that the real function of publishers and critics may be to save trees by keeping various unworthy efforts from ever achieving the dignity of print. Time does the rest. Just ask the ghosts of Arnold Bennett, of Theodore Dreiser, of Pearl Buck, or of Sinclair Lewis. Nothing can really aspire to be a classic that is not in print and read until the end of its copyright protections. For most books five years would be adequate protection from the anticipated threat of any pirated editions. It might have taken this long just to have written the book. The best as advice is to prospective authors therefore is to keep their day jobs. Those who wish for fame and fortune had best look elsewhere.

✳✳✳

To accept that life is ephemeral, uncelebrated, and largely unexplained may be the beginning of wisdom though it brings but cold comfort to the one who has discovered what everyone else knows but has the good manners to avoid enunciating, even in the silence of their private thoughts. Instead as we age we take anti-depressants and medicines for erectile dysfunction and hope that a padded bank account and a hot car will overcome any natural reticence to stall our decline by affection. Old age is a good time for spiritual renewal because we will meet little competition in this final race to attain the virtues. Instead many people seek a chance for one last score in their long battle for recognition and self-redemption. The true contemplatives meanwhile surrender regrets, honor the unused prospects of the young, and gracefully step aside when death comes. Even before we die we realize that it is just not our world anymore.

✳✳✳

The storm came nearer as the days passed. I was glad that it was coming from the south and was arriving in October rather than November. It would be nice to live in the city and hear the storm knocking over garbage cans in the alleys rather than to live beneath trees in the suburbs or as I do on the waters of Liberty Bay. A direct blow is the worst but waves that break on distant shores still eventually reach us. I know that the sands deposited over the month of August will soon be clawed away by the autumnal breakers. The sea spume will go hurdling over the highway at Depoe Bay. I know that I would not find many people now along the beach. I am grateful that the Olympic Mountains stand as a shield between me and the full force of what is coming. For the rest I hold my breath and wait.

I went up to the church this evening and caught the end of a Hispanic retreat there. As usual children were everywhere and I felt the deep devotion of the people that makes language unnecessary because the general goodwill is sufficient to leap across any language or racial barriers. I begin to see how seduced I have been by ideas and by the written word when blood ties and cultural resonance can be sufficient to sustain people's sense of the value of their lives. The dialogue across generations of authors may have its use for writers but it is hardly missed by those who spend most of their days simply living. Theirs is the experience that writers only imagine because solitude breeds a deficiency in precisely those areas where humanity is most clearly articulate: through eyes, embraces, and the many ministrations of touch. All of these share the qualities of immediacy and exchange. There are no winners or losers, no thought is wasted on who benefits the most as in trade; instead a sense of mutuality and community is created and from this a new life-form that exceeds its individual constituents.

Nothing in life is really merely a totality; each new element added takes what has been encountered to a higher classification as new relations become exponentially realizable. At the highest level all things coalesce into unity. Perhaps this is the long sought image that explains the Holy Trinity. Where communication in love is total unification is inevitable. Even creation, dispersed as it is, appears to be engaged in realizing possibilities that were in some way present in conception at least from the beginning.

In this sense time runs backward in the reminiscence of the divine mind that seeing all finds a common thread of intent so that as each new thing is realized it is seen against the fabric of the whole. Its modification may even appear inevitable as it finds its particular place in the whole so that even evil deeds are seen to advance the good that manages somehow to encompass and transform them. In this direction the devil's frustration must lie: that willing evil he only works the ultimate good of all things.

***

To entertain a sense of universal compassion recalls my experiences over the summer when things began to merge and to awaken again to life. This reflection makes me think of she who cannot be named, the one who was always impervious to my every reassurance. Is she doing better now in other company than mine? Is the membrane of silence and distance between us a wall or merely the distance created by a number that is not dialed day after day? Why are the simplest things the hardest? There are no words that can reach her where she dwells in her immense distance encased in the adamantine force of her refusal. Our two magnetic poles push us apart by our identity. We would each do better to love a stranger where the mockery of expectation is replaced by mere good manners. Perhaps pleasant always exceeds ecstasy in human life and adequate trumps perfection.

***

As the days passed the storm finally showed its teeth. I woke in the night to see the clouds being driven before the winds and a cold full moon shining through the broken edges. The scene was unearthly in a way that no artists from the old Universal Studios could have imagined. I had listened carefully to the news broadcasts all day and had mapped in my head the key hours of the storm in its course over the following days and the direction and probable speed of the winds. I was as prepared as extra lines on every available cleat could make me but I still wondered whether we are ever prepared for what life throws at us. To factor in disaster is to spoil joys on those sunny days granted to us while to maintain a hidden anger at fate is pointless for it is not dismayed by our displeasure. It does as it pleases, swiftly, incorrigibly, and without appeal. The brooding novelist wakes in the night and gazes through the breaking clouds in search of meaning. Random misfortunes leave us gasping, "Why?" Only by seeing in every person the same special qualities of the beloved is universality of affection possible. But is this spectrum of regard natural? Isn't it precisely the uniqueness of our personal losses that makes human love real?

Our soul cries out, "You and only you, so that no one else may fill the gap that was yours and reserved for you alone in my life. Give me back only yesterday? Allow me one more chance to tell you what I have already told you a thousand times. Let me see your eyes alight and know that your soul is so close to mine that I can almost touch it. Only do not give me this, this DEATH."

***

I drifted off to sleep at last and the storm boomed about while I slept, uncaring that I had not noticed its passing. The news that day had spoken of a gorilla in a European zoo that had broken loose until it was "subdued." I recall thinking that perhaps it thought that its own dear jungles and familial group was just on the other side of the walls that imprisoned it. Why was it there in the zoo "to be subdued" in the first place? Did it ask to be abducted and transported to Germany? Why was it asked to bear the costs of an imposed exile instead of its abductors? Why do these disorders keep breaking loose? Is there a connection between a storm ravaging the Pacific coast, an escaped gorilla, and a sudden death or illness among my friends?

Does it matter that I have been reading recently about the advent of AIDS and the making of the Names Project Quilt? Is there a subtle witchcraft to events or is it all the turning of a great wheel grinding us like grain into paste?

I had gone up to the Church that evening where I sat alone as the rain fell outside. I was reading and the lights were on when some late worshipers arrived. They had no sooner entered when the lights went out with a flash. I heard them later saying a rosary by the light of a flashlight and I wondered if they had seen my still form up by the altar when they came back from their car with their flashlight. In the darkness I thought how easy faith must have been when no technology could obstruct the forces of nature, no heat in the vast high vaults of the Gothic cathedral at Cologne but only the dim comfort of candles and the dark harmony of Gregorian chant thrown up at God through the darkness. After a time the people left and I was alone again. There were no sounds but those of the storm beating against the walls of the Church and the rain from a leak in the roof dripping into a receptacle placed in the isle. I was alone again in the forlorn and partially used church while in their homes people prepared for what was to come, while I like Victor Hugo's Hunchback of Notre Dame sought sanctuary there. I wondered if the lights when the power returned would shine all night in spite of my efforts to turn them all off when I was about to leave. At last weary of the darkness I got up to go. But first I would say a prayer for a peaceful night and a blessed end:

Hail Mary Full of grace

The Lord is with you

Blessed art thou among women

And blessed is the fruit of thy womb, Jesus

And at the word "Jesus," suddenly the Church was filled again with light, the timing to a split second after over an hour that I had spent in the darkness. Was there no meaning in this? No force trying to tell me something? The lights had to come on sometime, so why not then? If contingencies can be so finely tuned to coincide with meaning, then is anything accidental? Was the path of transformation that I have been tracing real? Is there an ur-novel beneath the text guiding first perception and then articulation towards some wider form that would embrace all things? That which I had formerly thought of as merely an innate underlying sympathy with the human condition might be a substantial unity in fact – all things may be connected and weaving a pattern out of seemingly accidental events aligned by an artificer whose hand is so subtle that it cannot be perceived, acting with what might be called the grossness of cause and effect to achieve more subtle ends.

***

I woke again in the night and this time I had. I dreamed that I was teaching a class but had never taken the trouble to come to it so that the class for all that I knew had long since abandoned coming to sit in an empty classroom awaiting someone who never came. But this night I came and strangely they were still there. I spoke to them and apologized for having so neglected them:

"You have not been gathered here without a useful purpose because no doubt you have spoken to each other over the course of this semester and in doing so you have acted the part of philosophers because that is what philosophy is: a long discourse of many voices on the subject of the great perennial problems. Even time is no burden here; it not too late because one session would suffice to tell you what in essence each of the great philosophers has said. If you have developed the instinct for questions, then the answers, even if briefly stated, will already have occurred to you in some form. Each great thinker has one central message or insight. It is precisely because of this that their conclusions are so fundamental and why their solutions recur in age after age with only slight modifications. Philosophy as a result is never old and never new; it simply is.

***

To change into what one has not been before – that is transformation. Once that change has occurred it is not possible to return to what one once was. This is the nature of all loss and all gain. It is not merely, as Thomas Wolfe once said that it is not possible to go home again – home itself is the illusion, it never was a place where we could abide. Time presses and we cannot stay; our chariot awaits us.

Bob Dylan was just awarded the Nobel Prize because his lyrics made a difference to a generation; isn't that a good enough reason to award the prize? Americans recognized his voice as their own. How complex does a message have to be?

✳✳✳

Bodies are breaking down around me. I hear talk of supplemental insurance everywhere. Out beyond the circle of firelight there is menace afoot. Maybe this is why this storm has been more than merely a climatic event for me. It is evidence that things are neither safe nor stable in my world. I cannot through sheer grim willfulness push my way through. Do I recall my birth in some strange way so that I think that I can find my way out of all of this and find light and air on the other side of our present awareness? I am looking for an altar candle burning in more than the church to show that God is everywhere. Perhaps I have blundered into life from the 12ᵗʰ century when the great Gothic Cathedrals were first built; but no, I need more intimacy than this. I would like to knock on the tabernacle fondly to remind God that I am here. I need to feel warmth like the light from a red candle flame. I go to the Mediatrix of all Grace knowing that she is the chosen vessel through whom to distribute all of the results of the redemption of Christ. I draw up to her with the quiet confidence of a wounded child. I see that I have been drawn back into the use of the present tense in recounting these experiences. Will the reader see that for me past, present, and future interpenetrate? I have forgotten nothing; my present is off-center and partially realized while the future is hidden in the darkness of the storm. In "Pacific End" themes are announced and then abandoned and like a symphony the further notes continue to develop and modify prior motifs. How long will my candle burn?

✳✳✳

Pope Innocent III in the 12ᵗʰ century, before his election to the exalted office of the papacy, wrote a fulsome book on the miseries of the human condition. His later actions were in many ways indicative of his prior beliefs. Once souls become mere fungible commodities the value of the individual vanishes. The only thing particular about us is our sins. The task is to die in the uniformly defined "state of grace." Joseph Stalin adopted a similar generic standard to apply to the Russian people when he followed Lenin as the Chairman of the Communist Party. Party loyalty became the equivalent of the total submission of the soul to God. What are the deaths of any number of workers as long as the worker's state prospers? This business of achieving the final realization of an idea is responsible for most of the deeper atrocities of human history. For this reason I have often wondered to what extent we should pursue the development of our own personalities, our private stories, a pattern of events and loyalties that are ours alone. What is the value of the particular the singular when laid against the sheer multitude of all who have lived before us and the vast number of our contemporary denizens of the earth?

One of the most invigorating ideas of the Declaration of Independence was its affirmation of the individual. It was an affirmation that subsequent American history has seemed bound to deny to the majority of its citizens. Every effort to emerge from the mass has been resisted as a threat to their station and power by those who have managed to reach a point where their time is not the primary commodity they possess that is available for sale. Even high wage-earners and professionals must fall behind what land and capital are in principle capable of producing. Americans are determined not to recognize this basic truth. The political system that sustains the present economic order aids and abets this denial because to admit it would be to plunge the nation into despair. Instead our collective resentments are focused outwards at various alien threats to our "way of life" and to anyone drawn from our majority classes that can be portrayed as getting a free ride.

As is the case with most widely held delusions great energy must be expended to repress what at one level everybody knows to be the truth. This in turn has generated the peculiar penchant for violence and death that have made most of our international actions of the same category as those of the Vandals and the Huns. We export misery and call it our national interest. We each own a small share in the guilt of these general actions perpetrated in our name. Freud called it the death instinct; we call it the defense of freedom and the American way. Students of nuclear arms call it meta-death, the excess of thermonuclear power beyond what it would take to kill every man, woman, and child on the planet.

***

The day when the second half of the great storm was to come ashore began quietly. I was glad that I was not out on the coast now because a tornado had hit the town of Manzanita, one of the first assaults of the storm earlier that week. Trouble was everywhere as that day's edition of the New York Times made clear. Haiti, a nation where suffering seems to never stop, was dealing with the flooding caused by a hurricane and a resultant epidemic of cholera. The proximity of Haiti to the United States is a constant reproach to the wealthiest of nations, one that was willing to risk nuclear war over Cuba while failing year after year to manage to aid this poorest of nations in the western hemisphere to a stable political and economic future.

Meanwhile, in its own sector of the world, Russia is stirring to life again like a great and surly bear. Displeased with the economic sanctions and still feeling the shame of not being one of the primary arbiters in the councils of nations, Russia is playing the only card that seems to draw world attention, its strength as a fearsome nuclear power.

American warships are currently engaged in shelling Yemen near Russia's area of regional concern. Suddenly my inchoate fears have a discernable focus in the state of affairs that prevails in the world while our major candidates bicker and reveal that probably neither should be president. The worst part of this is that the voters are increasingly of this same opinion. Why are we being dragged along by a governmental apparatus that few people believe can ever serve their best interests? Patriotism is only invoked successfully after a period of peace, but since Americans now exist in a virtually constant state of various armed interventions the concept of a just war, one requiring major sacrifices from average citizen is beyond our credulity. Instead we simply acquiesce grudgingly to the expenditures that plunge us year by year ever deeper into debt.

The young seldom protest beyond simply plugging their ears with various electronic devices and try and forget that these huge debts will be left primarily for their generation to pay. People of my age look towards an impossible dream of longevity combined with the desire to retain the full former vigor of our working years. The reality will probably entail being stretched out on a rack of mere length of days with bodies that are too damaged to be viable candidates for genetic reconstruction with purloined stem cells. Even cloning is not really an option because nobody really wants us back unless we are as beautiful as Cindy Crawford. (It would be nice of course to resurrect Marilyn Monroe and give her one more chance; she would fare better now than she did in the salacious and repressed fifties). The rest of us may as well face it; this is all we get; if we didn't buy Apple or Microsoft in time, if we contracted AIDS when it was still called GRID and died, if we went to Afghanistan on our four terms of duty: well, we were just unfortunate victims of history and it's just too bad that's all.

Of course we could clone Bush/Cheney/Scalia/Thomas and bring them back to make amends to the nation, but who wants to see their faces again after they pass on and the guillotine is out of style. No, we are stuck with whatever era coincided with our one and non-repeatable life. In fact in this year of grace 2016 we should give thanks that the real storm is still hovering offshore. The great Chinese foreclosure sale on America has yet to be declared. These *are* the good-old-days.

***

The storm eventually took a lucky bounce and vented most of its wrath northwards into Vancouver Island's sparsely populated west coast. I went down to the boat to pump the bilge dry and found that a rat had come aboard. Past experience had shown me that they always return. From the first encounter with them fate decrees an ensuing battle to the death. I went out immediately to buy a trap of truly serious technology, the grizzly bear version of rat-traps.

I then proceeded to set up a cunning maze leading the unwary one to destruction. I constructed a virtual highway of death that offered early rewards, gentle foreclosure of other options, and a logical progression leading to death. I tried to think for once like a Republican. The result was a dead rat. The only thing that might have saved him would have been an inner intuition that a boat owned by an obsessive- compulsive is a dangerous boat to board. Once on the trail I am indefatigable.

I had made years ago a study of rats, fleas, and their attendant diseases. My ears prick up at the talk of every new virus from the AIDS virus to ZIKA. Whole areas of the earth are off limits for me due to various indigenous threats, from the Brazilian Wandering Spider to filarial worms in Guinea. If I use caution with the humble doorknob and foreswear easy and familiar handshakes it may be imagined how I will react when my veritable living space is traversed with tiny rodent traces. I maintain a zero-tolerance policy. All of the aids of technology are brought to bear on the problem and the result is a foregone conclusion.

Now if all of my problems could be dealt with by such a direct and instantaneous reaction, then all would be well. But all is not well. I am writing "Pacific End" twenty years beyond the era when it should have been written, at a time when insight still had ample time to alter a life-course and produce fruit. Nothing is more common than for the aged to complain and to regret their lost opportunities. No writer enjoys being predictable. We would all start our own small revolutions by virtue of a sense of prophesy combined with ample persuasion. Novelists enjoy being popular even when decrying fame. It is a positive pleasure to imagine, even while writing in a lonely room, that soon the halls of power will take heed of the masses at the door waving flags and carrying the novelist's latest manifesto. Wealthy hostesses will seek out the novelist to adorn a dinner table along with statesmen and society beauties.

But then I am speaking of yesterday's novelists, not those who write today for a dwindling readership of aficionados or for a mass market of the linguistically challenged. The age that recognized the novelist as a public intellectual has already come and gone. We don't get interviewed often because we are boring. It takes us too long to make our points. We like to qualify our statements and quantify our assertions so as to give what we say proportionate worth. We also assume a nodding acquaintance with the tradition of our art form in those we address. We presume and that is the whole trouble; we aren't sufficiently important to be allowed to make any presumptions. We are lucky to be read at all. Who are we to dream of transforming the world into one that better accords with our particular vision? The result is that we are increasingly represented by paid pessimists. We are assumed to share the general quality of disillusionment that floats like a foul film over the Thames or the Elbe or the Hudson.

Where could the novel go after Kafka and Beckett? Where can history go after the war against fascism and communism? Has anyone thought up a new cultural idea in ages, one that will provide the adequate reason for future wars? This is how bad it is: we have been thrown back onto the middle ages for our revolutionary ideas. What is ISIS but an effort to import religion into a world that hasn't taken religious wars seriously since the 16th century? Where is our Marx, our Freud, our Einstein, or our dark triumvirate of Hitler-Stalin-Mao? Instead we are merely drifting like a crouton in a post-modern soup of partial articulations of problems in hermeneutics. Only theology has had a late flowering in works of Karl Rahner, Bernard Lonergan, and Teilhard de Chardin. These were big simply because theology had been set on simmer for years under various popes, most of them named Pius. The long delay caused a sudden leap forward after Vatican Two.

Islam meanwhile has possessed only two unifying characteristics: disproportionate oil wealth and resentment against Israel; neither is enough to expand its initial insights into a world phenomenon without an appeal to force. National epics like the Koran provide a weak basis for global appeal ever since Hitler tried to build an empire on the vision of the Nibelungenleid as filtered through Wagner. We are all casting about today for a cause worth dying for and not finding any we are content to simply survive.

***

Short is the new long where novels are concerned. Just make your point quickly and clock out like a good workingman and save the company money. Not much plot, less description, few characters, and a good cover: there you have it, a book. Sold by the pound like lean ground-beef; it is a good deal. Why sell a big burger when "sliders" are the thing?

We novelists try to talk art and publishers talk about return on investment; a short book is an easy read. (The unwritten message of course is, "Why not save even more time and don't write or read at all?)" Maybe the award of the Nobel Prize in literature to Bob Dylan reflects this new reality: words without music just won't fly anymore. The novel isn't just dead; it is bad form, a trial to the nerves, part of a world where publishers are just one of many industries owned by corporate conglomerates with each industry judged by the bottom line. Owning a publishing company jazzes up the image, gives commodities an intellectual flair; people think you aren't just in it for the money.

✳✳✳

An attorney says, "I read Ulysses. I was proud of doing it, but I didn't like it. The thing I'm most afraid of is being killed by a grizzly bear while jogging … or having to read Ulysses again."

I think to ask her, "Then how do you feel about "'Finnegans Wake?'"

Of course the jury is still out on what "Finnegans Wake" really is. My choice is: secular scripture. No one works for seventeen years on a literary joke even with the aid of a sponsor. I think it may be the best book since Dante's "Divine Comedy." This presumption that people appreciate your bragging about what you haven't read or understood is the most indicative characteristic of our age. It shows our collective pride in being shallow.

✳✳✳

The third Presidential Debate was held and I only caught excerpts after the fact. When Donald Trump ran out of words I noticed that he either repeats himself or adds adverbs as a means of emphasizing the degree of his certainty. Everything exists on the edge of apotheosis for him. It is not a good quality for a President to have. The Chief-Executive must learn how to quietly diminish tension not only in foreign but also in domestic affairs. Tension leads to precipitate actions that could extinguish all life on the planet. In contrast Hillary's strategic smiles often led her to score easily off of her more hysterical opponent. The country is already showing its weariness though with the whole process and Putin is gearing up his various threats in anticipation of a democratic victory. He is running scared; he seems to like Trump. After all, it is always so much easier to deal with a predicable blowhard than with a woman.

I checked the boat and no further signs of rat infestation were present, although the bilge was awash after a night of rain. I am isolated with my manuscripts for a time which will be a relief to my publisher. Bursts of creativity are only welcome when they bring the anticipated profits. Sales diminished for Henry James precisely when he felt that his writing had finally met his own elusive criteria for perfection. Genius is by its very nature limited in its appeal because it must by definition be in advance of the critical opinion that would presume to understand it. Any proclamation as a classic is the result of the revival of obscure works when conditions change so that they finally can be apprehended. Of course by then many great works have been lost. It is not necessary to burn the library of Alexandria to lose a classic; it only requires neglect at a key period so that the author will consent to keep silent.

It is hard to imagine today that books were once considered to be a threat. People lived in fear of Spinoza. Today authors are remarkable only for their public insignificance. To be listened to requires another avenue to achieve celebrity status. Persuasiveness is less important than imposed force or as it is better known, national-security. Never have Americans been more security conscious or more determined to secure it by arming themselves in order to kill their neighbors. Trust is a rare commodity perhaps because for a complex social order to survive it needs either uniformity of belief or a stable legal order and we possess neither.

Diversity has only produced a new level of mistrust. It is precisely here that a novelist can sometimes heal the breach by the use of his synthetic intellect, but if the novel is in decline as an art form then all that remains is the partial articulation of the sitcom and the feature film, and the currently dominant media formats, the talk shows and the news commentators of our day. One looks in vain for wisdom amidst the testimony of various experts, consultants, and therapists. We used to turn to our novelists to provide these rather than sociologists and gurus.

If writings are merely neutral discourses until a fatwa, formal or informal, is issued; where is competent aesthetic authority to be found? Sometimes in the form of book reviews by questionable sources, these confirm their value than less my reasoned argument than by proclamation. Why submit one's deepest thoughts and convictions to the scorn and noise of the multitude? This decreasing stature of the author as author is mirrored in the narrative technique of Kafka who erases himself even as he speaks. If this is true for Kafka then how dare I hope to sail a common sea with them? The world of verbal assertion is confined mostly to twaddle and demagoguery and amidst this the novelist is advised to choose silence as George Steiner has advocated. James Joyce did the next best thing. He wrote as he damn well pleased and asked the reader to step up to his perceptions or just set the book aside. This is the risk that every novelist takes of course, that he will remain unread as he approaches the achievement of his own highest standards.

This risk is always present, even for the patently clear and obvious, so why not dare to be difficult? If a book cannot stand on the same shelf as a work by Musil, Broch, Mann, or Kafka it can at least aspire to the same degree of query addressed to experience. Why should one do again what has been done better before by Sinclair Lewis, Theodore Dreiser, Jack London, or Emile Zola? The continental writers, from Ibsen to Maeterlinck, from von Hofmannsthal to Schnitzler, these alone knew what was happening to 20th century man before the great wars.

America meanwhile was remarkable only for its naiveté. A possible exception was Eugene O'Neil. The best artists are always tragedians because life is a tragedy for anyone without faith. King Lear's cry of never has not been surpassed as a summary of human life unless, and upon that great unless all else depends, a tomb was found empty in ancient Judea.

The novelist is by necessity allied to the prophets because he seeks to unite what has been to what alone he can foresee. He is great by virtue of this calling rather than due to his realization of its demands. Failing as a novelist his next best option is to follow Nietzsche and be an aphorist.

Comprehensiveness is the Everest of authors and few will ever attain its summit.

***

"Formless and discursive into obscure regions of the mind and heart;" I can hear the reviews already.

Or perhaps this: "Often willfully obscure as if he challenges the reader to follow him; don't bother!"

My measured and gentle response of course is: "And may you die in agony at the hands of an obscure group of zealots."

***

"Job description?"

"I'm a novelist."

"Would you call that being a writer?"

"I have nothing to declare except my genius."

"What?"

"I was just quoting what Oscar Wilde said that to the customs officials upon arriving in New York for his lecture tour."

"Who's Oscar Wilde?"

"Or for that matter, who's afraid of Virginia Woolf?"

"Can we just move on with this?"

***

Our City Council has just decided that homeless people should be treated as criminals. Of course I'm not homeless, I'm simply land-poor. I have lots of equity and little cash flow. It is all quite complicated just like most of my affairs. It is part of my appeal. Just ask she who cannot be named if you can find her. I think of her daily; part of the old obscure ache has come back since I returned. Her eyes are her best feature and she knows it. She plays them for effect like a musician. Her face could be molded by the memory of my fingers. Thoughts slide in like this if I leave my mind open. It takes discipline not to think. I have waited day after day for the long sought for transformation to occur. The storm has come and gone. I have caught the rat. The weather has become nice again and the trees still have their leaves, all red and gold.

I have packed things up so that when I am ready to do so I can establish a beachhead (literally) in Oregon. She will still be in Washington and things will be easier. I can start again. I would be going to Oregon because I couldn't afford to go any farther away. I needed to prove that I could forget, leave my sordid little town behind me like Thomas Wolfe did when he left Asheville behind only to go on writing about it, just as Joyce had done with Dublin.

It isn't that we can't go home again; it's that we carry it with us everywhere we go. Joyce carried Dublin. Hemingway carried the mid-west. Flannery O'Connor carried the dark dreams of the south. To the novelist place carries an ethos. It gives the novel texture, density. It creates a mood that pervades the whole oeuvre. After awhile you can hear an author's abiding voice in a single paragraph of his text. Words like eyes mirror the individual soul.

✶✶✶

Over the summer I had tried to forget the regulated world in the prospect of the unfettered sea. It is not uncommon for the novelist to push limits in his art and in his life. Of course the world has its sanctions for this attempt. Spontaneous creativity is not a virtue in a world that values conformity and predictability. Trying to be the unacknowledged legislators of the world, as Shelley recommended us to be, can be costly to the poet or to any writer. It all comes down to ticket sales, audience appeal, and that audience is seldom to be found on the knife-edge where the best minds attempt to balance themselves somewhere between accepted rules of construction and creative genius.

In an attempt to find relevance, many novelists have tried to portray the very world that holds their best efforts in contempt like Jack London in his novel, "Martin Eden." Novelists often write about their anger as they seek out readers in a savage world. George Gissing wrote his "New Grub Street" from the perspective of the author who is paid just enough to enable him to keep on writing. F. Scott Fitzgerald wrote about a class that he could never quite manage to join while Truman Capote was taken up like a mascot. The more assiduous Gore Vidal became the social historian that Capote's more precious talent could never reach. William Faulkner became the Shakespeare of the South by relying on a Hollywood salary to support him while American readers learned to step up to his Joycean fictions.

More popular novelists like John Steinbeck made the pathos of the common man as noble as an Arthurian romance and Hemingway showed that simply to endure was a source of triumph in a bitter world. Hemingway turned his life into legend until the actual books that he wrote ceased to matter, people bought them because he had penned them and he was regarded as a god. Americans love winners or people that can look like a winner even in defeat.

Meanwhile Conrad Aiken and his pal Malcolm Lowry are barely read at all because they take us into the same naked human condition as Camus and Celine have done by telling us just how grim things really are in a world without faith in God. It takes the cold analytical eye of a Zola to tell the truth without frightening people away. Most of us can stand squalor as long as it is not looking back at us from a mirror. The precision of Conrad Aiken is like that of an ice formation on the pole of a dead planet somewhere on the dark edge of the Solar System. Jack Kerouac meanwhile celebrates the idea that Buddhist nirvana is as near as the nearest bus station or a train pulsing through the dark fields on its way up to San Francisco.

But these are all yesterday's novelists, writing of conditions that may long since have been supplanted by our new temporary eye-blink of a world. I could carry all of their books now on a thumb-drive dangling from a set of car-keys or the key to open the storage unit where their physical books are stored, all marked-up and annotated by my admiring and critical hand. I have tilled the soil of my cranial cells with their words and images at the cost of countless hours of an unlived life simply to imitate in my fashion their often tragic and disappointed lives. Of course that assessment is a premature judgment, the very type of judgment that does not belong in a novel that aspires to be spontaneous, so the universe sent me an immediate corrective in the form of an Alaskan oracle.

He says, "We don't see things as they are but as we are. The universe is writing our lives everyday and it's not within our ability to foresee or control."

These ideas seemed to me to confirm my own initial hope that in writing "Pacific End" I could in some way transcribe the quiet and still OM of God breathing through his creation. Here was the Newport oracle again but from another place and gender, but with the same gentle willingness to leave things affirmed and not judged or reduced to what could be owned and controlled. As he went on to describe his early life in Alaska and how it was to live on the edge of sustenance where everything is just enough but not more I thought about the ideology of perfect security and control for America of the Trump campaign and of that same ethos as represented by the local goal to legislate away the homeless by viewing them as criminals.

Any real community of Norwegians clinging to life along the fjords of Norway in the 19th century when the city was first settled would have been more like our homeless ones than they were like the members of the complacent city council with their pretended and paternalistic sense of what the welfare of the homeless demands. The homeless were defined as a cause of local resource depletion. So buy just them into invisibility. Take our housing vouchers or be arrested. Your very presence violates our aesthetic of mythic small-town uniformity as mediated by 21st century commercialism. This is the same logic that decrees that a former grocery store now long vacant of a major grocery chain shall remain empty year after year when it could house the homeless rather than using jails to accommodate them. Is it any surprise that the city government and the police inhabit one building: the source of ordinances and the means to enforce them, all in one place? Fortunately the city hall looks as ridiculous as what comes out of it. Only people with no sense of humor would be immune to the incongruity of its aspect and its location. Its architectural design shows the essential cubical-mindedness of those who inhabit it, just another case of life imitating art.

How swiftly suburbia and strip malls have become the aesthetic imperative of American urban planning. The faceless public is allowed three minutes to speak as the façade of democracy demands before the various self-regarding apparatchiks mumble their yeas or nays to be recorded for the minutes, all correct and according to form and finally without any real meaning.

***

"I want to know everything or I don't want to know anything," from a former message from she who cannot be named.

If I can't control you I don't want you in my life. Maybe that was why I was still so angry with her. The refusal to be appropriated to an outside use has always been part of my personal design while at the same time I have never ceased seeking accreditations from some outside source to refute and overcome the evidence against me for the offense of simply existing. Gregor Samsa woke up one morning to discover that he had been transformed into an insect and I had sought transformation into a person that who could be approved by those who still withheld their recognition.

"Good luck finding someone who will listen to your stories and care to count every one of them."

(What she never understood was that no one's opinion but hers really mattered to me).

***

Transformation isn't necessary if things are alright as they are and free to change according to their own inner dynamics.

We were going to stage Mary Shelley's Frankenstein for Halloween this year, but there is more money in musicals the board decreed.

Homelessness, no lutefisk, and no Frankenstein; all are out this year – all are monsters driven from our village with torches blazing, like in an old film by Universal Studios. "I could always find jobs," claims a rich lady from Florida who recently moved here. She approves of the council's new regulation. Naturally her personal experience is assumed to be normative for others differently situated.

"How nice for you; maybe you could teach others your secrets."

"I've retired."

"Then I guess your secret will die with you."

A new sign is called for as you enter town, "Hospitality we ain't; drop some cash here or split."

It is the nature of our world that it makes impatient demands: contribute or perish. Everyone is afraid that someone else will obtain an unearned advantage. Meanwhile those who are master appropriators of other people's talents, beauty, time, and property are ignored or aided in their predation by the existing institutions. The techniques and professional aid expended in behalf of those who can pay others to help them steal go unnoticed while sidelong glances are cast on anyone getting a free meal even if they are hungry.

"Who are those little bugs scurrying about in the street below my office tower?"

The really rich used to complain that they could not find good help; servants today are superfluous because they savor too much of the domestic model. We prefer greater anonymity from those who serve us like invisible helpers in some sweatshop overseas. Drugs are still our largest import category where profitability is concerned, over gambling, over prostitution, over pornography. But over them all is the area where the biggest money resides, not in trade or commerce but in manipulating the blood-supply of the body politic banking; money, making money by trading money or money substitutes. Nobody is jealous of these guys because so few understand what they are doing. The governing structures help them to do it. The interlocking institutions keep the supine masses in check by distracting them with illusory symbolic values and glitzy entertainments. Even Emile Zola couldn't hope to tell the tale because it is everywhere and nowhere at the same time. Local democracy is the biggest lie of all because it could be different but isn't.

✱✱✱

After being distracted for several days by our little local sub-drama of the greater police state I returned to writing "Pacific End" bearing in mind that artists are judged according to their aesthetic rather than their social contributions. I still had the same sick feeling though and it made me want to find a way back to the older America of my youth. I thought about going back to places where I had once lived only to reflect that they also had changed with the times. The freedom that Thomas Wolfe dreamed about was as elusive as ever if it was sought in the outer world and not as I was doing in the novel that I was writing.

I have developed a habit of sitting in the dark at the local parish Church and listening to the raindrops falling in the aisle through a series of holes in the roof. I receive smiles from our Hispanic parishioners who, just like me, know what a good thing it is to just have a building where the authorities won't come and get you because who hangs out in churches anymore. This habit is a last remnant of Quasimodo crying sanctuary to the seething Paris mob in the old Charles Laughton version of The Hunchback of Notre Dame.

I have been reading a life and commentary on a neglected 20th century saint, Gemma Galgani. She seems to be the right saint for what I am feeling lately – abandoned, alone, always misunderstood, and maybe a little bit crazy. She thought that love was so important that she could get by on love alone. She took the love of God literally and bent her every effort to that one end. She got close enough to Jesus to share his stigmata. Evidently, taking religion this seriously is not such a great thing, even in pious Italy, because her Aunt choked her and commanded her to stop all the nonsense. Artists, even in the medium of love, always have their critics. But the Church for all its faults seems to know sanctity when it sees it, even in a dead girl of twenty-five who never did much besides love God intensely. Of course a cynic could argue that she was the perfect subject to be controlled by the hierarchy to perpetuate its mythologies but I am not a cynic.

Besides she had a lot of character to stick by her guns against all doubts and opposition. Of course this is easy to do when you talk straight across in complete familiarity to Jesus every day and your guardian angel mails your letters for you. Some things are so patently incredible that they must be true. Just ask Blaise Pascal who discovered the calculus, a stern man of reason and mathematics but also a man of passions who proclaimed that the heart has reasons that reason knows not of.

***

After writing several drafts of an op-ed piece I decided to return to the novel and to ask myself where in this world it is ever safe to simply exist unless one is ready to enter religious life and live in a monastery or try and find some residual hippy-commune and just hope that the skin-heads and vigilantes don't show up. I had just finished a book by Clive Jones about the days before AIDS ravished the Castro District in San Francisco. For a short time an urban enclave of freedom and self-definition for gay people appeared to exist although it took the death of Mayor Moscone and Councilman Harvey Milk to show how readily the forces of mandatory heterosexuality and middle-class conformity can reassert themselves.

Americans will gladly elect people who seem to promise them a way of life that keeps them tied to their credit-card debt, excessive mortgages to pay for artificially inflated real estate, and exorbitant health-care costs. Community is so rare that Americans are as likely to rely on privately held guns as on the official police force for protection against their neighbors. At times like the present various totally futile acts are called for so I thought of dressing up like a witch and using my three allotted minutes at the next city council meeting to put a curse on the council and its proceedings, but besides making myself a person to be watched I might be burned in the village square. So upon reflection I decided that literature is its own proper resort for those who find it difficult living in the real world, the one that has been co-opted by various persons who know how to play the system to their advantage. After all I had always in a sense lived in various volumes whether on the Yorkshire moors of the Bronte's or in the London of Conan

Doyle's Sherlock Holmes. The only recourse in times of unreason and greed are simplicity and reflection. The mind eludes pursuit as the resistance proclaimed during the Nazi era by whistling the tune of the song, "Die Gedanken sind frei." The real trick is to slip through the cracks by eluding location; "taking it on the lam" as the old movies of the 1930's used to say. If you can avoid getting yourself pumped full of anti-psychotic meds or lithium you can even be crazy and get away with it. If neither of these solutions works, then just act the part of "a beautiful little fool" and most people will forgive you anything.

As for writers being crazy is okay as long as you are articulate. Publishers won't care unless you start skipping promotional tours. Since people don't favor intellectuals, it helps if you have a gimmick or can read the public's desires before somebody else gets there before you. Nobody cares to read about fifty shades of yellow. Even the Marquis de Sade can't compete today in the arena named for him. Who reads "Justine" anymore without laughing? As for poetry it is so avowedly personal that only fellow poets read poetry to remind each other that others are just as lonely and incomprehensible as they are. This leaves novelists with some hope but not with much. You need a subject, something that has not been adequately discussed or better still some taboo that has yet to be broken, the great American incest novel for instance. It would fit nicely on more night-tables than people think; just ask the psychotherapists.

Absent a new subject or just a lucky-strike you take your chances with a novel. But what's left after all: short stories, screenplays, or the legitimate theater. Lots of people resort to tattoos to gratify the literary instinct, anything to differentiate the thronging bodies, the seven billion contemporary souls jostling for space and recognition on planet earth. There is always the danger of sifting down through the layers, of being appropriated to someone else's enterprise. The body is the ultimate ground for all politics. You know when you have reached the bottom when all that is left to sell is your body; at higher levels all you have to sell is your time. Leisure and discretion (the right to say no without having to put a gun to your head) are the truest measures of wealth.

***

Maybe the answer is not to write or read anything, just return to the blissful joys of the illiterate and talk a lot about nothing. So we circle back into silence as the only option open to those who refuse to communicate as the only way to assert themselves. Why talk to anybody about anything? Let's just leave events as we find them. Who cares if the whales die? Maybe rhinosaurus horn is an aphrodisiac, just ask a horny Chinaman. He thinks it's okay if they go extinct. Just follow the dollars and act accordingly. In a few years they will have virtual reality and three-dimensional television and we can kiss the real world goodbye. Maybe they will keep our brains alive with a computer that can simulate our personalities and then just run the circuits together; endless orgasms in a sort of biological feedback loop. Who will need novels then? Unless we could clone Tolstoy from some old flaked-off piece of his leg bone. We could bring him back and strap him to a lap-top.

***

I caught myself being cynical again, a trait unbecoming in a novelist, one of those to whom we entrust the synthetic function to write another "Middlemarch" or a "Vanity Fair." So I come back to the virtues of the human body. Maybe novelists should describe heads and shoulders or just do cameo portraits in light and shadow. Maybe novels should just be shorter or maybe shorter. Who am I to say? Nobody forced me to write about writing about novels after all. The world can get along without another discourse. So should I stop?

But then even the Canadian writer who committed suicide finished her last book first. She may have despaired of her life but not of the value of the printed word. So I decided to keep on writing...

***

Why not just bag subject and concentrate on style and stylistics. There are entire broadcasting networks at the present time dedicated to the worlds of style and fashion. High cheek-bones and pouty mouths are combined with flowing fabrics that would have been the envy of Kublai Khan in the pleasure dome described by Samuel Taylor Coleridge. Youth is presumed to be the best talisman against death as long as drugs and self-indulgence does not freeze celebrity into a premature death and by so doing add one more legend to careless youth who thereafter covet fame or at least notoriety as a substitute for survival. Meanwhile, those who exist to gratify actuaries and earn profits for insurance companies will settle for an additional year purchased by careful diet maintenance and judicious aerobic exercise.

If a diplomatic compliment subtracts a decade or even two from our real age we preen ourselves as if when we were actually that attributed age we were not carping already about the inroads made on our faces and figures by time; no doubt when we are ninety we will be immensely flattered to be taken for an eighty year old stripling. Another decade makes such a difference in maturity as we learn to lower the bar of our expectations to accommodate a new dermatological vintage. As a novelist of course I am immune to time because I stand outside of it as an observer and recorder of other's lives carefully distilled into words and paragraphs. Anyone can be appropriated as a character and have dialogue forced like a dental-dam between their teeth.

Style allows us as novelists to trim insights into clean packages of observation. Put enough of these together and you are William Makepeace Thackeray. Composition works against decomposition at the cellular level. I have been told to moderate the sugar in my coffee, but I point out that the brain's circuits demand sugar as a basic fuel and caffeine in the absence of absinthe has been known to stimulate genius, at least if the example of Balzac is to be taken as evidence. Artists of all sorts are noted for burning the candle at both ends; who after all can tell when the muses may depart?

Vincent van Gogh was not chary of his pigments and often went without food in order to afford them. Words being far cheaper than pigments and paid for only in time may be slapped down in abundance and the worst that may be said is that the author is overly garrulous or that he tries the reader's patience by assuming that a Renaissance hunger for experience is still common among the populace.

We are living in an age of the short-sell and the summation. The author, according to this view, should have a penchant for simplicity and the declarative statement. He should round off his calculations to the nearest whole number, even if he sacrifices accuracy by doing so. After all, style is really merely a fancy word for seduction. Speaking of seduction I have rather lost track lately of the candidates in the great election of 2016. After the three debates and a good airing of scandals the electorate has enough information to choose between the twin malefactors.

My present outrage at the city council will doubtless also pass. No doubt my anger has been partially motivated by the discontent that I have felt in general since coming home. My sister called me yesterday to tell me of the death of the husband of a friend of hers from a sudden heart attack that happened with no preceding signs. If he could have taken a break from his thriving business the sum of his ready assets could have placed him in Venice or Trieste by the next day to contemplate the glories of the Aegean Sea. He could sample pasta and wine served with a local fish before adjourning to his five-star hotel room and now nothing. If life is so insecure then why make any plans at all? Why not turn from precarious life to the novels that whatever their flaws may still manage to get the reader to the end with a proper sense of closure and not simply present him as life so often does with a series of twenty blank pages at the end.

This problem of unlived possibilities is not confined to the prematurely dead. In looking for some books the other day I found an old alumni magazine about traveling to do social service in Thailand. It is the sort of thing that I usually pass over quickly as a life-option for me but then perhaps the criteria for my life-script are themselves faulty. I dream of returning to an England that I knew in 1977, long prior to the incursion of Syrian refugees, when the greatest threat was from the recalcitrant Irish across the short sea from Holyhead. Why had I never thought of doing social service in Thailand or among the aborigines for that matter; then I might be sitting here today writing about the fascinating Dutch girl that I met at a remote government station in the western deserts of Australia. Instead I can only report that I have yet to hear from she who cannot be named and although I am tempted to offer a proposal that a truce in honor of the harvest season be declared, I have not called her. If I have not done so it because even to suggest this would constitute an infringement of her last request of me, one that I conceded to immediately and without discussion or dispute, not because I thought that this would be our final word to each other, but because by acceding to her wishes, even this one, I could prove that I do in fact love her.

***

I keep waiting for the anticipated transformation of events. If things don't come together but instead drift apart, as the law of entropy explains, then at least I have always hoped for a transformation of the meager constituents of my life before they drift off like stray cosmic rays into endless space.

It is assumed that the novelist always owes his reader a happy ending so as not to end like the famous painting entitled "The Scream" in an exclamation of frozen horror. After all, there is nothing particularly dreadful happening right now in my life as I write. This famous painting was later stolen, although reproductions of it are seen everywhere; its point has been made.

To enter the realm of hyperrealism for a moment: what if the cause of the scream in the painting was the prophetic sense that it would someday be stolen? Was the painting crying for help? Is all art prophetic, a warning? Or to put it in sixties terms, "It's about telling all of us what's going down." But that was when all of us thought that it would be so different than it has turned out to be in America after 1969. Now we live differently and expect less from life. We have our actual past rather than the dream version that once seemed so securely in place before Watergate, before the spectacle of exploding space shuttles gave the lie to the belief that "space is for everybody," before the Savings and Loan Crisis, before the Gulf Wars, before the events of 911. In a couple of years will we be eating each other; the zombie apocalypse will finally occur. Where then will be the girls in tie-dyed T-shirts and jeans with their long-lashed eyes and iced-pink lipstick listening to The Mamas and the Papas and dreaming of an endless summer in

California?

Science fiction used to be a genre until science became omnipresent and technology came to run our lives. Gothic novels are passé now since governesses ceased to arrive as virgins at the dark and scary mansions. Naturalism was always a safe bet as was regionalism but travel has deprived almost anywhere from being an exotic location and people are no longer stressed by change; it's just how things are.

This leaves romance and metaphysics. A historical novel is still always a good bet; we can imagine that in remote times things were better. Why not write about imaginary cave-people; after all they had feelings too. Or maybe just probe the psyche, "I was a Victim of Dementia Praecox." Learn the rules of the genre and then tweak them a little. Get some good reviews and you're on your way to three or four weeks as a best-seller before your book sales fall off, books like candy-corn, books as intellectual gummy-bears for people on buses or high-speed trains between the neon-lit metropolises speeding through a sterile countryside.

***

Maybe transformation is less my goal than integrity is. Integrity of form is one that is true to its own definition and aims. We know good stuff when we read it. This is the author's hope, that what he writes will awaken an answer in the reader from his own inner sense of how things are or should be. Recognition or resonating of word and thought, word and image in pursuit of artistic comprehension and the pleasures attached to it. Or was that what I was really after in "Pacific End?" Was I in pursuit of a novel or in pursuit of a new way of life? I could sit down and write a novel but how to create a life that would pass muster to my own critical sense, let alone the judgment of God, with the time allowed rapidly diminishing? Instead I have created a vast La Brea tar-pit of half-realized aims and my reserves of salutary denial are in a depleted state.

Death will always be a minority cult because it doesn't really answer the problem of how to live. Pessimist novelists are really just engaged in passing the buck. Just read "The Plague" by Albert

Camus or the novels of Samuel Beckett. No matter how tough it gets you are instructed to just go on. If you can't find meaning then make some meaning. We are expected to do what novelists have always done: keep our faith in the human enterprise alive. You can be sad or angry, but don't quit; we need you.

***

I think the first half of the sixties was the best, say from 1960 to 1964, if you don't count the Cuban Missile Crisis or the Kennedy assassination. Johnson gave us the Civil-rights Act in 1964 and he would have done great with his war on poverty if there had been no Viet Nam war. Then he would be thought of like FDR instead of leaving office and doing public penance by drinking himself to death. Things were going well for awhile in America with the Peace Corps, the Freedom Riders, and color television.

I always loved the westerns because the good guys always ended up on top in the end. Johnny Crawford would toss Chuck Connors his rifle and the bad guy was toast. There was lots of good father-son bonding in the television shows then; no long-haired hippie sons spurning hard-won access to suburban housing and the long-awaited consumer society. As for feminism, men would say, "Ask your Mom; she knows. You just don't know how good you've got it."

None of us knew how good we had it. We thought the future would be like, "The Jetsons" or "American Bandstand." Then there came the great watershed of Viet Nam and a sense that a generation was to die to fulfill an antiquated dream of patriotism rooted in a struggle against Germany and Japan; not the peasant farmers and irregular soldiers found in bamboo forests, rice paddies, and caves. If everybody was going to die young then it was unnecessary to plan a life. Everything that happened later was just a gradual unraveling of my generation's early illusions. Maybe we didn't have a new explanation after all. Maybe we were as violent and greedy as every other generation had been before us.

But then this isn't a historical novel, at least not in the traditional sense. It belongs to that in-between class of experimental fiction that tests the limits of an established art-form by seeking to define them. Much of my life has involved testing borders and limits while simultaneously seeking an established orthodoxy in which to find repose and a secure purpose to stand behind my endeavors. Simply to trust my own instincts or finding pleasure adequate to ground my actions always came up against by simultaneous awareness, and a metaphysical one it was, that I was not the ground of my own being. I wanted something that would bear up under the pressure of radical doubt whether applied from an outside source or from my own insecurities and anxiety. Any assertion regarding content in a novel is subsidiary to a prior choice of form. Although the critic can later attack the novel from many points, the choice of form is an act of pure freedom. It is the single God-like act of the artist is to say, "Let there be light." Suddenly a world of sorts appears where there had before been only blank paper.

***

The days of October advanced towards All Hallows Eve. I dreamed one night of a house that was pulled apart by a landslide and on other nights of other images of dissolution. This was not strange because I was suddenly hearing from many quarters of the deaths or recurring illnesses of loved ones, spouses, brothers, and friends. I saw how quickly the sands filled in around their vanished footprints in the place that I had called home now for twenty years and suddenly realized that these tales might as easily have been about me had a sudden collision occurred on my travels or if I had encountered a rip tide or a shark or even a nervous patrolman with a ready gun on the Oregon coast. The pressure of events is such that no vacuum long endures. The one exception might be the case of she who cannot be named. The silence bred of our estrangement persisted day after day. I still thought of her and kept the gifts for her that I had accumulated, carefully setting them aside and preserving them against any fortuitous opportunity that might offer itself to deliver them to her.

Unsought acts of kindness still came my way from time to time. I felt stitched into the fabric of smiles. Maybe I was part of things after all and not a mere flickering candle before an abandoned shrine. People cared enough to remember incidents that I had forgotten. A woman from the library brought me pictures that were taken three years ago on Halloween, a mechanic recalled how my car had unaccountably stalled and then seemed to heal itself several years ago based only on a quick phone call that I had made to him seeking advice and reassurance before calling a tow truck. In these tiny unrecorded events my life was preserved in their memory. If they still remembered me then what of she who may not be named who had claimed to love me so much that she must needs control every aspect of my life as evidence that I would never leave her? When this proved to be impossible she demanded the complete eclipse of my solstice moon, one that never crossed the sky without thinking of her.

I kept reading about Gemma Galgani who was dead by the age of twenty-five. She had begged God to take her to heaven because her body was being consumed by the divine fire of love. She couldn't eat anything but the sacred host. It was as though anything of earth was already too tainted to nourish a spirit weaned through suffering to feed on God alone. With every favor of grace granted to her she condemned her own dispositions the more as being entirely unworthy of such incursions. But she kept inviting God while deploring what these supplications entailed for her as God's willing victim. If she had been a harlot and not a saint her openness to be ravaged would have been more to be expected. Her smallness and obscurity did not protect her from enduring the full force of love that can be generated by the dynamo of heaven. The sensualist only dreams of such raptures. Millions of addicts seek it at the end of a syringe while Gemma found it in prayer.

***

I told people that I was writing "Pacific End," welcoming them to my mind purling like a stream down from the mountains taking strange channels by the sea. Every new death was a reminder that I too would someday die. Strange concept! I who was made up of various texts drawn from the world of the great minds of antiquity was too much of the past to ever perish? I who scorned the trivia of being just one more link in the falling dominos of flesh would end by being just as dead as other people, those who were more beloved and worthy of enduring because they had quarried a home and family through the labors of their days and nights. Where there was not death there was affliction. Good people suffered from various failures in bodily systems like a car on its way to California from Oklahoma during the depression leaving rusty parts strewn along the road on the way. "Always time for a rebuild it once we get to California!" But bodies are necessary to keep us glued to the earth and upright rather than supine and buried beneath six feet of soil.

If you can't change it throw a tarp over it; refuse to wrinkle, fight the good fight. Dress well and no one will notice. I think of Donald Trump beneath his orange hair, puffed up like dandelion fluff if you dyed it. I think of Hillary. If she ages in office as fast as most male incumbents of the office have done she won't be a pleasant sight in four years. I think I can account for the changes observed while in office. Perhaps every President who has been elected since Ronald Reagan has been replaced by an animatronics figure. (This was not necessary for Reagan because he started out as not quite real).

For most of us age starts to tell by sixty-five. We just don't bear up well after our recall date. That doesn't mean that we want to be pulled from the shelf though; just move us to the bargain area. You have to be dead of course before you qualify for nostalgia status. Your reputation has to be at the lowest ebb before you can be rediscovered. It helps if you can be classified as a classic for a revival to begin. Even then some publisher will say, "Hell, nobody even read him when he was alive!" Shakespeare has never died because we are still trying to figure out what he was saying. Not rich, powerful, beautiful, talented, or notorious? Then don't hold your breath and hope for enduring fame. Snuggle up to the few people who have loved you or you can be holy like Gemma Galgani and be satisfied with God alone. But for recognition you've got to have friends in Rome willing to get behind you and push and evidence of miracles done by God through your intercession. What all this adds up to is: either be a star or start thinking about other people and make their losses your own.

***

Halloween was past and still there was no word to the wicked witch from she who cannot be named. It was time to reflect on death in earnest because November was here, the month when the Church celebrates the virtuous dead, invokes the Blessed Virgin's motherly compassion for our afflictions, and celebrates the feast-day of Christ the King that ends the liturgical year. The leaves lie upon the ground and winter sets in. This jubilee year reminding us of the Divine Mercy is coming to an end. America will choose a President. Putin in Russia may wonder whether if Chairman Khrushchev had been stronger he could have made that arrogant Irishman Kennedy flinch during the Cuban Missile Crisis. Let's roll the dice one more time and see how it goes! (Of course we'll all go with it). I suppose that the ultimate historical novel will be the one that ends with the end of history, but who will be around to read it? This will be a definite hard-sell to a sensible publisher. "If you're right nobody will read you because they'll be drifting ash and if you're wrong all you will have done is frighten and depress people."

***

I want to be relevant to the times we are living in because I think what we decide now could just decide the whole damn game. I think we are all living in the most critical time that humanity has ever faced. We act like somehow we don't have any stake in history's outcome. I want to remind people. How's that for a plea for the continued relevance of the novel? (But then the novel must always veil its underlying purpose: show it don't say it).

A big group of people just came in to where I am writing with a baby in tow, one of countless babies I have seen this year. I like to think of babies as a quiet colonizing force. Don't be fooled by those social smiles. Like Putin they've got a lot of ideas and most of them are beyond what I can conceive trapped as I am by all the ideas that I have been shoving into my head for 65 years. Meanwhile babies are sets of percolating cells with long telomeres. They may look red and wrinkly now but just give them time and they will be running corporations and modeling tomorrow's fashions on catwalks and writing books to rival that long forgotten experimental novel called "Pacific End." I managed to digest last night's big dinner at the casino buffet. I kicked my diet a few more days into the future relying on the good numbers on my last blood test. Tomorrow I get my teeth cleaned; no more of my self-scaling with a nail file just to save money. I have seen the light when it comes to dental care. Good news though! My C-reactive protein score was below one; no sign of chronic inflammation and all the plaque on my arteries that may have accumulated will likely remain quietly in place. This means no blood clot producing a massive heart attack. I can keep churning out words to justify my existence.

But back to those babies … it is really their world I am writing about here. After all, they have a bigger stake in the future than I do. I hate to warn them. "Smile while you can baby; we've left you one hell of a mess."

✳✳✳

All Saints Day is where the Church celebrates its acknowledged winners. If the purpose of life is to save your soul, then these are the ones who never forgot this central truth. The rest of us figure on being a holy old person after a life of being somewhere between "not such a bad guy" and being "a total son of a bitch." I figured I'd write some tough sounding stuff here. After all, I don't want my readers to think that novelists are wusses; what would Ernest Hemingway or Norman Mailer say if I allowed compassion for the human race to censor my manner of showing it? If simply saying true things was adequate the art of novel writing would be superfluous.

We look to the saints for the answers while we proceed to seek happiness or security in our usual ways. One of the most common reminders, to give cold comfort to those who experience disappointment in the results of pursuing their goals, is to remind them of their essential limitations by saying, "You know the universe does not revolve around you." The problem with this truism is that in point of fact the universe *does* revolve around us because we are the focal point of our own attention surrounded by a great non-us.

The sun and moon move across the sky, cars surround us on the freeway threatening at every moment to plunge us into an insurance mess through a moment of impatient miscalculation on the part of their drivers, people that we care about disregard our well-meant advice and misinterpret the intent of our actions, and a vast sea of strangers of foreign race and tongues seeks admission to our little island of dearly purchased capital prosperity, one that was once guarded by oceans and protective tariffs.

The more compassionate among us feel diminished by other's losses and the more anxious ones ask about the cause of deaths, injuries, or illnesses in others so as to augment their grid of suspicious symptoms to be checked out daily. Many maintain a daily status check before they even venture out of bed.

"Let me see, I was really worried about something before I fell asleep...hmm, oh yeah. How will I face this day? Why did I bother to wake up?"

Others are bothered by people's misfortunes because it proves that this world is not to be trusted while others still take a grim satisfaction that their ill prophesies have been confirmed.

"I told her not to have children; they just ask for money and break your heart."

The more generous ones spring into action with unsought solutions to situations that they cannot truly understand. They feel a tremor on the outer edges of their presumed world-responsibility and try to assist while their own lives are a mess through benign neglect; anything rather than force introspection and the inevitable clarity that might result.

Some members of this latter type like to write novels and thereby create a world more to their liking. A few like Count Leo Tolstoy even become spiritual leaders while unable to find enough charity to ensure domestic tranquility in their own homes. Others like Dickens are all fuzzy and heartwarming in their works while remaining tormented within. The novels that Dickens wrote grew darker and less sentimental with every year.

Life has a habit of catching up with all of us. Joseph Conrad's character, Kurtz, in "The Heart of Darkness" speaks for more than himself with his dying words, "The horror, the Horror!" As I grow older I am convinced that to be fully engaged in earning a living is the one great anodyne to despair, that and the walking of dogs. People like to be busy because it exhausts the faculties of thought and reflection. Maybe the happiest of all people are those who have been rescued at sea by a chance encounter and are sitting afterwards on a chair, naked and shivering but enclosed in a rough blanket while a compassionate crew member feeds them soup. They thought that they were goners and behold, they get another chance at this unsatisfactory life of ours.

For a similar reason the most salutary use of the air time of the local news is in the recitation of disasters. Afterwards people heave a sigh when they realize that they have been unaccountably spared for one more day. From the Godlike security of their couches they watch while fires gut buildings, flood waters inundate cars, or various shootings are described. One of the greatest reasons for rejoicing remains the simple realization that, "Today I didn't have to see the dentist or call a lawyer." Beyond that we always have an available novel for comfort, "I am so glad not to be Oliver Twist or Little Nell."

✳✳✳

It is often said that we were never promised a rose garden but were we then promised a briar patch instead? A little kvetching is good for the soul. The afflicted man says to God, "Why me Lord?" And God answers, "Would you rather that I visited another with your terrible affliction?" To which the afflicted man replies, "I have the list right here!"

My grandfather was always planning on writing a book with the title, "So You Think You had it Tough." Maybe I am engaged in writing it for him.

Of course we could always lower our standard for happiness. I remember assuming an aggressive attitude when I took the bar exam: "I eat bar exams for breakfast!"

It helped; over 50% failed to pass the bar in that particular testing season. I don't like doing predictably nasty jobs twice. The exception is when I fall in love. Then all my chips are out on the table ... well maybe not, because I didn't like to let the one who cannot be named know that she could draw blood with every unkind word. I still don't know if that was really the whole point. She could never be sure that I really loved her until she could break down that last reserve of my self-esteem, flood every compartment, and see the ship sinking in fire and steam below the water. We were engaged in a dark game where one or the other of us had to hurt more than the other to justify the win.

∗∗∗

Some people like to make deals with death.

"I'll embrace you willingly if you promise to leave me a little window of consciousness afterwards."

I don't think anyone really commits suicide expecting the end of all sensation; they just want to obliterate a set of particular memories and start over. To will nothingness is metaphysically impossible because we have no real knowledge of non-being. It is like putting all your chips on double zero in roulette; it's still a bet. Once you are conceived it's too late to back out of the sweepstakes of eternity; it's heaven or hell, so you may as well ask for a little help. That's why we pray.

"Well I don't believe that!"

"Then what do you believe?"

"I think we're all on our own."

"So the universe just coughed you up like a ball of mucus?"

"I didn't say that."

"Then maybe you matter too much to just die. Maybe you owe somebody something as well."

"Death cancels everything out."

"Or maybe you just realize fully what you owe when it's too late to pay. In purgatory you learn to ask for the help that you refused while you were alive. You pay there in proportion to your residual pride."

"I'd rather go to hell first!"

"Well that's up to you."

***

I thought I had a pretty unique idea in the ideas of "Pacific End" until I realized that Andre Gide was up to something similar when he wrote, "The Counterfeiters." This raises the whole question of whether writing fiction is itself duplicitous. Oscar Wilde and Plato agreed that art is essentially about passing fraudulent merchandise to an unsuspecting public. Of course in today's economy, one based on reciprocal national debts that will never be repaid, even genuine money is counterfeit; so why shouldn't a poor novelist get a few bucks for his scribbling. After all, words are free to be appropriated at will. Novelists are at least honest about writing fiction while governments issue paper and call it money. Federal Reserve Notes admit as much if you read them carefully. They simply say that they are legal tender to settle private or public debts, in other words you won't be prosecuted for fraud if you can get some sucker to share the publicly shared delusion that they are really money after all.

American bank notes are not even pretty. I guess they figure that the illusion of security is furthered by attaching photos of grim statesmen to a drab green background. It's all so pragmatic; these notes will serve until something better comes along. Americans have learned to accept delayed gratification as a way of life. Someday we'll patch up the bridges and fix the interstate highways and defuse the atomic weapons and pay off the national debt; meanwhile work hard and be sure to vote. After all, we are a democracy.

***

So you see novelists are actually shining examples of comparative virtue. Far be it from us to pass off a phony novel for a real one. Besides, publishers make sure that no junk ever reaches the shelves. Just check out the titles at any bookstore or look at the list of bestsellers. No publisher is in it for the money. Every editor is just as selfless as old Max Perkins was at Scribner and Sons. No beady-eyed little accountant at the headquarters of the conglomerate is watching the bottom line. It's quality all the way for a literate and sophisticated reading audience. "You're being ironic aren't you? Why do novelists get so bitter?" Of course we are bitter because as novelists we wonder why life is not more like a novel.

Life unmediated through art can be intolerable to the artistic mind. Life proceeding as mere duration or as a chain of loosely linked incidents, some pleasurable but most of them alternating between the painful and the merely inconvenient, just doesn't measure up to our exalted expectations. Novelists demand order and purpose, plot and motivation, crisis and climax, and hopefully from all of these a gentle dénouement leaving an abiding aura of aesthetic satisfaction and wisdom.

Novelists are, among other things, miners of dialogue and professional eavesdroppers. Yet for all of this we are not inordinately attached to life's organic processes. Our goal is always to be preserved in a leather-covered volume with golden binding, to be lined up along with the other classics on a walnut shelf in a properly lighted library of a late Georgian mansion; or at least such was my ideal. I was not prepared for the artist-as-prostitute era let alone for the era of artists as hucksters at the fairgrounds. Publishers once provided generous advances and avuncular editors with salutary advice when the novelist's peculiar madness led him into problems that might interfere with his writing. Reviewers might lie in wait to attack the newest offering, but whatever his short-term judgments, these could always be smoothed out later by discerning university faculties and doctoral candidates.

Of course I am speaking of the classical writers and not those who merely aspire to achieving bestseller status or receiving lucrative film offers. Words alone were adequate to justify the novel's existence so that even a creative cover design was of secondary importance, let alone aggressive marketing or promotion on the Internet. My role-models were always those writers applying Joyce's formula of "silence, exile, and cunning." Silence because the novel stands between the novelist and the world like a wall to keep the barbarians at bay; exile because no prophet is honored in his native place; cunning, because novelists are more innocent than we appear to be. We need cunning in order to stand firm against the predators.

Life tends of necessity to become a full-time occupation. Writers are forced to adopt a measure of solitude merely to apply their craft to the resisting medium of a blank sheet of paper. This lack of life experience in the realms of the mundane among writers demands that we behave as animals must if they wish to survive. Publishers avoid this problem because they apply to their writers the same evolutionary strategy applied by opossums: large litters, a quick life-span, and a quick turnover due to the ever-hungry wheels of motor vehicles. Books are not expected to have a permanent shelf-life anymore than breakfast cereals. Paper can always be recycled; ideas less so. The novelist then is primarily a thinker and therein his cunning resides. The discerning author must manage to scorn quietly the deficiencies of his audience without forfeiting his sales among them. He must be connected to his times without being strictly of them. He must stand apart and yet be representative of his particular place and era.

Seen from this point of view many of the best novels have remained unwritten simply because the writer decided to let the masses go to hell in their own way. Most people will pay readily to have their illusions confirmed but are reluctant to subsidize ideas that are too abrasive or deflating to their pretentions. The surprise is that so much quality has managed to accumulate and endure in literature; but even at that most nations can create a respectable anthology of a hundred years using only a score of names. How many people have lived and died in that same period unrepresented? Where do the thoughts and words, oral or written, of the multitude go? Most lives vanish in a puff of smoke. Small indeed is the village that recalls its dead and visits its graves for longer than a decade. If Thomas Grey was to write his famous elegy today the uncelebrated life would be even more obscure: diminished by the grass, mocked by the grasshopper, and no more one of a kind than a can of sardines.

***

We have lost any belief in the abiding significance of our most sacred emotions. Nothing echoes in the cavern of the common breast of humankind. We are sets of data, entries in someone else's ledger so that even Kafka, were he to write today, would not speak of a trial but of an automatic assessment. He would not write of a castle but of a summary hearing in a room at the end of a long hall in an administrative building. A truly communitarian existence leads less to justice than it does to anonymous classifications. A nurse enters a darkened ward, "Are you in pain? We can increase your morphine. There is no need to worry about developing an addiction when you are dead."

So where is human dignity still to be found if not in literature? I read the play, "The Iceman Cometh" in the evenings when I drove out to the San Francisco Bay area from Michigan back in 1979. I stayed a week with a friend and then set off northwards to the Oregon coast on my way home to Washington. I had wanted to get across the Rocky Mountains before the snows set in for the winter. I remember seeing Wyoming by frigid moonlight and the wet November after I arrived home spent studying for the Graduate Record Exam. I needed a similar relocation now or homecoming now.

I recall how I settled into Lakewood again and re-visited all the old places. The mists closed in around me and the world for me was no bigger than the outer limits of Tacoma. The best part was that I didn't mind the restrictions. I have always known as did Henry David Thoreau the value of the familiar. Even now I wish I could recover the first warmth of the house as I entered from the garage by the back door, placed my books in the study, and met the smells of cooking and the sound of a sit-com re-run in the family room. Any world beyond the Seattle-Tacoma nexus had seemed almost mythical such was the intensity of the gravity applied by familiar memories and a restricted zone of acquaintance. Our family home on Lake Steilacoom growing up was my equivalent of Marcel Proust's Combray. We cannot recover such places and that vast reservoir of unfilled time that only the young possess. What remains for us when our reservoir of memory is more extensive than the pool of time remaining?

My hero of those days, Eugene O'Neill, summed it all up when he lay dying by saying, "Born in a goddamn hotel room and dying in a goddamn hotel room." It was as though nothing else had ever happened to him. Now Anton Chekov is my hero because he took life as it came without needing to draw a moral from experience. He demonstrated the universal compassion that heals all wounds and tried to make everybody he encountered feel a little safer and able to face up to whatever fate might bring to them.

You can usually tell the jobs that do the most good, few people want them and the pay stinks. Of course the real money today is in residuals and endorsements and if you are the President you get Secret Service protection for life so that no disgruntled citizen will end up killing you. The consensus is that our Presidents are destroying the country. A comfortable obscurity in one chosen place isn't such a bad thing, whether it is found in places like Stratford-on-Avon, in Trieste, or in Oxford, Mississippi.

✳✳✳

When I was in Dublin I sought out the city library just so I could feel in my hands the works of the great gothic writer, Joseph Sheridan Le Fanu. It has taken me all these years since then to finally get around to reading the Dover Edition of "The Rose and the Key." O got through my lonely freshman year in college by dwelling alternately in the two mansions of his masterpiece, "Uncle Silas;" such is the power of great literature.

It is Le Fanu's atmospherics and precision of diction and character that make him a master and worthy to be in the company of the more famous Charles Dickens and Wilkie Collins. A quiet undertone of the tragic quality of life pervades his prose accompanied by faith and resignation. His noble families carry secrets and time, that great equalizer, moderates their wealth and glamour by showing them against the proper perspective of the fleeting years and the swift succession of the generations. His novels are pervaded by a gentleness that would make possible a pacific end, one that is conscious to the end, resigned but not prematurely embraced, and withal carrying a sense of dignity but not of pride to our final breaths.

The best writers can often create a sense of ambiguity without being amoral. I thought of this as I read a passage recently from

Andre Gide's great novel, "The Counterfeiters." I read it standing up in a Bremerton dental clinic today. No cavities, pockets for the most part only twos and threes, and only one tooth gone, my lower molar; all in all not so bad after chewing with them for over fifty years and grinding out my frustrations while dreaming. Literature allows us to share the salutary company of the minds of people we know well through their books but will never meet in person because they are dead.

✳✳✳

The sun came out today and allowed a soft frosting of mold to settle in my various living spaces. Now that I drink less milk I can actually breathe through my nose again and perhaps avoid the onset of sleep apnea. I should so hate to die in my sleep. I want to great death while I am still conscious of its approach. Henry James' last words were, "Well here it is at last the great and noble thing," the first statement he ever made without any qualifications or revisions. But then ambiguity is held to be evidence of a subtle mind. Maybe life does not admit itself to generalizations on serious subjects. We should allow ultimate facts to speak for themselves. But who can say what qualifies as a fact? Now there's subtlety for you.

Kierkegaard says that truth is subjectivity. By this he means that you have to give a damn about the outcome. Objectivists are for the most part liars as are metaphysical skeptics. I always felt that David Hume could prove that cause and effect relations existed by simply catching his little toe on a piece of furniture at night on his way to the bathroom. Humor depends on the tension between double meanings: one of literal expression and the other an underlying truth. Humans love laughing at discordant appearances. Ambiguity on the other hand begins where two meanings coincide and it is impossible to decide which one is being asserted by the author.

In the end a book must speak for itself. It means what the reader thinks it means until another reader disputes that conclusion – then both turn to the critics. Every novel is in this sense an invitation to arbitration. What did the author really mean? Sometimes he or she is the last one to ask because the temptation to special pleading can be irresistible.

"The correct interpretation is the one that makes me look like a genius."

***

I listened to my voice massages on my cell phone yesterday and found that although I had faithfully kept saving the ones sent to me from, she who cannot be named, to prevent automatic deletion, they were all of them gone. Probably it was due to a new phone company policy.

"Why torture yourself, just move on, it's over."

Still, I wasn't happy. The universe seems bent on making decisions for me if given enough time, and it has all the time that there is. Of course space and time are both just part of the space-time continuum that is affected by mass. If I had thrown my cell-phone into a black hole time would stop and the messages would still be there although retrieving the phone would be problematic. The better choice would be to throw the entire cell phone company into the black hole and I would never get another monthly bill.

I feel lately like a car in a freeway back-up; every time the car in front moves up more than twenty feet you have to look up, put the car in gear, and close the gap or get honked at. After awhile you just enter the same agitated zombie state as the other drivers. What makes us all so patient when hours are being stolen from us daily, as though we were going to live forever? Does everybody else have more faith in time's reserves than me? Who writes novels about what life is really like, even when things are, by and large, sort of working out? To tell the truth, to be a real realist … nobody would read such novels because they are engaged in living them every day.

***

It is dark now and the people at adjoining tables are getting up and hugging each other; evidence that human community can thrive without novels, at least this one. Nobody paid much attention to the assiduous author in the corner writing a first draft in real time let alone the distant and still hypothetical future readers. By the time a book is read its progenitors and models may be dead. This is the irony of life and of physics as well: that the stars that we see in the heavens may not exist anymore by the time that their light reaches us. Is an event to be registered though by its causal instant in time or by its delayed effect?

Certainly for the reader the book happens only when it is read. Similarly, did my life happen when it was lived or when I recollected it here? Do we ever reach a position from which we can turn around and judge ourselves? If the answer is negative then how is repentance in the theological sense ever possible? I think that we blunder into eternity like a runaway horse, to use a homely 19th century image. The act of contrition I would like to make can only be made when I am already dead.

(N.B.: If God is reading this I am only kidding; I'm sorry now).

To whom must we render our final account? As a Catholic I believe that this matters, as a writer I am engaged in playing with life-alternatives as though they will always be available to me.

"Sorry for the delay in making a choice God. I just wasn't sure who you were amidst so many opinions and in a world so contrary to the best definitions."

Novelists have two original sins: the first is the one that goes with descent from Adam and Eve and the second is in trying to interpret the world-order according to their own conceptions."

***

Stable societies tend to favor vast novels that can encompass many types of persons and trace the broad currents of influence on events, novels such as George Eliot's, "Middlemarch" or Anthony Trollope's, "Barchester Towers." These sum up a composite picture of a given time and place. As their societies age though a spirit of uncertainty can come to dominate them and the novel becomes more introspective as the author comes to depend on his own intuitions and desire for order. It may take a turn toward fantasy or toward the exploration of morbid states of mind as the confidence and forward momentum of entire social orders slows down, classes become intermingled, and the life-paths of individuals become less dictated by outward circumstances. The novel turns then to individual dilemmas and morbid perceptual processes as in Gustav Flaubert's, "Madame Bovary," Fyodor Dostoyevsky's "Crime and Punishment" and "Against the Grain" by J.K. Huysmans.

When the historical sense reasserts itself it does so either by taking a satirical look at the norms of the past as in Samuel Butler's, "The Way of all Flesh," or by imagining a future society to be built on the ruins of the past as in the novels of H.G. Wells. If actual fragmentation occurs rather than the slow decay of a social order, the novel itself must fragment in order to encompass the dissolved elements into some type of container. The result is seen in the novels of Robert Musil, Samuel Beckett, or Anthony Burgess.

Some novelists retain a residual didacticism or nostalgia for whatever has become rare or has perished and are as a result already non-recoverable. These turn sentimental or seek to revive the old order by new techniques as in the works of Herman Hesse, Flannery O'Connor, Walker Percy, Henry James, Herman Broch, and James Joyce. Without a frame of reference provided by reading such works one's mental equipment is for that very reason deficient because one is compelled to adopt a frame of reference without contrast or depth, one mediated only by the prevailing mores of the times in which one lives and the people with whom one associates. The result is worse than mere provincialism; it is the complacency manifested by those who cannot even imagine that alternative perspectives could, even theoretically, exist.

In my own reflections on my novel, as it exists at the present moment of its spontaneous composition, I have become aware of certain deficiencies which will be pointed out to the reader from time to time. As an instance, my use of the point-of-view of events recorded as they are happening has already denied to "Pacific End" the classification of the novel-as-memoir. When the sense of time of the narrator is altered or displaced the reader is apt to lose a stable sense of where he is in the text. No doubt a careful editor would point this out to me. But then this is of the order of an experimental effort, so rules are bound to be broken as in a painting by Rene Magritte.

Self-contradiction after all may be cited as evidence of broadmindedness. After all, Ralph Waldo Emerson once said that "a foolish consistency is the hobgoblin of little minds." So it is that I press onwards to express how we live in this memorable year of 2016, the year in my life when everything came together, then gradually fell apart, was eventually subject to transformation, and then ... but that is to anticipate part four of this novel which is still in the process of gelling in intentions of the author. (As an example of foreshadowing though allow me to say that at the time of which I am writing I am becoming convinced that no transformation would be adequate to rescue that state in which the world is currently languishing, judging by the persons to whom the human race is entrusting its future; nor for that matter will the current writing efforts sustain the weight that is being placed upon them by history).

***

Even Christianity is ambivalent regarding the degree of transformation that will prove adequate to achieving salvation. Something more than the merely human is required. So to come to the point I will simply ask this question, "Can what cannot be transformed be redeemed?"

The very form of the question immediately invokes religion and religion of a peculiarly western cast of mind. Millions of Buddhists have managed to side-step the question of redemption through the simple medium of a series of rebirths – what is unfinished or flawed in this life may be remedied or improved at least in the next life, but as a Catholic I believe that we get only one shot at life as we know it and then... well, we get something else.

Atheists meanwhile say you get one shot and then... nothing else. It doesn't take much reflection to see that a poor rice farmer who is a Buddhist might be more sanguine about the future than a ninety-year-old billionaire who is an atheist. The Buddhist might anticipate returning as a rich rajah, while the atheist can hope at best for round-the-clock nursing care. He may in addition already be anticipating the potential havoc and squabbles that his last will and testament may cause among his heirs. Reincarnation of course merely passes the buck because at least some among us must have been here many times before without having really learned all that much. The world is still a mess, with the exception of Jesus, Mahatma Gandhi, Confucius (although he was sort of a company man), and a lot of very patient elementary school teachers and nurses. Human nature doesn't get much better over time and people are for the most part pretty resistant to change.

So it is that Catholics turn to grace and pray for the dead. Who knows, maybe even Mafia dons say as they lie gasping out their last breaths like caught trout in a bucket, "Mama Mia, I really made-a the big-a mess of my life!" He may make it to heaven after all.

Friedrich Nietzsche figured it this way: you better love this one life of yours and the decisions you have made because the universe has recorded it all on its best-hits album and it will sooner or later get played again just like it was and then eventually again and again forever. That means that you will have to learn again how to factor quadratic equations. The only people who will like Nietzsche's idea of the Eternal Return are those who are multiply orgasmic.

Soren Kierkegaard meanwhile figured that if Christianity makes sense to you, then you still haven't got it right and moreover you don't deserve to call yourself a Christian.

Baruch Spinoza figured that we are all just part of the big one totality and as long as the sum is infinite who cares about integers – as long as the cola bubbles who cares about each individual bubble you just dissolve back into the atmosphere or into a sort of 17th century vision of humans as humus.

This wasn't all that comforting to Leibniz so he figured that we and everything else are all simultaneously attuned monads, each linked up in a sort of 17th century version of the Internet.

But then philosophers considered as a class are bothered by things that the rest of us prefer to ignore until we have to apply for Medicare. Life finally catches up with us then and we look at what we have accumulated, all the great investment chances we have missed out on, and say to ourselves, "You've got to be kidding; *this* was my life?"

Right about then you start thinking seriously about redemption...

✱✱✱

But I have yet to exhaust the possibilities of transformation in this world before turning to the possible intervention of what stands outside of the created order, I the possessor of a sovereign freedom to which our contingent choices bear only the slightest resemblance. Eternity and its inner relations are simply beyond what our imaginations can supply and therein is their deficiency to provide adequate motivation for out acts, absent the guidance of faith. We are less created in the image of God than we are created as very poor analogy of Him. To infuse the divine essence into humanity requires lots of stooping on God's part. But then novelists are always a little Calvinistic and apt to want to spare God any affront to his dignity while being simultaneously disillusioned about human nature.

Transformation differs from redemption in two ways: first it conserves the primal matter of its former existence while relying on a change of form to alter its character and function; second the change may proceed from within its own inherent capabilities rather than proceeding from an outside cause to work the change. Redemption on the other hand looks to an outside intervention to complement and alter what could never originate sua sponte from within the thing that is redeemed. There is also a sense to the term, when it is commonly used, that one nature is exchanged for another and by doing so the redeemed reaches a final goal or valuation (as in redeeming a coupon for a prize).

To redeem a life then is:

1. to exercise an option for renewal;
2. to complete what is fundamentally lacking;
3. to cancel a deficiency or pay a moral debt;
4. to reinstate a soul to divine grace.

Can a novel redeem anything (unless it implies performance to fulfill a book contract as in: "We have an option to publish your next three novels)?"

Novels are expressive in nature rather than redemptive. Novelists do not save the world; they may at best instruct, edify, inspire, or amuse their readers.

(The reader is asked to forgive those instances when the author is being unduly didactic, but it does save time and in small doses is permissible by way of providing a summation and thereby shortening the text.)

***

To write one's way out of a life-crisis is after all precisely what allowed Kafka to be prophetic.

Kafka raises the whole question of whether an omniscient narrator is always reliable. Is the K in the novels Kafka? Are his novels parables based on his own emotional experience transmuted to another and more universal level?

Am I engaged in a similar task here in writing, "Pacific End?"

(A hint to students for an extra credit paper if this book is ever taught in a high school English class)

***

So if you really want to know the truth, I was pretty sick and tired of everything this year. I'll admit sounding rather like Holden Caulfield here, from J. D. Salinger's novel. I just wasn't connecting since being home from the coast. I kept hearing about illnesses and deaths which didn't play well to my sense of the omniscient author of my own life and the general arbiter of fate wherever I chose to take a hand. Not that I'm a narcissist, because after all I just want things to work out so I can get back to what really counts, which is being beautiful and intelligent and loved by everybody and selling lots of books.

***

At an imaginary book-signing event: "Your book was a real trip. You remind me a lot of Daniel Defoe if he lived in Algiers and drank coffee with Oscar Wilde and Albert Camus and they put absinthe in their coffee everyday and talked all afternoon and watched the stars emerge at dusk when Paul Bowles and Jack Kerouac would show up and..."

Advice to authors, "Don't bite the hand that feeds you; remember we are really trained seals."

***

I had a girlfriend once who loved the novels of Tom Robbins and used to correspond with him. She wanted to be a writer and I thought we would have a house together someday filled with manuscripts and be the new Scott and Zelda. I guess I have spent my life looking for the light on Daisy's dock or even trying to be Daisy, a beautiful little fool.

***

My sister is in San Diego this weekend my Dad says. She is looking into a new business. The housing market isn't what it once was and it is unlikely to improve much until the economy collapses and the people in the east migrate away from the eastern cities where riots will be taking place daily. The Cubs did win the World Series though; Chicago could use the morale boost right now.

It's less than a week now until the election and the Catholic media are all for Trump. Trump will trumpet that the fix was in just as he said it was id he loses. Republicans will win either way; Barack and Michelle will leave the Whitehouse. Putin will grumble a bit and a big chill will set into America's heartland and the Deep South and the coal companies will say, "Well boys I guess that's it; now we'll never get our coal to China." Americans will go out and double down on ammo just in case. The gays and lesbians will know that their marriage rights are safe. We'll just all have to wait and see what happens. That's the news folks. Now how are we going to go about transforming America and making it strong again, bringing the jobs back, and making sure that black lives matter? The doomsday clock seems at least one second closer to midnight, but that sure beats two seconds closer.

***

Apparently we humans share above the 95th percentile of our genes with chimpanzees. This is not a surprising discovery to anyone who has spent much time in a male locker room. The compulsion to pass on our genetic heritage has become a constant preoccupation among at least half of the species. The more civilized of the two sexes filters this desire by diffusing at least part of its imperative by reading romance novels. Love as a partial guarantee of fidelity also serves the purpose of turning mere mutual liquefaction into something oriented to something beyond the gratification of a momentary impulse. The result when formalized by marriage is what Americans sentimentally refer to as family values. Of course no nation has proven itself to be more opposed to the advancement of the lower classes than supposedly egalitarian America. The vast income disparities between classes are not only tolerated but aided by every means possible from credit traps to low wages. Only the influx of cheap foreign-made goods and the big-box stores that merchandize them have allowed Americans the illusion of permanent prosperity, one that is floating precariously on our vast national debt and the potential for inflation that may be triggered by sovereign decisions to be made beyond our shores. The stale nationalism that has been the hallmark of Donald Trump's campaign is in reality due more to a lack of historical memory and the simmering brew of unfocussed class resentments than to current political needs. America is the source of its own problems. Terrorism is a straw man to distract is from our unjustified sense of global entitlement. We ask, "Why do they hate us?" The answer of course is because our bill is long overdue. We romp and rampage and expect that the world will enjoy what is for us just another Wild West Show. Trump promises a return to American greatness; alas, we have already had our brief hour of accidental supremacy granted by the old European Empires; the ones that just a hundred years ago 1916 were busy tearing each other apart over the spark of Serbian independence and their own need to maintain a credible threat to the others.

✳✳✳

Soren Kierkegaard assures us that a repetition is impossible just as Thomas Wolfe has told us that we can't go home again.

This means that whatever has been is etched irrevocably into our past; human life being what it is as we grow older, we end up with more past and less future and our prospects to transform are proportionately diminished. It will take a wrenching effort to achieve a reversal of a life's course and set it off in a new direction. We will tend to fall in love with the same type of person, even if she should appear in a new skin. We make the same mistakes. We simply discover that we are unable to forget. This is why getting a good start in life is so important and why a society that is callous to the needs of its children will never create a true civilization. I have been long of the opinion that in the face of a tyranny it is better to be a victim than a mere survivor. A false prosperity leaves all of its beneficiaries tainted to a degree. This is why being an American isn't easy for novelists and why ever since Nathaniel Hawthorne our literature has had a dark edge.

Edgar Allen Poe and Ambrose Bierce caught in their works a great deal of our underlying illness. There is a savage side to the American habit of conquest that makes all talk of progress and morality merely proof of our desire to efface what has been evident everywhere but here. If immigrants still flock to our shores it is only because remaining at home is even worse.

***

But this is speaking historically and it is my desire to be more singular here as well as more abstract. If we cannot retrace our steps and effect a reversal then where shall we look for a transformation? We might be tempted to believe in predestination if we felt less guilty about it all. How did things come to this? Where was the essential nexus, the crossroads, the intersection of tracks that once begun was sustained by any number of successive choices so that character was formed for good or ill and even our bodies were bent in one direction rather than another?

George Orwell said that we get the face in middle-life that we deserve. He may have been grimly humorous in saying so but his statement becomes even more evident in old age. There are exceptions though. Perhaps the reason why "Uncle Joe" Stalin could look so benevolent when he smiled was, that like a spring in a desert, a smile on his usually grim and pock-marked face was like a miracle. In golf it is called "taking a Mulligan." It means taking a second drive after a lousy tee-shot. A repetition in the sense meant by Kierkegaard would be to either to relive a past joy or to efface a past sorrow in the case of a significant life-event. The problem is that by the time that we can see our life in perceptive we are already too far down the road to easily retrace our steps. Even if we get to the magic spot where the error occurred we will likely find that the whole terrain there has changed. There may be a strip-mall on the corner and the open fields and meadows that were once there will be only an uncorroborated memory of the way things used to be.

✷✷✷

A strange experience: I was at a store and suddenly looked up to see an unusual little figure looking up at me and smiling, a little girl of that indeterminate age that might have been six or ten. Her expression was imprinted in my mind in an instant remarkable because for all that she had smiled at me there was an underlying theme of sadness in her face that touched my heart. The skin surrounding her eyes had a delicate bluish tinge as though she might be one of those cases where tragic illnesses like cancer strike the youngest among us, illnesses that summon up certain souls out of life at its very dawning hours when the elements of heaven still cling about them. I was distracted for a few moments and when I looked up again she had vanished from sight.

In reflecting back on the incident I began to wonder if I had in fact witnessed an apparition and not a child at all but a ghost or perhaps an angel. Was she one of those ministering spirits that remind us that our actions are observed and accounted for in a parallel celestial realm even while we go about our prosaic daily tasks? Or was she a wandering force, a sort of remnant of earth's sorrows, embodied in the natural goodwill of children towards a social order that lays snares for their feet and spoils the orchard of delights that might more appropriately await them?

Later that same day I was reading about the planet Mars and gazing at its cold desert surface as photographed by space-probes. There is evidence that at one time water existed there and an atmosphere that might have sustained the delicate processes of life. Its present desert aspect is the result of a low level of gravity that allowed its precious atmosphere to be blasted off into space whenever an asteroid would collide with the planet, Mars the God of War as victim. Could this bleak aspect be a prophetic vision of the earth if our foolishness should upset the balance of forces that sustain us? No mere temporary political solution should be able to exercise a deleterious effect upon the miracle of the biosphere which is our collective trust. Perhaps my ghost-child was a visitor from the future sent back to see the world as it was once inhabited by the generations that sealed her future doom. Perhaps it was a mute appeal that I had read in her eyes: "Please allow me to live."

Did she ask that among the more abstruse points in my novel I might point out the obvious: that human culture requires as a precondition the physical substrate of our existence, a planet of precisely the right size not to crush us by gravity located at a precise point from the sun, with a moon to move the tides, and oceans to drop rain upon the land?

Was she a presiding fairy-creature, one that had come to me to say, "Write thee oh novelist of the greensward at dusk. Hear the music of the spheres as did the bards of olden days when words were first being uttered as the Angles and Saxons mixed with the blood of the Norman and Viking invaders. Hear my Druid appeal and remind your contemporaries that when all human overlords have passed that we, the faery guardians of the earth remain. Let it not be to weep at the ruin you have wrought."

And I answered her, "Child of the future, wounded creature, whether admonitory spirit of the faery world or angel, whatever you may be, in obedience to your mute appeal I, a latter stage novelist, practitioner of an archaic craft in a digital age, have entered again the darkened smithy of my soul (as Joyce the great artificer once described his own creative process) where I can begin the quest for a way to connect to the earth again.

Part Four

All Things Redeemed

It has always seemed to me that the best proof for the existence of God is the existence of radical evil. But I personally think that the devil has recently been overplaying his hand. There is an aesthetic to evil that should favor the delicate touch of malice, the hidden resentment, and the quiet poison of gossip over a vulgar display of rank brutality and shocking atrocities. Why then do we witness every day such things as the following: the mother who shot her two young daughters down in front of her husband as a way of getting back at him, the young girl who broadcast her suicide on a long-term web-cam, feeding it onto the Internet in real-time for the delectation of the public, or the mass slaughter that is happening every day in Syria, the place where St. Paul once encountered the risen Christ and received his commission as an apostle? Just what is going on here? Are we witnessing the results of international rivalry, of conflicting social forces, of the mental stress produced by institutional decay, weakened family structures, or is all this the result of the loss of any sustaining belief in transcendence? Perhaps all of these are in play, but why add that little tincture or moral cyanide that leaves behind it the sharp and acrid stench of the diabolical? Where are the workers in the vineyard sufficient to oppose things like this?

I came to maturity in an era where religious vocations were considered to be cheap and plentiful. The prevailing idea by the 70's was to create a downsized but fanatical cadre of zealots to replace the larger monastery-like classes that had formerly swelled the ranks of the religious orders. There may have been some wisdom in this; after all, it only took one St Francis Xavier to spread Christianity in India. Why not take a chance on the exceptional ones to get the job done and cut costs in the process;

it works in the industrial sector. The world is accustomed to getting by on the minimum of saints while the majority of souls hope for some little saving codicil or last minute conversion to get them through the narrow gate to heaven. Others seek to find a way to attain reconciliation with this nasty world as it is or to find a way to selectively oppose it and still have a pleasurable life. These publish works like "The Plague" by Albert Camus. But can any novelistic treatment diminish the sheer impact of the daily march of sordid events, particularly when they affect the young to whom the rest of us look for hope and renewal? We need more than a zone defense to employ against losses like these; we need guardian angels.

***

As the summer energy wanes away and winter proper begins it is not unusual for me to pass into a state of semi-hibernation. I need to feel more than a mere sense of homecoming. I need to feel encompassed by warmth and familiarity when winter approaches. In recent years I knew that at least one other shared my immediate reactions to the seasonal changes, so her absence has been felt keenly.

I returned to the local casino, not for the thrill of winning, but for its capacity to create a technologically induced womb-like environment of lights, food, and an attractive fireplace in the adjoining hotel. I am not averse to feeling the world shrink around me until it forms a sort of protective skin.

One night I went up to the local parish church at a time when our active and large Hispanic community was holding a retreat. Rather than being confined to merely inspirational talks or the tight ritualism of the sacraments this evening was devoted to song, movement, procession, and dance in a way that I found simply hypnotic. The church grew warm with people of all ages and the evidence that children were welcomed and that procreation was seen as regular and natural, as the budding of leaves in spring. The music was brass dominated and fiesta-like and the whole presentation was as far as can be imagined from the somber manner that redemption is enhanced in a typical Anglo community setting. I was reminded of what America has lost in being dominated by the cultures of the white colonists, the somber Puritans in the north and the fire-and-brimstone Baptists in the south.

American Catholicism was dominated in my youth by Cardinal Spellman's brand of simplistic orthodoxy, one that was inquisitorial, anti-communist, suspicious of sexuality, simplistic, and ultimately sterile. Its primary character was a complete absence of joy. Its concept of God was completely alien to ordinary human concerns, a brutal judge dominated by the elaborate jurisprudence of Church history. God was so other as to almost undo the primary Christian doctrine of the incarnation. The Church was a realm without appeal, understanding, or compromise; all had been settled long ago and the heretics had been soundly anathematized. Most of the books that have been the backbone of philosophy had at one time or another been on the index and it was forbidden to read them. It was the duty of Catholics to work hard in a Protestant dominated nation, to raise lots of kids, and use any spare dimes to keep the Church going at the parish level, sending their children to be taught by the shrouded nuns and later in the sex-segregated Catholic High Schools.

Heterosexual activity was mysterious and perilous, a concession to our vile and humiliating status as the rational animal, one that cannot procreate by concepts alone. The Church admired the rational and despised the animal base that formed a sort of unworthy pedestal for elevated thoughts, for careful Thomist distinctions, and the mystical prayer among those so favored by grace. I think that the general climate of dread and my need for warmth and community stems from the vast loneliness of my youth where even redemption was more about threats than reward and love for any creature was predicated on a constant habit of recalling that one did not deserve to be saved. After all, we had our chance in Eden and we had blown it. The rest of us ever since were born already in debt, unworthy, an affront to the pristine angels and ready prey for devils. We piled up prayers like bricks to negotiate trustee status in the jail of purgatory by working off our sentence before we died by suffering when it was easier and cheaper than the flames we would later encounter would be;

pay-up now or pay later. At least we had the comfort that we were Catholics and not like the heathen Protestants whose very services of worship were considered with contempt, an affront because there was no belief in the Real-Presence of Christ in the Eucharist. Add to the terrors of religion the vague nuclear dread of post-war Americans, the upsets and redefinitions of the 1960's, and a sense that various American dreams were little more than the indefinite deferral of a truly just society and my background as a novelist in the mold of Huysmans makes sense. When our ideals are the source of our anguish and disappointment we turn to decadence and that fin de siècle spirit that the reader may have discerned in "Pacific End."

The western states are separated from the east by the fact that their roots are in the Spanish conquest and the legacy of the French trappers and missionaries rather than a mere extension of the ethos of the original thirteen British colonies. The entire west was only a century old when I was born. As a westerner I share that desire to break away from history and to ride the waves of gold and silver to untold riches. Only the coastal states retain this radical spirit unscathed and even they possess their own aristocracy.

California remains though as the mythmaker of the nation in film, music, and architecture. I spent part of my life on the road to El Dorado and the Comstock Lode and it still remains inside me. Like many Americans I am still waiting for the lucky strike that will set me up for the quiet years of letting go that we call retirement or senior living. Of course what is really involved in aging is a culling process as various genes manifest their relative efficacy at holding cancers at bay and blood vessels decide whether to block-up with cholesterol or rupture after our lifetimes spent eating red meat and downing various drinks at bars and lounges.

All of the above of course is merely my effort as a novelist to explain why my thoughts are turning to redemption at a certain stage of life, just as a depleted treasury will result in efforts to negotiate a loan from a central bank to restore its liquidity. The best current candidates appear to be Christianity and Buddhism the sacred canons of both have been long decided. Others today adopt a sort of vague syncretism of all faiths and try to be good, or at least no worse than most people, and figure that God, if he exists at all, is more understanding than he is usually portrayed.

Then there are the "we work harder religions" like the Muslims and the Mormons. Both have borrowed extensively from prior belief systems but have the advantage of brand-new books of revelation, actually penned in heaven and only transcribed on earth by an authoritative prophet. The Koran undoubtedly reads well in Arabic and even the Book of Mormon might have some poetry in it if certain tedious repetitions had not sounded particularly biblical to Joseph Smith. (I speak somewhat slightingly of both because their emergence had more to do with geo-political issues prevailing at the time than with any initiative by God). Both are radical off-shoots from a solid Judeo-Christian core and as such are novelties, examples of divine literature on a par with the Iliad and the Odyssey. This is not to disparage the personal virtues or sincerity of those who adhere to these faiths or to claim that we can learn nothing from them. It is only to put their supposed revelations in a proper place as derivative when they correspond to orthodox Christian beliefs and as poetic persiflage when they do not. If redemption is to be found it is in purging mere political accretions from the true faith as taught by the Doctors of the Church, by the councils, by the mystics, and by the daily witness of the body of believers whose simple trust makes complex novels superfluous.

I have always envied people who seem to know intuitively what life is about and who can live at peace with what fate has thrown to them. But then novels thrive on conflict, suspense, and foreshadowing. The future is always vaguely grim and the path to get there strewn with obstacles. Things are not here as they are supposed to be. Then after various twists and turns and alterations the protagonist is seen to grow or shrink or become noble or complete his fall into his unique moral morass. Throw in a few thrills or sex scenes to keep the reader going and some unique gimmick or two and, there it is, a novel, the poor-man's path to redeem the lost days and hours.

I have not surrendered a belief in redemption but I am troubled by the sticking-plaster concept of sanctity that seems to invalidate precisely the elements of the human-all-too-human in our lives that are the very meat and drink of novelists. Novels are always in the nature of an exposé. Novelists thrive on conflict and tragedy for their themes and to retain the reader's interest. Happy endings, when they are tolerated at all, are deferred to the end of the novel when it is too late for reader to throw the book aside as dull and vapid. Until the end the crafty novelist keeps suspense alive by adding misfortune to misfortune and enlisting the reader's hopes things will improve, which they quite often inexplicably do, except in the works of Thomas Hardy.

I have always wondered who Hardy's readers were. Did they expect that just maybe in this latest entry things might just work out and the human condition be seen as other than irremediably bleak? Or did Hardy's rugged readers enjoy seeing that basically redemption is as impossible to achieve as the aforementioned repetition? Fate in the works of Thomas Hardy seems always to prefer the disproportionate actions of the furies; the scale is invariably weighted against us. Try as we will, nothing will work out. Worse still, happiness toys with us only to make its eventual loss more unsupportable. Yet a poem of his makes it clear that he possesses all of the instincts of Christianity but simply cannot believe for some constitutional reason. Catholic novelists use their works to support the truth as the Roman Catholic Church proclaims it to be for all of humankind in age after age, world without end. The Church and those who look to it for redemption still await the coming of the Bridegroom and the restoration of all things in Christ. Until then we live, we pray, and we even may read a novel or two to pass the time and maybe for instruction and inspiration.

***

If Thomas Hardy has plumbed the netherworlds of depression and despair, the novels of Thomas Wolfe celebrate the hunger of youth for the sheer variety and compass of experience. Thomas Wolfe always spoke as well of the cycle of wandering and returning as the basic rhythm of life. This would certainly be true of my own life, a series of partial realizations, all of them directed towards reaching the proper starting point, to set a standard from which to calculate the moral longitude and latitude of the earth, my own version of Joyce's "uncreated conscience of the race."

Humans have always sought to express beginnings before all else: how can we know where to go if we don't know where we came from? Genesis will always be the first book in any Bible aspired to by future religionists. It is just no good saying that we just got dumped here, woke up, shook our collective heads, and started looking around for food and someone to share a bed with us when the night came on. But, as a novelist I know that there are people, often quite wealthy and apparently happy, who don't go much beyond this primitivism in the course of their metaphysical questionings. I don't write for them because they are unlikely to value what I say. The question must exist before the answer is meaningful.

For this reason I thought it might be a good idea in writing "Pacific End" to explore the primary conditions of my life in the year 2016 before suggesting any general solutions as we expect novelists to provide. Besides, the novel has long since abandoned its primarily didactic function as practiced in the 18th century. We don't expect novels to have a moral ever since Mark Twain threatened in his novel, "Huckleberry Finn," to have those seeking a moral in it to be shot. But then I'm not Mr. Twain and besides I'm Catholic after all and I figure the only safe water is to be found in the river Jordan and environs. I didn't want "Pacific End" to resemble Mark Twain's bitter final diatribes in his "Letters from the Earth." So it was that my prospective readers were to be led first from innocence to experience as things initially came together and then fall apart for me this year, then to explore the options of transformation as we cast about in middle-age for solutions to problems that we did not even know existed when we were young, and thus having put to rest the middle years of life to clear the way for the great reassessments of old age, that season of summing up a life, all of this very systematic and novel-like.

***

While I was engaged in writing today the Basque Princess entered and came tripping over to me like an elegant flamingo.

She is lately from Santa Barbara where she did some modeling of sportswear for a magazine designed for the elegant horsy set. As one who inherently mistrusts those with money almost as much as I mistrust those without it I heard her story with the predictable mixture of envy and caution. Thank heaven I have so far managed with adroit skill to avoid a lucrative Hollywood contract as a screen- writer or a career at any one of the big established publishing houses in New York that work their talent to the bone and then cast writers off to bewail their former greatness. I much preferred to follow the Emily Dickenson route to posthumous fame leaving my manuscripts sensibly in a drawer. Now here was the Basque Princess, fresh from a recent film screening and a modeling assignment with her brown eyes flashing and wearing a tailored leather jacket, whisking about me like the tail of a California Palomino in the annual Rose Parade. Well, I figured that grace and dignity, the most valued of the personal characteristics of the unknown, would best become me and recalled that one writing of redemption should be above a level of mere nostalgia combined with sour predictions regarding the fate of the contemporary world. The radio playing background music began to play the old hit, "Brown-eyed Girl," just to let me know that the universe has a sense of humor at my expense.

✳✳✳

I would have written more about her before this, but it is hard to reduce to print a young life that is still in prospect. No one has ever written a novel about the young from a young person's own partially-formed perspectives and passing enthusiasms. The Bildungsroman is typically written from the perspective of presumed maturity by middle-aged authors. Notice that the middle-aged do not write about being middle-aged with a similar facility. There is always at least a ten year gap between experiencing a life-event and the ability to convincingly portray it in a novel. By the time that it is possible to write about life as a whole few writers have the residual energy left to do so, unless they are Leo Tolstoy. (He did write "War and Peace" as a young man but then he was *Tolstoy* after all).

Anything that I might say now about the Basque Princess

would be the product of my imagination. I do not know what lies in store for her. Instead, I simply hope that everything will work out well and in her case at least the gods may show forbearance. Sometimes everything just works out and there is a happy ending. I look at her and I see the human equivalent of a nervous filly running a first derby race and hope she can run without injury. Every day at this season of life is worth four of what will come later on. When you are young a one degree angle of deflection can put your life destination way off course forty years down the road. A chance meeting can alter a whole life's course. Glad to escape the tension of so many possibilities I return to the safety of my manuscript, satisfied that at least I know how it ended with me.

✱✱✱

The paths to ruin are ubiquitous. Some people go to hell all at once and by age thirty-five they already are talking about a crack-up. I avoided this due to my penchant of reinventing myself at intervals of one or two decades. I could then do my twenties over and over again, always hoping for a better outcome this time. I needed someone as timeless as I was to share my hear my tale and share my sorrows. I thought I had found her.

And now I wonder whether I am more like Lord Byron after all and not poor misunderstood Percy Shelley crying to his wild West-wind and lamenting his early fallen leaves. Vampires cannot see their own reflection in a mirror it is said. What though if everyone else can? The season of sap-running is after all a short one and worldly wisdom, even in novels like "Tom Jones" must finally end off coupling and discuss character and social circumstance. I think of the Basque Princess and of the timeless oracle of Newport and wonder about the full course of a woman's life. How much do I know of this life? So little in fact that faery-guardians or even angels are sent to me to smile in greeting and then just as swiftly disappear.

✱✱✱

November 8, 2016 was a day of sun and unexpectedly balmy air. It gave me a chance to catch up on things and then to ceremoniously vote before looking forward to a long evening of watching the election returns, able to finally relax a little knowing that the Republican Party had been thoroughly thrashed (a fate that they deserved after allowing their party to be hijacked by a loudmouthed vulgar lunatic because the other potential candidates were even more deluded, self-indulgent evangelical types of various stripes).

Imagine my surprise, when I arrived at a quiet bar where I could watch the results in peace, to discover that the lunatic was actually winning! By the next morning it was all history: America had been hung up to dry like fresh doe-skin tacked to a wall. I could almost smell the odor of stale beer being guzzled by all of the Joe Six-Pack types across Michigan, Ohio, and Pennsylvania who had joined the Mormons in the west, the wheat-farmers on the plains, and the old Confederacy to place in office a man whose long suit was nothing more than his xenophobia and greed, the very emotions that awoke an answering echo in the bottomless abyss of the American Empire.

The vast tides of the terminally mediocre were beginning to doubt that their era of collective exceptionalism was finally over so they decided to gamble on Trump. Rather than opt for the services in education and health care that their very survival depended on, they held out for some desperate resurgence of a national myth, one based not on policies to secure prosperity but on the mere exclusion of aliens and a willingness to go to war. The New England States with their sophisticated intellectual heritage were joined by New York, New Jersey, and even old Virginia while in the ever-optimistic West the Blue States held firmly with the Democrats. Everything in between (and of course Alaska, which never quite emerges from its polar night) went Republican.

America is really a political black-hole between the two coasts where alone reside the educated and the humane who favor reaching out to other lands rather than alienating them. In that black-hole various forms of malcontent rule the day: insecure males without blue-collar work who wish that they could get away with "grabbing pussy" at will, complacent evangelicals who only believe in the value of human life until birth (after that it is capital all the way because "God wants you to be rich,)" and the hard-line cynical business types who want anything that will pad the corporate bottom-line. America isn't well-bred enough to possess a real aristocracy so it substitutes a tower-climbing dullard with a bevy of trophy-females to balance out the gender equation.

Working-class girls of course are fair game and now firmly reminded that they better be careful who gets them knocked-up because they will be on their own from here on in. But then why be bitter? When America, "takes a selfie," the result is now the well-fed visage of "the Donald." The election results are playing well on the world markets though today with the people that matter and even Russia is delighted. Idealism is always bad for business and the Russians know well that even emancipated serfs still know their place. If Americans should get out of hand and try to renege on the deal Putin can always tell Trump a thing or two about public relations and policing the electorate. Ruling might become so nice for Donald that he may just decide to move into the Whitehouse permanently unless the Rapture comes first and he goes whirling up into the clouds like in a big velvet mural sold alongside a service station in Tennessee. It's time for that wicked witch Hillary and her philandering husband to leave the public stage having been taught her place. She should be grateful if the new President doesn't appoint a special prosecutor to pursue her as she fades from the limelight, never to return. That should teach other old broads about just how much use political experience is in a real Presidential race to the death.

✳✳✳

I beg the gentle reader's pardon. I got some of the spleen out of my system by writing the extract that appears *supra* and having written it I am beginning to lay plans again for a life that isn't plagued by sheer disgust with America. But I still feel that the final links are being set in place for the National Security State. A little tremor of terror has passed along the margins of my mind. I see how Putin and Trump could sit down one day and remind each other of their joint power.

Putin: "You know you and me and maybe a handful of Chinamen could end up ruling the whole damn world! Now here's the deal that I propose: we cook up a little international crisis so you can declare martial law at home; we scare hell out of everybody. Then you and me reach a compromise and everybody will be so damn grateful that their asses aren't orbiting the cinders of the earth somewhere in space that they will appoint you the Plenipotentiary of America. How's that sound to you? Even Genghis Khan never dreamed of such a deal! Now, if you're the man that I think you are you and me, we can divide the world between us and if the Chinese object we'll finally play our hold cards. Chinamen aren't stupid, just prolific. Survival is very big with them. When they realize that they are caught in a power vice they'll take whatever deal we are willing to concede to them. You can call me Vladimir. How about it what do you say, is it a deal?"

But then maybe I am just being paranoid. Just because a guy uses inane rhetoric to get elected to the highest office in the world's oldest, the most powerful country on earth, and is an ego-manic of the first caliber doesn't necessarily mean that he would want to become some sort of world-dictator. I mean does it? I'm just being way too imaginative. Novelists do that you know; they just imagine stuff and then use language and artifice to make us pretend that the world that they portray is real.

∗∗∗

So it was only forty-eight hours since the results came in and I had already begun to process the thought that maybe things just might work out. What's a little more coal smoke in the atmosphere, a couple of Supreme Court justices committed to Originalism except when corporate power is concerned, and maybe a universal right to stop and frisk anybody at any time just to remind you that the police are on the job? Why get all George Orwellian about it? So what if exclusion and deportation become a way of life? It will just remind the rest of us how lucky we are to be here in Republican America? After all, freedom isn't free; you have to give up actual freedoms if you want to have the big Freedom (whatever that is). Besides why ruin Trump's Cheshire cat moment while he is feeling generous and inclusive? Does anybody really want to sound like they just might be trouble and belong on a short-list kept somewhere?

Of course novelists deal in ideas and ideas aren't a threat unless the masses ever start thinking; so I guess I can write as I please here. Philosophy is the ultimate indulgence, like eating a cake that is almost all butter. America of course is very diet-conscious when it comes to feeding things into the mind. Even the women are not upset yet. "You know we say awful things about men too when we're in the ladies room," as one post-election interviewee said when she was questioned.

What's a little pussy-grabbing among friends as long as everybody is in the GOP?

***

What role has gender as applied to narrative voice? Lady-novelists have been masking their sex since George Sand and the publication of the first novels by the Bronte sisters. As I write these words the radio just played "Born to be Wild" and for just a fleeting moment I recalled how it felt to savor the rebellion and change in the air in 1968. I thought now of "Les Miserables" and that wonderful year of 1848 when country after country in Europe tried to shake off their shackles and to form republics.

Seattle made the national news after the election. Youth thronged Capital Hill to say, "Not my President." Poor babies, they are forgetting the four thousand miles of farmland dividing the coastal civilizations of the Atlantic and Pacific coasts and the ruined factories with puddles on the floor in Youngstown, Ohio and Pittsburg, Pennsylvania that will soon be humming away with non-union workers grateful for whatever they can get. They are forgetting the wall, to be supposedly paid for by the Mexicans as a sort of act of reparation for all the cheap drugs that they send to pollute our unwilling and innocent youth shooting up at the suburban shopping malls. A little old-time religion and a minimum wage job will fix all that.

I could go on and on of course but then diatribes are unseemly and grace in defeat is so becoming and so un-Hillary now that Big Daddy is securely set to take over the reins of government and start tightening the spigots of entitlements until they squeak. We can rearm our nuclear warheads, put Iran in its place, and let the Arabs know that our support of Israel is why God has chosen America to exercise hegemonic power over the world and chosen the Republicans to run the country. How else explain how the polls could have been so wrong?

***

Had I been looking to politics for redemption all along? If so I had fallen into a very common trap for the unwary reformer. I forgot that as a practitioner of the written word I was joining the likes of Lincoln Steffens, Upton Sinclair, and H.L. Mencken, all of whom learned that politics is the realm where the cunning play off the opposing prejudices of mediocre minds and of lives doomed to anonymity. The herd of blind buffalo has simply reversed direction as instinct, hunger, and fear tells them to do from time to time and moved from electing a young half-black reformer to electing an old, white fat-cat. The masses are always in search of a political solution to the intractable economic dictates of supply and demand. To this problem writers add a measure of consolation to the minority that can still take pride in knowing what is really going on although its members are equally powerless to change the course of events.

The problem for me was that probably most Catholic bishops had also lined up behind Trump. Secure in their essentially life-time jobs, if not necessarily in any particular diocese, they have been promoted for not making waves. For all their "collegiality" most steer close to the course set in Rome by the Pope and his administrative arm the Curia. The Pew-Catholics of course don't keep up on events or read encyclicals so many ships of conscience sail on right past various theological icebergs without even knowing they are there. This allows the bishops to keep their jobs and hold synods while lay Catholics instruct each other on the requirements of the faith as best they understand them. Through a process of self-selection and migration some parishes end up as liberal and others as conservative bastions and the average disaffected Catholics on either extreme quietly leave the Church behind for greener pastures. This has been considered a workable pattern for most of my adult life.

A little study has taught me a lot about institutional survival and how individuals can invade and infiltrate organizations like a mess of boll-weevils in tall cotton. There is a name for this phenomenon: it is called "a universal imperative." If you want to survive then you have to learn to play the game, sound out the phonies, to hide your cards from your enemies, and when is the moment to take the opportunity to destroy them utterly. Never leave a smoldering fire; stir the ashes and drown it again.

✳✳✳

What all of this means is that if you want redemption in America today you will have to seek it out; either that or join the widening circle of victims. Of course in saying this I am not speaking as a Catholic but as a cynical novelist, one who has wandered through Thomas Hardy, Emile Zola, William Makepeace Thackeray, and Herman Melville. I need though have ventured no further than Cervantes, Voltaire, and Swift to know that compared to some novelists John Calvin was an optimist in his assessment of human nature. This is why the saints sometimes need to hover on the edge of what we might call holy insanity with their eyes fixed on God and pity in their hearts for suffering humanity. These leave it to the novelists to bear the cross of revelations to their brothers and sisters, things which the innocent should be spared.

A novelist died and he was informed that his time in purgatory had been reduced by half in virtue of his occupation. He was delighted of course but was bold enough to question the reason for this unexpected largess. The answer was, "You poor bastards have already suffered enough with rejection slips, editors, reviews, and neglect, not to mention laboring just to say something worth reading."

The novelist thought about it and then called his agent and told him, "This 'half-off purgatory' deal stinks; I'm holding out for a free-pass straight into heaven and residuals."

✳✳✳

Of course the new President Elect already has all the accoutrements of success in America, a series of attractive wives, money, fame, an attractive family, and now the power that not even the richest of men possesses unless they are into organized crime; he can have people killed, millions of them in fact. Since America stopped having Congress declare wars, as it alone can do according to the Constitution, we pretty well let the President send our troops anywhere that he considers necessary to keep American power credibly regarded around the world.

Of course we wage our wars with borrowed money, mostly the hard-earned Chinese money, so there are limits out there somewhere; we just don't know where they are. So "the Donald" is now much more than a figure of fun and a real estate mogul. He is more than a connoisseur of pretty ladies; he is one of a handful of men who could write finis to the whole human enterprise and probably the planet as well. This is not the sort of power you give to a guy who takes gambles and likes to shoot from the hip and grab genitalia of strange women if he happens to feel the urge. Having a billion dollars in net worth and plenty of ready cash for any need close at hand can breed a habit of not liking to hear people say no to you. It can make you petulant, shallow, and even sort of dumb. Of course I am talking from the point of view of most scholars who tend to put too much emphasis on the power of the written word as an indicator of intelligence and culture. Words won't buy you towers in Manhattan. They may not even buy you a year's worth of good dinners. But writers feel like creativity is its own reward and having people perhaps care what we thought about long after we're dead. We all have our own brand of egoism.

Too bad that Ayn Rand isn't alive to watch as John Galt is sworn in as president. We finally have a President who can look at his term of living in the White House as his "Bungalow Years." The old mansion could really use a face-lift: get a little glitz and bling in there and no Mexicans allowed trimming the shrubs. Of course success in America always tends to look great until you calculate the costs and reckon up the body-count. The bedrock of American life is pretty seedy and it is bedrock because low wages support profits. The American Middle Class is really just a tight spectrum of micro-classes when seen from the very top of the pyramid. Nobody wants to admit that most Americans are really the equivalent of the serving class in England. We also have our share of serfs but with no landed estate on which to labor; no job security in that.

We have a police presence that has less to do with solving crimes than it does with keeping economic frustration in various ghettos from breaking into open rebellion and looting. The whole balancing act is to sustain masses of people just above the level of desolation and loss of hope. We are a lottery society with casinos and bingo as a way of life for the poor and the marginal as they look to the one big win for their salvation. Many people feel that this can't be all that there is to living, but for most of them sadly it is a treadmill existence waiting in long lines on freeways, hoping their job will not be downsized or outsourced, and seeking in drugs or dull sit-coms a little restoration at the end of the day. The simmering brush-fire of racial discontent, angry youth, and resentful age, all of these and more are bubbling away in the deadly brew of cauldron America. This is the America that President Trump must now lead.

✳✳✳

There won't be a big bailout for America from some lender of last resort anytime soon. The twin specters of inflation and dishonored debt grow bigger every day. Russia is making its play on the Black Sea region that was contemplated before the 1904 War with Japan forced a reassessment. Putin wants his little Riviera among the Balkans. He hopes that Trump will give him a free hand.

What we want in return is not to be unmasked and humiliated by countries like Iran and North Korea. We are like a tall tower swaying in the wind and hoping that the material stress-coefficients and probability analysis will allow us to add on a few more stories without having the whole thing tumble down. We know at some level that America can't afford to have anybody call our bluff. We have to keep calling and raising the stakes in a poker game that began at the time of the Spanish-American War during the McKinley Administration. If it all starts to come down it could well be in the next few years and it will be on a Republican watch that it happens. They better have some solutions besides just more guns, walls, and prisons.

✳✳✳

Of course you can't blame Donald for his own election. In the days that followed his victory I discovered by reading the comment columns appended to news articles on the Internet that his base might someday turn on him like a pack of savage dogs. Many talked openly of civil war had Hillary won and pointed out that they had been stockpiling weapons for years under the belief that a nation without its own equivalent of the Nazi Storm-troopers just isn't American. After about fifty paragraphs of reading this stuff I began to wonder how civilization here had been gradually leeched away while I was busy studying law. I suddenly realized that the reason that Trump had been elected was because nothing further to the right was on the ballot. It wasn't that voters liked him; it was because they hated a composite portrait of "liberals" in just the way that Nazi party members had elaborated their politically feasible concept of "the Eternal Jew."

The liberal is supposedly an atheistic urban dweller who has exported the jobs of hard-working-but-anti-union-conservatives-with-guns. But the liberal is also an effete, bleeding heart, pansy or bitch, one who loves bums, Muslims, and communists and wants to deliberately rip the Constitution to shreds starting with the Second Amendment (which you can bet they have never read). If they had they would see that a condition precedent of the right to bear arms is that it is to enable state militias to preserve the peace. The right in other words is neither individual nor absolute, *on its face it is not!* Every year demonstrates that the diffusion of private arms into our society is a cause of crime and innocent deaths to a degree that makes terrorism negligible in comparison. If walls are called for to appease paranoid Americans they are not along the border with Mexico but surrounding everything south of the New England States and east of the western coastal states where liberals are said to congregate. In the great basin that covers everything between the two coasts people are arming themselves against the urban enclaves where the people who can still read above an eighth-grade level are prone to gather and drink espresso and sleep with members of the same sex. I would be quite satisfied to let them have the right to idolize what, if they understood it they would deplore, a Constitution that was not designed to further either anarchy or a police state but rather to make a commonwealth possible. Until a second secession occurs the majority of Americans who voted for Hillary Clinton must share the nation with denizens of the red states that like arsenic salt dissolved in elderberry wine surround them. If President Trump doesn't foment their agenda and the wall doesn't get built, the Affordable Care Act survives semi-intact, and the jobs don't come back from China well, all I can say is: watch your backs everybody.

✳✳✳

Personally speaking, I don't place much hope in politics for redemption. Nobody gets redemption without atonement. The latter is the cause and prerequisite of the former. Atonement has always been understood as essentially payback or what lawyers call restitution: to put things back into the position that they occupied before the alleged malfeasance occurred. Theologically speaking this would mean putting God back into a position prior to any sin's commission. The idea here is that since God is by definition infinite goodness any offense against him is a sign of infinite malice on the part of the malefactor. Sin is the failure of a contingent being to align its will with God's commandments. If you are a Calvinist this occurs because our moral status after the Garden of Eden is inherently flawed and depraved. Only divine grace can alter this inherent deficiency and when it does so it cannot be resisted because it partakes of God's infinite power. We can at best only watch people's actions and infer the presence of grace post-hoc by what they in fact do. If you act like sinners do you are evidently not of the elect which means you are of those condemned to hell by retaining your residual unsaved status. The Catholic position in contrast is one that allows for alteration until death cuts off the possibility of human freedom as it is exercised in time. It takes this position because one who is dead and deprived of a body and the period allotted for meaningful moral choice has in effect exhausted his options.

"Time, put your pencils down and pass your papers to the end of the row!"

Catholics don't say "I have been saved" like the Protestants do. Instead Catholics pray for "final perseverance" and meditate on the four last things, on death, judgment, heaven and hell. Those with an undifferentiated Christian background just hope that God will grade us on a curve of misbehavior and that a make-up class in some sort of post-demise summer camp will take care of those who have not received good marks below. The Hindus dealt with this problem by figuring on a staircase of lives. The problem with this position is that anybody might say, "Well this is the one where I am greedy and make-out like a bandit. I'll be better the next time around." The Jewish position is, "Heaven? Hell? Who's to say? I try and do the Mitzvahs and I raised some great kids. I'm no worse than the other guy and after all, it has to count for something being Jewish I mean. I'd hate to have learned all that Hebrew for my Bar Mitzvah for nothing." While Muslims say, "God is one and Mohammed is his prophet. The unbelievers will receive a severe chastisement of that we are certain." (Just in case we recite it about one hundred times over while lying on our faces every day, isn't that enough?)"

∗∗∗

But what if there is no redemption and we are all stuck with this crazy world and this short life and all the unanswered questions and with no do-overs? If this is so then all I have to say is that even the winners are really losers because fate plays with them first before grinding them into dust. Only the terminally bored welcome death as long as things aren't going too bad. Anyone who ever sees a heroic child in a cancer ward knows that something is owed to her for her diminished and unlived life besides just a ribbon pinned to her bed after the little dead body is taken away.

Regarding the doctrine of hell, eternal punishment seems superfluous and degrading if no reform is ever possible as a result. Does God's love require vindication, as though holiness couldn't stand on its own without the aid of retribution? Eternal punishment is a contradiction in terms. God's justice is not vindicated by such indirect means as the deliberate torture of the damned. Only heaven makes any sense for a supreme being. If anyone is in hell it must be because he has looked over the accommodations in heaven and concluded, "This is not for me baby; I need me some thrills! I think eternity here would be a real drag."Another group might choose hell simply because of social status; living with the poor and obscure is a real come-down., "It isn't the place; it's the people. I just had no idea that *she* would be here. I hope she didn't see me."

If things can only be transformed by grace, well, judged by results not everybody looks too saintly. When will the great turning take place? A lot of people appear to be okay with going to hell and maybe figure they'll at least see a lot of familiar faces there. Of course that doesn't make things good, but what the h—l, maybe this life is all we get after all so why not grab a little gusto and bang a little p---y along the way?" Others covet hell as a sort of reservoir for their private revenge. "Hell is alright as long as that S.O.B. that I married ends up there too. Boy will I laugh. He can't stand pain. What a big baby!"

***

As a novelist of course I want to reach the big issues and find the big answers. It's part of my job. Albert Camus wrote a novel called, "The Plague," that suggests that living well and taking a swing at the big problems without the assurance of a lasting victory or a reward is the highest moral position we can take and in any case it is all the certainty that we're ever going to get. This has to be enough for us. It just has to be because it just has to be because it just has to be … generation after generation. I on the contrary line up with those who say that I'm not buying it. For one thing the argument is circular. There is no moral order because there is no moral order. The universe is then just like one big pub with the landlord calling out, "Drink up boys; it's closing time."

"Buck up chaps; think of England and it's over the top with us. Some spot of soil over here will be forever England."

Is death necessary just to add a little spice and urgency to human freedom? But so few of us really feel the full measure of human choice and dignity in the course of our lives; mostly we are just lonely and scared, like a child at night or one with a skinned knee hoping someone will bandage it up. Did Jesus really come just to make us feel how much we deserve to pay up for everything we have done to God? I think not. I think that salvation ought to be "the gift that keeps on giving" instead of more like an option and right of first refusal to be exercised in this life or surrendered forever.

But try and suggest that approach to the Catholic Bishops as both better doctrine and better pedagogy. They evidently figure: Lower the bar and just watch; people will stay home and watch football instead of coming to Mass on Sunday; collections will dry up and we may just be out of a job; far better to scare the hell out of them and hope that at least some of it sticks.

∗∗∗

I think that I may be forgiven for taking questions like these seriously and writing an unconventional novel about them because what I am hoping for when I die is a pacific end and one that I can live with for eternity. So where is redemption to be found? Maybe it can be found in the perfect lines of a Grecian urn or on the stage at a Las Vegas casino or at the end of needle. Check your lottery ticket purchased from a service station on a rainy winter night; redemption might just be there. Or you can sit before an altar candle and hope that something is there beyond a lot of empty pews. The floor-show of the liturgy has trouble competing today with I-max and with 3-D let alone with video games. Conviction is needed for us to hang from the slender thread of faith with little spectacle or elaborate staging. The bishops meet and exhort and meet some more, and the great unwashed masses of the laity stand, sit, and kneel for an hour once a week and drop twenty bucks in the basket when it goes by. The rest stay home and claim to be spiritual, but not religious. Still, Annie Lenox told us all that everybody is looking for something. Maybe salvation or perhaps just a brand new lover; it depends on whether you ask the philosophers and theologians or someone else instead.

∗∗∗

I am not asking for much, just a time when she who cannot be named will circle back like an orbiting comet to cross my midnight sky. I send out silent summonses now and again and wonder where she is and how things are going with her, but the fluid medium of thought on astral bodies fails to traverse the distance that now exists between us. Her invoked silence has hardened like dry clay over the weeks and months since. I will not find redemption there. Of course my situation can't compare to what I keep hearing that 2016 has been a year of sickness and death for many people, good people, people who just like me want their happiness back, even if it hasn't been all that good. Bittersweet to drive a Chevy to the levee and drink whisky and rye; I am reminded by the radio that Dreamboat Annie has been gone for a ling time; and the little lies become illusions after awhile that we just can't afford to lose. We attempt to custom-build an idea of the happiness that we are willing to settle for and hope that we live long enough to get a little of it or we posit something totally out of reach and spend our lives feeling as though we have been cheated because we didn't get it. The alternative is to stop assuming that God takes his cues from us; God is not bound by *stare decisis*. I have been thinking a lot lately about relinquishment as the path to redemption, not because I like to let things go, but because things that I counted on as permanent are starting to strip away like old paint on a rusty chassis, the rusty chassis of my life.

✳✳✳

I saw the Beautiful Couple again today. She is all curves, tawny skin, and white teeth and he is cute enough to keep her and is neither paranoid nor possessive. I hope they never forget how much they mean to each now if one or the other of them ever makes it big. I try and decipher her like a perfect formula for passing genes along and wonder why he doesn't look more tired and desiccated. I am certain that compass needles must follow her everywhere she goes and that the tides would be deflected if she was to walk along the beach at Rio.

I tend to envy people as though I could step into their flesh at will, as though I am not confined to my one life. I am astonished at the way that a look in a mirror can send me plunging back into my own flesh when I am still carrying an image of another in my mind. It is as though my borders can be infiltrated by the diffusion inherent in all perception, not that I readily abandon my immediate creative judgment or my ideas and values easily but rather that the embodied me possesses inadequate gravity to retain its own atmosphere. I can be altered by what I see or hear so that I become it by an involuntary substitution. As a writer I suppose that I should be grateful to show such sensitivity to my environment, but as a human being I wonder if I am a mere extension of what can first surround me, then encompass me, and finally supplant me with itself.

***

Writers proceed further into alternate values and states of consciousness than most people ever do if for no other reason than that they must inhabit their characters in order to make them believable. There must be that aura of a complete alternate subjectivity in the various personae he creates or the author becomes a mere puppet-master and the discerning reader is certain to notice the strings and the jerky movements.

Even ideas are to an extent a force that stands outside the author. He is as apt to discover them in the process of writing them down as he is to entertain them in even a germinal form prior to expressing them. In this sense the book exists primarily in the writing of it. Expression is drawn from the author just as oil is extracted from the ground. Who can say what proven reserves remain after several years or a whole writing career have been devoted to recording states of consciousness following various guidelines provided by the mandates of a given genre of composition?

Writers tend to like what they are doing or at least they grow accustomed to the demands and compulsions that over time have become second nature to them. The result is that many writers continue to try and publish their newest efforts to make some sense of the world until they die. No author wishes to leave behind unfinished fragments. This means that every new book is a gamble and a gambol as well. Will this particular romp with language proceed to closure and completion so that the author, even if no one else may agree, can say proudly that his design has been achieved?

✳✳✳

After completing a book there a period follows where the author may have caught up with life, at least as filtered through the author's personal vision. In fallow periods the author may go further out on the limb of imagination and write about people who are vastly different from the author herself. She may imagine a life that has proceeded along a radically different path than the one that she has chosen. A brief introspection may reveal that chance may have had more to do with the course her life has followed than any conscious design, just as a few broken strands can cause a run in a nylon stocking. Much of life is also determined by preconditioned states provided by environment and what are currently termed significant others. It is not unusual to arrive at a point quite late in life before a radical change can even be contemplated let alone performed.

✳✳✳

The right words may arrive too late to be fully tied to the relevant experience. I have somehow managed for instance to get through most of my life without knowing the definition of the word "quotidian" and was rather disappointed to discover that it is an adjective that refers to mundane daily routine. I had hopes for the word "etiolated" but similarly found that it also lacks vigor and means a state of feebleness caused by being like a plant that has been deprived of the requisite amount of light to ensure its ongoing photosynthesis. To live an etiolated life is to end up confined to a quotidian existence.

✳✳✳

I cannot express the urgency that drives the author to listen, to observe, and to imagine in ways that lead ultimately to a novel where "a strange newness" enters the world and we end up with a "David Copperfield" or a "Pickwick Papers." But to live our way into writing may be a dangerous proposition. I trust that I shall never entirely comprehend a terminal depression, what it feels like to be raped, or how the terrorist feels just before he detonates the bomb concealed beneath his coat. Experiences must be avoided as often as they are sought by the novelist.

There are as well certain things that should not even be imagined and it is well known that drugs, by virtue of their very artificiality, may be considered to bias ordinary experience and thus disqualify the judgment of the author and the reliability of his impressions. The objective world and the accurate workings of our senses prevent subjectivity from spiraling out of control. It is like pressing on the scale with your thumb while measuring goods sold by the ounce. We like to think that the author bears some relation to our quotidian selves. The author however, always fearful of running out of material, may be tempted to avoid an etiolated state by living on the edge.

*****

In my own life I recall the urgency that I felt to somehow get to Paris and London, convinced that human truths can only be arrived at by dwelling in one of these enriched milieus. Of course Flannery O'Connor managed quite well to plumb the human depths without trotting about the globe and the peripatetic James Joyce, for all his talk of exile, never really left the psychic region of Dublin. If there were not certain constants in human nature it would be impossible to empathize with the plight of Sophocles or with Job.

Some authors become famous simply because their own lives are so interesting. F. Scott Fitzgerald is fascinating as a cautionary moral tale of the decline from reckless idealism into disillusionment and failure. Yet, did he really fail if it was precisely this process that his fiction was intended to describe? Would Jack Kerouac have been able to write his "Visions of Cody" about skid road existence if he had not lived it? Would Fyodor Dostoyevsky have understood the gambling compulsion in all of its squalor and desperation if he had not been addicted to roulette?

Many authors live lives that cannot serve as paradigms of healthy and successful living. Their lives are seldom emblematic of that pursuit of happiness that our founding fathers presumed was among the set of sacred goals of human lives. Note that any concept of eternal salvation was likewise omitted in the presumed ends of life, liberty, and the pursuit of happiness. We must look then to the saints and not to authors if we wish to find models of morality or of eternal bliss. Authors may be as often found among scoundrels as among the virtuous. The drive to express ideas for the benefit of others may be among the few totally unselfish acts of the writer and even here he may hope to earn a few bucks in royalties when all is said and done. It is silly then to be scandalized by the life of Byron or to complain that De Maupassant died demented by syphilis.

My own sole claim to the typical pattern of the artist's life is having once suffered the ravages of tuberculosis. All that I have written, other than a few poems and prose fragments, has been conceived long after my diagnosis and cure. If I had been born in another era, I would long since have been dead of consumption. It would have been a natural end for one of my temperament. I felt the same frenzy for distant places that afflicted Thomas Wolfe and I shared the languishing moods of a Katherine Mansfield. I was meant to cough gently into a silk handkerchief and to look anxiously for the tell-tale spot of blood. Of course the poor and the obscure died like flies from tuberculosis as well, but I only thought about the company of Chopin, Stevenson, D.H. Lawrence, and of course Thomas Wolfe. My early deliverance is the reason that I could defer my end far enough into the years of maturity to leave something behind me after all. Certain diseases though carry their own cachet. They purchase allowances for extreme behavior.

"We must forgive her whims because after all, the poor thing is dying."

Artists actually suffer from an illness that exceeds the effects of any particular microbe. Our illness demands deliverance much as a pregnancy demands a birth. We must be allowed scope to develop our supposed talent prior to any proof that it actually exists in a manner sufficient to make the latitude that we demand in living to be reasonable.

In a similar way, she who cannot be named resented it whenever I appeared to be less obsessed with her than she imagined she deserved. I think she would have preferred more my silent contemplation rather what has actually happened. Instead I have tried to resolve our past by writing it into a form that could make her absence less painful and perhaps explain why living with a writer can be trying to the nerves for those who require that they be constantly affirmed before all other pursuits.

***

November proceeded to unfold and the last leaves of summer fell to the ground. The year would now trickle down like all the benefits that would soon accrue to Americans when corporate taxes are reduced or eliminated and the world's jobs come back from China and India to nestle in the green valleys and the coal-slag heaped states of Kentucky, West Virginia, Pennsylvania, and Ohio. The Republicans look forward to knocking people off of the medical insurance rolls and making sure that if you have cancer you move along the road to glory because God wouldn't have made you sick unless it was the right thing to do.

"Get saved and get along home and free up the living space if you can't afford to pay your own way. The lord said that we will always have the poor with us but he didn't say how long each individual poor person has a right to ask us for our charity. Get the fetus to the delivery room and after that the little bastard is on his own. It's the American way!"

I thought about our faith in our recent gunboat diplomacy, our failing to sign international agreements to preserve the environment or to punish war-crimes, and our general cultural illiteracy as a nation. How in light of these I had ever thought that a guy like Trump would lose? He is tailor made for the American male in decline: rich, snotty, rude, misogynistic, and always looking out for number one. He is part of America's grab and hold ethic - why he was is as American as a catered apple pie!

***

America would soon be transformed into an even more hideous caricature of itself as various Republican dinosaurs that I and others had hoped were retired or dead or engaged in hunting parties on the Cheney ranch lands came flooding back into

Washington to assume positions for which they were unqualified by anything other than the loyalty due to party hacks. It was to be the 19th century robber-baron days all over again, a gilded-age America electro-plated with zinc and copper because the Chinese have stockpiled most of the gold. India can be the new Hollywood as well and leave us to the running of old Judy Garland and Mickey Rooney films at a telethon to pay off the national debt. Wars are costly of course, but never let it be said that we aren't willing to pay the price of freedom by telling other countries what to do. Meanwhile Americans, who cannot see what is ahead for all of us, keep a wary eye on each other and keep the safety catch on their handguns off in case anyone is getting a free ride.

✳✳✳

I thought it was about time to head back to Oregon now that I knew that transformation wasn't enough; it was more likely to be a deformation. My lifetime was running short for the changes to take place that would make me into a proud American novelist. I am more convinced than ever that for an American to write novels he must be countercultural. In my writings I keep coming back to that descriptive adjective, "discontented." Is that what I am doomed to remain? Why have I enjoyed reading Daniel Defoe, Jonathan Swift, Nathaniel Hawthorne, and H.L. Mencken if not that I take a certain delight in bitterness? I savor the grim poems of Robinson Jeffers and his granite hard narratives inviting death and dissolution for the human race; any chance extinction will liberate the grand cyclic epic of animal and mineral life from our depredations. But can a poem exist without potential readers or a gravestone without someone to read and consider the epitaph? In spite of this flaw in his creative logic there is something bracing in the clarity of his condemnation and contempt for the human dilemma. If the author pushes bitterness too far he arrives at the position of the Canadian woman-novelist who wrote her book about suicide and then proceeded to act in her conclusions. In contrast to the literature of despair satire always contemplates reform even when it is most cutting and misanthropic. I spent this morning at the editorial offices of the local newspaper to help with the research for an article that might get the city council to withdraw its anti-homeless statute. Then I went for my morning coffee served with a smile by the Basque Princess who is on leave between modeling assignments. There is still beauty in the world.

***

I have been reading lately about Marilyn Monroe during her years involved with the Actor's Studio, perhaps the one time that she was happy. I recall how much I had once envied her when I was a child and how I could not understand how she could commit suicide when she was beautiful and famous. I only knew that I wanted to be Marilyn and have people watch my lips for any hint of a smile and see my full bosom making my sweaters pointy and alluring. Movies in those days of my childhood even more than books were real to me, vaulting over any critical disbelief. The problem was that life was all too often in black and white rather than glorious Technicolor. My dramatic emotions demanded an A-list director and to be filmed in cinemascope. I wanted widescreen combined with lots of close-up shots as I lifted my gilded nails to my glossy red lips in surprise or fear or passion. I wanted a license to be dumb and beloved at the same time. Marilyn wanted only respect as a professional. As for me I just wanted that little gasp and the hungry eyes focused on me as I walked across a room and then to look back once over my shoulder with a little smile and sniff that says, play your cards right and then, just maybe…

I would be up to any attempt at a put-down, "You wish, as if, fat chance, sorry buster, in your hat, not in a blue moon, no way Charlie, I'm more than you can afford, call my agent."

***

Is power the road to redemption? Is sex power or submission? Some things when once given away cannot be restored. This is why we hide our past like Blanche Dubois when she lived at The Flamingo in Tennessee Williams' play, "A Streetcar Named Desire." I think a lot about the past as well as the present. Were things always this bad or was it just the gloss that I put on them at the time and my sense that I always had plenty of time ahead when I could still change that allowed me to keep my illusions alive?

The further I went into my life the more I sensed that I was now caught in a narrowing funnel. We all need a reason to get up out of bed and face the day and if the novelists don't provide this for the multitudes then who will? We don't have any great national poets lately to show us the way up and out; epics are out of style. The last ones have been rather pessimistic and they were written on the Continent, not in England or America. Gabriel Garcia Marquez is still writing as if epic novels are possible and I have a Hungarian work called "Parallel Lives" to show that Europeans are still in the business of writing big books. I even tried my own hand at the epic. I don't have time to write another so the result is this humble set of notes for a novel that may never be written in the way that it deserves to be. Instead I am collecting fragments throwing them together willy-nilly in four semi-equal parts designed to give them some sort of order and direction. And always over my shoulder I feel the dark grimace of the graveyard at Newport and the thousands of miles of Red State territory, a vast mental wasteland that begins with Idaho and reaches to the Mid-Atlantic seaboard south of New England.

✻✻✻

If the epic fails what's wrong with a little deliberate triviality? Why even seek an underlying principle of organization in the novel? If life just happens without moral reasons or any regard for our imagined dignity why not simply record its disorder and randomness just as the universe does? If the earth was without life but of roughly equivalent mass so that the various other planets stayed in their relative orbits what would mourn the loss or even notice our absence? It's a question worth asking just in case extinction becomes our announced national policy, "Death 'R Us." Of course that would still leave my aesthetic questions unresolved regarding how best to write a post-modern novel. I have raised the expectation of some sort of deliverance here by virtue of creating an apologetics for the writing of such novels. When life becomes an example of surrealism then the surrealists have to get more deliberately creative. Of course it is surrealist dogma that any deliberation will cut off the unconscious sources of inspiration. But then novels have a certain obligation to be expository and not merely suggestive.

The novel should usually tell a story. We need to affirm in it our customary sense of time. A novel should have a discernable beginning, middle, and an end. So where are we to find the collective American story for this year of 2016? Is America no longer the source for world stability? Wouldn't it be strange if America made such a mess of things that the other countries ordered us to sort of stand down? Try and pitch that idea, even in liberal Hollywood, let alone in those places where the real Americans hang out, in the cheap prairie truck-stops and taverns of the heartland and in the statehouses of the old slave-owning Confederacy. Of what use is a sophisticated response in a country bent on pursuing a policy of knee-jerk diplomacy?

***

Sometimes the author is too far into a book to turn back and skipping to a premature conclusion doesn't help because the author has interlinked the parts so as to create an organic whole out of what at first appeared to be a chaotic mass of discrete data. Form begins to emerge out of the formless like amoebic life in a rich organic sea. "Should I continue? Let's have a show of hands. The ayes have it!"

(Besides what else would I do but leave early to go to the casino and chow down on clams and prime rib and wonder what she who cannot be named is doing tonight?)

So back to redemption: is it a mere idea or is it as Christians believe it to be the divinely revealed purpose of the whole visible universe? If we are this important to God maybe we shouldn't blow ourselves up. Perhaps that would be sort of disrespectful to God.

"Yeah but what if the Iranians decide to invade Israel, I mean that's worth blowing up the world, right? I mean God is not going to stand by and see America-Israel defeated. How about if we have to destroy Russia over the Crimea and the Ukraine? Why don't we just nuke North Korea and kill that little fat kid who runs it now that his little weasel of a father is dead?"

"Yeah, ain't nobody gonna dis the U.S. of A."

***

The raven discovered the world but coyote runs it. The jubilee year of divine mercy is closing soon so a procession was held at the Indian Mission at Suquamish. The wind that day was high on the waters of Puget Sound and environs. The sun came through the clouds at intervals to gild the tree tops that swung about above the grave where Chief Seattle is buried. The green that surrounded the humble cemetery was that incandescent color that invokes a sort of hyperrealism as though everything had a hologram-like intensity with tight firm edges and colors that vibrate along an edge of exact definition rather than that of more generalized experience.

History is made of moments like this that stand apart from the dull flow of time. The past and the future fall away and only the present remains. This graveyard did not appear in the cold blunt facticity of the one in Newport. Here it was truly like the inhabitants were sleeping denizens of the community, not pushed aside beneath the soil as though the dead inhabited a land-fill. The Suquamish tribal land surrounds the graves and the tribal spirit reveres them as though the dead still lived among us. The Suquamish offer their hospitality to the mission so that it is hard to define the direction of the influence of missionary activity between the races.

The early missionaries never really "got" the Indians with the result that rather than building upon a truly spiritual and mystical sense of being they sought to substitute doctrinal formulas and clothe them in a simplistic primer-like catechesis that was at once condescending and ineffective. This approach is still seen in the crude instrumentalism that pervades the American spirit and that has just resulted in the election of Donald Trump to the Presidency of our compromised nation, one with only the moral authority imposed on their subjects by all conquerors. We own it because we were able to take it and hold it.

Sooner or later the barbarians end up on top but the spirit of freedom, un-extinguished and immortal, endures. The more precise our definitions become the more they appear artificial and ridiculous because they are disproportionate to mystery and as a result unable to awaken awe which is the essential religious perception. When we add to this a rigid hierarchy of administrators who claim to direct grace as though it can be channeled like some well laid-out irrigation system it becomes clear why people are loosing not simply loyalty to ecclesial demands but even any sense that those demands further the course of redemption. Without an experiential core faith becomes only an overlay like vinyl-siding to a house to keep the water out and to prevent rot. Triage Christianity cannot sustain a Christian civilization let alone make it attractive to cultures that do not share the Christian perception of the necessity of redemption.

The Indians see life as essentially paradoxical and filled with trickster figures drawn from their daily experience. Compare this to our sense of the devil as almost equal to God, a view that betrays the residual influence of Manichean beliefs (derived from Persian Zoroastrianism) that are still present in Christianity. The demonic only manifests its full power in the presence of the Holy; possessed persons and the saintly often manifest similar paranormal behaviors while for most of us evil is less dreadful than it is merely sordid and disappointing. One senses that things should be so much better than they are. Most lives lack the necessary grandeur for sin; they are merely selfish, petty, vindictive, or misled. They are at best qualified to be the crabgrass that surrounds the vast estate where the truly evil lord it over their supine minions. There are few Borgia's in the suburbs but there are quite a few Marie Antoinette's who are callous out of innocence and lack of imagination rather than cruelty.

Life flows in and flows out past the Suquamish people who felt no compulsion to migrate or to cross oceans and assert a spurious set of claims based on mere acquaintance. We sail our ships in and claim the land as ours because some French trappers in canoes came this way once and we are their successors in interest because of the Louisiana Purchase. Is this evil or merely an illegitimate extension of a jurisprudential metaphor beyond mere reasoning by analogy to a leap of faith; this is ours because we can make it so. Does the novelist do something similar when he claims that life is like this not by virtue of proof or authority but simply by writing it down or having a sympathetic character announce it in dialogue? Where does creativity cease and delusion begin?

***

I often write surrounded by what are apparently very busy people. Business deals are concluded, moves discussed, special occasions celebrated, and not because I am writing at some café in Montmartre but because I am at a coffee emporium in the northwestern United States in the early part of the 21st century when America was still the global hegemon. When this book is read vast alterations may have reduced it to an inadvertently historical novel. It may be discovered someday, discolored by age and with cracking binding in a used bookstore in some town in South Dakota and be read while a tire is being changed if the age of the privately-owned motor vehicle has not been supplanted by moving conveyer pods. The author cannot choose his stage and lighting, only his text and maybe a cover design.

I sure wasted a lot of living-time writing. If I am ever diagnosed with cancer I will wish I had these days back. Where did I ever get the idea that I could explain it all here? I could have been eating a pizza in Pioneer Square or trying to get in touch with she who cannot be named, just to give it one more try. Was happiness waiting for me on a street corner in the rain or should I have moved to Maui? What I always needed was a greater variety of outside influences.

Maybe I was always a little too sure of myself. On the other hand for all my pretensions I am not universal. I am confined to one skin and to one set of experiences. I have been plunged back into my individuality recently, only without the comforts of a partial viewpoint. I want it all and in pursuing it will end up with the panting mouth of Tantalus, always just short of achieving ... what ... what, perhaps an aesthetically satisfying whole, closure, a conclusion ... or perhaps an epitaph. Is writing living or just something to make coyote, the trickster figure, laugh at human folly?

***

I see people every day with the signature of their fate written in their bone and flesh. Yet the merits of their stories may exceed all of those contained in recorded literature simply by being real and not a post- hoc summation, human relations rather than books, procreation rather than composition.

I talked to my Dad today about a new business scheme and bought some Plexiglas to repair the trailer sky-lights. These tasks were real. They were not reduced to print before now and having just done so I ask why record what is just one more life-incident unrelated to larger themes. Would an editor peel this away "because it does not advance your story?" But what is that story absent the qualifications promoted by the keynote speech of an old retreat-master speaking on the topic of the old fire-and-brimstone days warning me that life is short and uncertain and eternity long and terrible in consequence of the very real chance of going to hell and beginning the long and vain reparation of sinners to repay an infinite God for an infinite debt incurred by a momentary act?

"That little orgasm is going to cost you, because it was not oriented toward the natural end of being open to transmitting life. The same God who ordains that volcanoes bury whole cities will not ignore that sticky effusion that had far better remained securely in place in the prostate gland unless ordered to its proper end. So delicate is the celestial balance that one deviation can place a planet tumbling into the abyss of the infinite coldness of space and the soul us no different. The thin membrane that separates mercy from great and terrible justice is only held at bay by the feeble breath that fills your lungs. Mercy ceases on the instant with your brain waves. One tiny blood-clot in the wrong place and eternity begins for you. A collection plate will now be passed so that the savages in other lands may be awoken from their errors and heathen ways. May share the comforts of our faith and the means of grace be spread so that merits may be acquired. Absent faith man is helpless before God, plunged in primordial sin and justly suffering the effects of his vileness and disobedience."

✷✷✷

Is this a proper exposition of redemption? Is God's announced desire, to share life more abundantly, only achievable by navigating this narrow channel? Is God really so nonplussed by his own creation to be offended at us? Or is evil somehow greater than we can imagine; even God is called in to suffer its consequences. Maybe we just don't understand the full dimensions of events when they are set against a background of the Holy. If even Cherubim shield their faces from the presence then a tomb in a garden to house the dead Christ is beyond inadequate to contain divinity.

To take these doctrines seriously is to be plunged into many difficulties. Nevertheless, I wish to be a Catholic novelist and to reclaim the faith from the sanguinary ministers that make us dread God too much to ever love Him.

***

Or am I guilty of false reasoning on a path that once determined the lives and deaths and politics of nations? Just how serious is this religious stuff? Is it like dealing with an IRS audit, a cancer diagnosis, a failing head-gasket on your car, or the loss of she who cannot be named? On a scale of disasters, how bad is bad?

In a world that finds even believing in a supreme being a difficult task how hard will it be to ask them to buy into a conception of the divine that begins with the proposition that it is all our own fault the way things are and only a very narrow avenue of escape is offered to escape an eternal cataclysm?

It may purify our conceptions to strip Christianity down to its functional terms and look at the way that we presume too much when we act as though its workings are like a vast machine, a mechanism for processing souls, or a particularly tightly drafted contract with hell as the liquidated damages clause. How many have been turned away from God by just such imagery!

Flaming bodies once lit-up the city squares in Germany and Spain as evidence that God is not mocked and just to be sure Catholic prelates did not wait for natural death to reveal the errors of the heretics. From these ramparts of civilization various outshoots were sent off to the mission lands and before long there was slave-labor in the silver mines of Peru and diamonds were dug up in Pagan Africa by the Zulu's. King Leopold turned the Congo into his personal slave plantation and no royals cut him dead with scorn if they happened to encounter him at a wedding or a coronation; after all, it was all in the family. Maybe the historical answer to the current "Black Lives Matter" movement is simply the question, "Have they ever mattered?"

James Joyce once said that history was a nightmare from which he was trying to awaken. That view applies to most of Christian history as well. I think about all of the regions of the world where the evils that were formerly committed were no worse than might have been predictable for frightened primates, those flowing from a scarcity of goods or the dictates of our bodily desires, then I compare these to the slaughters and atrocities, the moral terrorism of threatening people with the fear of hell while barely touching on the attractions of heaven, and all the other things that have followed the Christian conquests. I think of how moral theology has often become one vast catalogue of all the ways that human beings can be exiled from the face of God from missing mass on a Sunday without a proper excuse, to masturbating, or for that matter to killing millions of human beings in gas chambers.

I deplore all of the many ways that various conservative prelates have managed to build-up barricades around the cross, to fail to encounter actual human behaviors, to codify what is demanded of us, and to tighten the spigot of mercy until only a few drops of holy water can ever leak through.

So why do I keep coming back for more? Why do I leave its nasty history behind me on the shelf and hope only that God will look in mercy on poor unrepentant but hurting souls, the very ones that can never quite manage to summon up what is required for a complete re-birth in grace, the ones that will be confessing the same sins over and over again until they die because these sins simply are the human condition?

Why do I value the testimony of the erring over those who have frozen themselves into immunity to the common lot? Do I cheapen the sacrifice of the ones who used to wear the cilice and plunged into icy streams to purge visions that might have caused their bodies to contract with pleasure?

Should we do our best to worship God by abusing ourselves and covering ourselves with dung and ashes? Maybe we can even someday getting to the point where we can gaze at a baby, as St. Augustine managed to do, and still say that just moments before its Baptism it was only worthy to suffer a vicarious exile from God forever.

Are God's intentions so easily frustrated by human accidents? Are most sins indicative or dispositive? Wasn't there already something in us worth saving as St. Paul assures us? "While we were still in our sins God loved us."

I wish someone would tell me where fallible ordinary human love has been displaced in all of this emphasis upon doctrine straining to exclude the unworthy no matter how technically correct it may be. And yet I know that I will keep coming back to the Church until the end because I have never been able to find any other way home to God.

***

Where else shall we look for redemption, unless we are content to run the present program for the human equation through a few more times by reincarnations, while always coming up with the same error notice on our computer screens. Is the error in the universal operating system or in our software?

The historical disk could certainly use a good defragging. It is hard to forget all of the millions of dead in wars and famines. We all want to believe in a kinder and gentler version of God than that which once prevailed, when plagues of cholera and small pox were a yearly occurrence and a quarter of all children born were dead by their eighth birthday.

"And what do you want for Christmas, Honey?" a parent asks.

And the kid answers, "I'd like to still be here at the Christmas after this one."

Nobody likes seeing life in all of its potential horror or to recall that in the pre-industrial world life was every bit as nasty, brutish, and short as Hobbes claimed it was. If we are to reckon up redemption though it can only be by asking what remains for us when all of our coping mechanisms fail.

"Isn't it the truth I'm tellin ye? Lots of fun at Finnegans Wake..." James Joyce told us about life in a language that we could all understand because it both communicates and withholds communication by its mixed and hodge-podge language and yet it is all a vast comedy, life-affirming, filled with love and resignation combined. I think that "Finnegans Wake" is "The Divine Comedy" of our age – Joyce as Dante for unbelievers.

I made "Finnegans Wake" the focus for my Master's Degree, the ultimate anti-novel because it is both closer to life and more refined in its format than the average novel – life presented as an undigested mess while simultaneously the novel itself is as elaborate as the Summa Theologica of Aquinas. Where does one proceed after having read Joyce? Had he lived would he have written a sequel?

Here comes some more in the endless cycle of actions calling for redemption when they can only be recorded against all of the similar events, all of them the result of the uncaused cause of our own malice towards the unglimpsed and incomprehensible Holy of Holies."

***

It always comes down to holiness in the end, to burning bushes, to temples, to a cross on a hillside, and to fathers offering their sons in sacrifice to purge sins. The Japanese keep a running record of malfeasances from generation to generation and do their best to repair past damages at Shinto Shrines. The Moslems place it all on one vast clearing-house of judgment on the last day.

Catholics look to the sacraments to infuse grace and Protestants ask if you have signed up yet for the big annulment of guilt by being washed in the blood of the lamb, something that you don't get as a Catholic without confession, communion, and a Plenary Indulgence.

All share in common this desire to make good on a past debt while the unbelievers do not believe in debt; in this world "you just takes your chances and things are what they are, period." If you blunder into a holocaust it's just tough luck from this point of view. If a little girl with blond ringlets gets hit by a car, she's just another unlucky kid with no meaning, no recompense, and no making it any better. Who can live in a world like this?

So I keep coming back to redemption even when it seems impossible and to the holy even when it seems obnoxious to a world where I like many others have gotten used to accepting things as they are but with just a small metaphysical reservation: a maybe that could just swing the whole cosmic election towards victory.

✱✱✱

So where do novels fit in this scheme of things? Am I trying to write here my own, "Concluding Unscientific Postscript to the Philosophical Fragments?"

She who cannot be named might say,

"Why not write, 'The Diary of the Seducer' instead. You wanted me to die! You planned it. You wanted one big immortal love that you had and then lost. You would have encased me in immortal prose as a testament not to me but to your vanity. I was your Frankenstein, your Golem, your idea of the kind of girl I might have been but wasn't. It was too late for me before I ever met you. You wore me down with your hopes that I could be better. Did you ever think how painful it was to me to entertain possibilities? I kept on wanting you to come back at me. You shamed me with your kindnesses. They were like little darts in my skin. I needed you to hate me. It would have proven that I was at least right about something. That would have left me something that would have been just mine, something that would not be able to receive a parting gloss in a latter-day commentary after the fact by you. The only thing I'm sorry about is that I ran into somebody who would take me on as a project and was too proud to just let me go when I struggled to escape your everlasting love! Did you ever think that some people prefer hell just to get away from people like you?"

Grace was never mine to bestow. I did care for her I see now, but not in the right way. You don't do anyone a favor by denying them a chance to make ultimate choices. I left when I knew that

I couldn't stand between her and her own decisions. If hating me is the price I had to pay then it was worth it.

"See, even now you are trying to take the credit that I decided to live!"

"But you aren't here. I haven't even named you in the novel."

"But I'm part of you now, don't you see? Try and escape my accusations and recriminations! I wanted to tear you down so I could feel worthy. I see now that I was such a fool as to believe that you were what I needed you to be. I see salvation everywhere because I feel so empty. *But you,* I mean how dumb could I have been?"

"Well as long as we're talking, are things better now that we're apart?"

"Why don't you just read, "After the Fall," and find out how I am. Don't you always look to books for your answers? Arthur Miller and Marilyn Monroe – he with his ethics and her with just her beauty and her pain - sound familiar?"

"You still sound mad at me. If everything now is the way that you wanted it then why should you be angry with me?"

"Because you got one thing right about me; once I start loving somebody I can't stop. You knew that and I hate you for it. You authors bleed your ink that other people read as though you know something they don't. Well you don't know anything! You aren't even fully alive without me!"

"Is that what you want to leave with me? Words like these?"

"Change them then if you want; after all this is your damn book. You could write it anyway you want to, make people hate me, I don't care! You can always sign books and get sympathy. Why don't you?"

"Artistic integrity…"

"Why couldn't you ever just be what I needed you to be?"

"And what was that?"

"Someone who would die for me because you couldn't possess me, because you couldn't be me; I wanted you to pine as I had pined, bleed as I bled, waking up night after night wondering if I was enough that you would never leave me before I could leave you first. I want…"

"What?"

"I want you to call me."

"What could I ever say?"

"Nothing I guess. You could call by mistake and then hang up."

"Then you would have to decide…"

"You're right; it's better this way. Only…"

"Yes?"

"I don't want to read what you said about us."

"I thought you might like knowing that it matters … you not being here. It is in me everyday so that I can't even write without having you there in some way."

"Well you'll figure a way to feel better; you always do."

"Not always."

"Stop it!"

"I mean…"

"I know what you mean. You see we do understand each other after all."

I must be getting near the end because I am hearing her voice in my mind again. I see us on that rainy night in the graveyard where she used her cell-phone to illumine the headstones.

"She feels so deeply," I said to myself. "She cares for their tragedies. She would make it up to them if she could. I can trust her to preserve me and to remember me when I am gone. In her eyes I matter after all."

A Fleetwood Mac song has just begun to play. It is all about rain. I must be on the right track because the universe is talking to me again. I hear the song I need to hear today. Is some choreographer following this dance of distancing with us, stepping in our footprints or showing us the way? Is the novel showing me a way back to life?

***

RING

"Yes?"

"One more thing; have you stopped wearing that damn blue lip-liner?"

"Well…"

CLICK

"Hello? Hello? Well I guess we're back to normal…"

Even an imaginary contact is disturbing so I guess I'll just keep writing, trying to catch life as it passes.

***

It's Taco Tuesday and my stomach lining has no doubt grown back overnight since over indulging at the casino buffet. The afternoon is waning and since she who cannot be named has no idea about the course of the imaginary conversation we have just had in my mind I need to figure out whether to keep on writing or call it a day. Writers do their best writing when they are fresh. Words are precious and not to be wasted. But swift transitions heighten dramatic contrast, anything for effect, and she is still talking…

"Good luck finding anybody who will care to listen to your stories and remember every detail of them."

"Oh come on, you were always the mistress of effective staging. You already knew in advance where you wanted the play to go. The director's chair had your name on it."

"Yeah, but the script was yours."

"You brought the cast in though, tons of extras, a regular Greek chorus of your ex-lovers."

"I don't want anymore of your Catholic guilt!"

"I never accused you of anything."

"But I saw your disappointment."

"Well, it didn't matter to me."

"You aren't all that pure yourself you know."

"Who cares now? What do you still want; you can go anywhere, do anything!"

"I wanted you stripped of everything before you knew me."

"So I could fill a role in your production; an endless stream of rats and super-rats."

"I could have cast anybody. I chose you."

"Why did you choose me?"

"I never chose you; you just wouldn't go away."

"I thought your play demanded eternal love.'"

"That shows what you know! For your information it is called... No, I won't tell you. You would only claim the credit. It's part of your narcissistic nature."

"Come on, we're all alone here. And this is only a first draft after all."

(With enthusiasm)

"Alright, the play was to be called, 'Pay Up you Bastard You Owe Me Big-time.' It was supposed to be a sort of a film noir, all black and white with lots of violence and sordid scenes."

"Um, you know that black and white thinking is symptomatic of..."

"And you've read all the books right. You can't let anyone else take the lead for awhile. It's just like with you and your father, each of you looking for the other one to mirror them. You can't just listen, surrender first place and let things go."

"I let you go when you asked me to..."

"You wanted out as much as me; I knew it was only a little time before you would leave me. I got my sell order in while it still had some value in your eyes."

"I would have waited."

"Yes, but how long ... probably until I had nothing but ashes left to build on."

"And now it's me; I have the ashes."

"Well, you're the novelist. You will turn them to some use I'm sure."

And then she was gone again, back into that place where she lives inside me.

I stirred my coffee and felt the stitch across my back that a long writing session can cause or was it my unprocessed feelings. If she was here I would ask for a shoulder massage and to read what I have written for her and maybe see a tear again, as precious as a pearl, trickle down her cheek.

✸✸✸

One of the most difficult questions for the novelist to answer is the question of how to maintain an optimum distance from his characters. Total involvement robs the novelist of the omniscient outsider stance that allows for portrayal rather than mere transcription. Lack of critical distance in composition will be punished later on when critics accuse the author of special pleading, of being enamored with his own characters losing as a result the ability to let the characters speak for themselves. Characters come alive to the degree that the author can pull himself back and see the situation from multiple conflicting presuppositions and motivations within a highly charged situation with consequences for all parties.

Duplicity may exist in the characters' relations with each other but we generally assume that the author is always being straight with us. Of course if the book is written in the first person style of narration we will naturally wonder whether the author has assumed a different voice; the speaker and the author are not necessarily or even usually one and the same.

As the author retreats behind various veils and disappears around various corners of technique he may essentially disappear and we have then what has been termed ironic narrative voice. By speaking directly the author may reveal his narrator's delusional sense of time, place and person. He may allow other characters to have all of the advantages and sacrifice the supposed teller of the tale. Of course the text does not announce its technique in advance but rather embodies it. The reader must guess by internal clues whether the happenings in the novel have any direct correlative in the author's life.

It is considered a breach of trust and etiquette in the writer/reader transaction to try and look behind the curtain at the wizard and to deconstruct into its constituent or contributing elements the novel that has been constructed with so much labor into an integrated whole. Of course most authors are like method actors; they use their own life experiences and emotions to sustain a realistic performance. What must be avoided is the assumption that a one-to-one relation exists between the world as it is lived by the author and his creation of a mirrored yet distorted world in the novel.

I mention this among other reasons to explain my own intentions. She who cannot be named has just evidently spoken and in doing so has entered a frame of reference that she has made every effort to leave behind her in the real world. The narrator did not challenge the appropriateness of this cameo appearance put into the novel, one that is supposed to be dedicated to the building of a new life after she has broken off contact. What is she doing traversing the bulkhead that keeps the less successful episodes of our lives from breaking loose and rattling around in the hold doing no end of damage? How is the poor narrator to move on if she who cannot be named insists on popping up at will to let the narrator know that she has been following the composition of the novel from the citadel where part of her still lives and speaks? Isn't this a classic example of life's inexorable tendency to invade the containers that we devise to give it order and meaning? An author who cannot keep an offstage character in line is running a loose organization and may as well surrender his position as chairman of the board.

A subtle exorcism may be called for here? Perhaps I should protect this humble writing table by surrounding it with a circle of salt to keep any dark forces at bay. I mean to say, well, just between ourselves, I can tell you that…

"I'm back."

"You are interrupting a point I was just about to make."

"It'll wait."

"Why didn't you just text me?"

"You can't tell me what to do."

"When did I ever try to force you to do anything that you didn't want in order to fulfill your own master plan?"

"You were just as controlling as I was. You just used different methods. You knew that I needed you and when you didn't get what you wanted you would withdraw into one of those silences of yours instead of engaging in a little honest sword play."

"I didn't want to fight with someone I loved."

"No, you would rather just freeze me out. You knew that drove me crazy. I would sit there with the phone in my hand and know that all the angry things were backing up inside of me like a servo-mechanism gone awry. I would have to spend the day feeling dirty and bruised inside until you condescended to speak to me again. Don't pretend that you didn't enjoy my helplessness."

"How could you be helpless with all of the nasty things that you had at your disposal to say and..."

"Stop it! Were you too dumb to realize that I didn't mean them? I just wanted to reach you any way that I could. I kept feeling that you were going to leave me any minute. My anger and my fear are one and the same thing. I was in a panic because I saw you as everything and I felt that if you left that I would just die."

"I never did leave did I?"

"It wasn't whether you would or not; the point is the fear I felt, not whether it is reasonable."

"So all of my proofs of devotion meant nothing?"

"Of course they did and I loved you for them. In fact I loved them so much that only a constant stream of them could make the bad feelings stop inside. Why weren't you there always?"

"Half of the time you would call me when I was on my way to see you and tell me to turn around and go back."

"Because I didn't know what I would say or do; I didn't want to ruin everything!"

"Well what was I supposed to do then?"

"Understand! I wanted you to tell me my thoughts and show me a way through my fears, instead you…"

"What?"

"Why go into it now?"

"Because we are broken up; you aren't even here. What have we to lose?"

"I'm still inside of you. I can still hurt you and I don't want to. That's why my last words to you were, God bless. Why didn't you answer me?"

"I gave you immediately what you asked. I haven't contacted you have I?"

"Why didn't you care enough to try and change my mind?"

"Because you made your wishes so clear; you didn't leave me any ground to protest, no firm base to other than to beg you to stay."

"Would that have been so terrible? What would it have really cost you, the always poised you, to feel what I feel everyday and sink into the wet and muddy mire where I have been treading water for years? I wanted to see you dirty for a change, feel a little desperation, cry until you wanted to vomit, cry until your eyes hurt and you had no more tears to give, to feel like me. Have you ever cried like that, perfect, legal-minded, Catholic guilt wielding you?"

"If you only knew how it really is with me. How do you think I survived all those years? You might have been afraid that I would leave, but you made it a habit to leave and come back, again and again, one more turn of the screw. The lashes dug deeper each time. I was always so glad to have you back that I forgot how much it hurt and tried not to think that each time you played your little game you left me with that much less to repair the damage that you were doing inside of me until it took a novel to tell you and you aren't even here to hear it… Well, are you here or not? Are you?"

Silence

"I thought so. If you knew how the pain is back again between my shoulders; it feels like a nail."

"And I'm supposed to feel sorry for you I suppose...poor brilliant writer."

"It got you back didn't it?"

"Hah see! You are a seducer after all, you with your big innocent eyes."

"We never talked much about what we wanted from each other."

"I was afraid you would judge me or that you would laugh."

"And I was afraid that you would be scornful."

"You can tell me now."

"I wanted to protect you and have your admiration and esteem and have us be everything to each other, to leave the world behind us and be legends like Scott and Zelda. What about you; what did you want?"

"I wanted you to die for me, to drag you into the sea with me and drink you in until you were part of me and also..."

"Well, don't stop now."

"I wanted you to … to pay me back, to punish me so that I could feel purged and clean again and I could show myself to you all clean and renewed, glistening like the sun."

"That's how I always saw you anyway. I would light up whenever I heard from you. Your name was like magic to me, so magic that I don't even use it here."

"Well then you were a fool. I'm poison."

"No you aren't."

"I know now that I need someone who is just like me; we'll be immune to each other's poison. Could I have ever had that with you?"

"You could have if you would have just dropped that guard of yours a little… Come down with me to the coast."

"I would spoil it for you. You want to weave me into your dreams of a happy life. Shall I tell you what you want?"

"Please."

"You want it to a glorious summer day and we would be walking arm-in-arm and you would be telling me about your new novel, "Pacific End," and I would be fascinated as always and we would find a place in the rocks and you would read to me and while you read I would see myself as the mermaid that I always wanted to be. I would look out at the sapphire surf, all clear and transparent breaking on the headland, and think how I had finally found my way to land. I would not need to swim with the sharks or dive into abysses to feed on dark weeds along the bottom. I would live with you and try to make it up to you for all of the pain that it takes to write novels. Your words would be like a spell cast on me and suddenly you would be the mermaid and not me. I would see your sweet green scales shining in the sun and your breasts cold and wet and beckoning. You would comb your long hair then with the dry ribs of a fish and shake it down over your pale shoulders while looking admiringly at me where I now sat reading to you from my novel, a novel all about this horrible year of 2016, all about dying things and a graveyard on a hill. Well do you like my story?"

"It can't have been that terrible, this year 2016. We both made it through to the end."

"Well, we aren't into December yet."

"Did you say that to scare me? I think you're going to be okay you know without me... I wonder if you are alright today though."

And just like that the spell was broken and I returned to a November evening, clear and cold, with a cup of cold coffee at my side and the pain between my shoulders and the old familiar sorrow deep in my heart.

✲✲✲

She was only partially right about what I had wanted, but then our dreams of happiness tend to coalesce and then part again, lonely and in opposition. Maybe the only people who can bring us happiness are the ones that we do not love. We might meet them by chance on a street in Vienna and go to a café to drink warm plum brandy against the chill. I would tell her about my latest novel and she would describe a film location in Morocco that she had just left and how the desert was white in the moonlight and the hotel where the film crew all stayed. In the evenings they would be served iced prawns on a bed of saffron rice. I would note the tiny lines at the corners of her eyes and be grateful that she did not comment on how gray I am becoming. We would walk later along the Ring just like old friends do who have given up everything to their art and in consequence have never found love. We would know what it is to smell the leather seats in the old lobbies of theaters and to always leave a chain on the door in hotel rooms before falling asleep. Maybe she like me would wake each night at 4:00 A.M. and be happy that she was not a cold corpse in a strange city to be found the next day when the hour ticked past check-out time and the do not disturb sign was still there on the doorknob. We would leave the street after a time and climb the cathedral steps and push the great doors ajar and look up at the illumined ceiling with its baroque scrolls and the angels.

"I suppose that you still think of her," she would say.

And I would hesitate before replying, "I wrote it all out of me years ago."

"Is writing ever enough to purge our pain?"

And I wouldn't answer her because I do not know the answer, even now.

✳✳✳

I guess I should say here that I was finally able to find out the name of that song that has haunted me all summer long. It is called, "Stable Song." I wonder if she who cannot be named would like it. Music and films always formed a bond between us. We tended to be obsessed by similar lyrics. I think we would have liked to catch a freight-train someday and ride across the moonlit country and hear heartbroken country songs sung in little one-horse towns like I did that summer in 1981 when I traveled all over the west looking for the real America so that I could write about it just as Thomas Wolfe had done. Some songs capture a time and place for us so that ever after, when it is played, time tends to disappear and we traverse the years and seasons. We return as we once were, even if our bodies have withered and altered like fallen leaves.

The days passed after the election and it became terribly cold. My normal body temperature is only 97.4 degrees with a pulse beat of sixty beats per minute so it takes me a long time to get warm again if I get cold or become upset. My emotions always manifest as darkness and cold. I like to sit in corners with a hard surface on two sides of me for support and protection. These are especially necessary for me now as the country begins to settle in to its own Siberian winter. A vast abyss of solid red states stretches between the two coastlines of America. America has settled into a sense that by electing our first billionaire president we are about to return to some sort of golden era, one where a victorious World War America could pose as something more than what it has really been since the 1870's: corporation-ridden, militaristic, and self-deluded. I started thinking again of the countries that might just survive a nuclear war. There would be a few days there before a general blotting out of the sun, time at least to realize that the human race had finally done it, time to get any last tweets from America saying, "Hell it was worth it, America rules now forever."

I could move to New Zealand and sit by one of the southern fiords and maybe see one of the last of the Tuataras sunning itself before all light was blotted out by the firestorms raging across the northern hemisphere. It would look up at me and blink its ancient eyes, the very eyes that had once watched as the great dinosaurs perished around them, eyes that had watched millions of years of time hurtling by them until human beings arose, the same that were now perishing forever.

I would see in my mind then the owl-like eyes of Robert Oppenheimer and the lowering brows of Edward Teller and hear again that first newscast about the bomb where Harry Truman announced that since God had given the bomb to the United States we had "naturally used it." After all, he reasoned, we had paid for it; it would be a shame to not use a perfectly good bomb.

I would see again the eyes of the horribly burned Japanese children trying to make sense of the fact that they were bruised, bleeding and vomiting. Soon they would begin to die of radiation sickness because their bodies had been shredded by tiny-holes caused by speeding gamma particles, smaller than any shrapnel could ever be.

I knew that a group with a terminal mindset was about to move into Washington, people who were just as impatient for Armageddon as any ISIS suicide-bomber. They would get all teary-eyed with patriotism as the gigantic face of Donald Trump, all red and rosy, would blossom over us like a mushroom cloud.

Grateful Americans would watch their television screens announcing that the state of the union was just fantastic, in fact very, very, fantastic.

The Mexican families that had been split-up as parents and grand-parents were returned to Mexico wouldn't share the enthusiasm. Muslims would be banned from entering America. Affordable health care would return to being the luxury that it should have remained in our meritocracy. Poor people should die quietly as they did in India and be taken to the nearest refuse disposal site. America has become a nation where poor men in uniform defend the wealthy as has been their proper role in every empire since the world began.

America could now be great again; in fact it already was; it was very, very great.

***

I went today to pick up some black-lace and satin high-heels. It might be fun to go out as Betty Paige for New Years. I went next door to see the one who cried on the night of the election. It was her world that was about to be consolidated into a tacky nightmare more than it is mine. Our relative ages make all the difference; she has more to lose. She deserves better. I looked at her all fresh and clean and perfect, her eyes sparkled with passion and faith and dedication. I wondered if she would be able to repair and rebuild whatever would be left after the parade of "Trump, Trump, Trump" with its noisy bassoons and tubas had passed.

***

I am all caught up lately in reading about Marilyn Monroe and what Arthur Miller endured from her during their short marriage.

I am surprised that she even made it to 1962. It's funny how I once thought that the bright aura of the movies and comedies of that era reflected reality rather than just commercialism and the last death-rattles of the studio system. I guess nobody has ever had it made in life, not even Arthur Miller and Joe DiMaggio.

Before she went to the Golden Globe Awards Marilyn took a bath in ice-cubes to firm-up her flesh for the evening. Skin gets tighter when it is cold. All of the fat caused by lying in bed eating chocolate pudding and drinking can be pushed down and out by a properly tailored dress. You can never have too much of a bosom though and kisses thrown by a small white hand from deep red lips are always welcome. They say, "I am terribly, terribly, happy and so glad that you love me."

It's all about body language, all body, all…

***

I was sitting in the Church this morning. My little, seventy-five year old ex-librarian friend came in to pray. She told me about a friend who was dying in a Seattle hospital.

"Ten days ago she was fine. They say it's a very rare brain disease. It causes the cells to suddenly die. She is in a coma. She wouldn't even recognize me if I went over to say goodbye."

Was it my imagination or was death still cropping up everywhere around me? Is all of this being caused because I am trying to write about a pacific end? Is my book the ghost that kept coming back in the poem that begins Thomas Wolfe's first novel, "Look Homeward Angel?" This was the book that I began to read so many years ago on the front steps of the old convent school where our novitiate was temporarily located. Those were the years when the Jesuits were "trying to get back to our old charism." Vocations had dried up and even vowed scholastics and priests were leaving the order left and right. Somewhere between the days of the stiff pre-Vatican II location of the novitiate on a remote hill outside of Sheridan, Oregon and the liberal, justice-in-this-world theology that they picked up later at Alma, Berkeley, or Boston their sense of mission changed. It wasn't anymore about teaching the dangers of concupiscence and keeping people out of hell; now it was about dictators in South America and ghettos in America.

The younger Jesuits were now always talking about the poor and compassion for the sexually confused, while Ronald Reagan was trying to keep a lid on the AIDS crisis and Nancy, his wife, claimed to have sex and drugs all figured out, "Just say no." The Jesuits were in trouble though with Pope John Paul II with his twin initiatives against communism and condoms and making sure that everyone knew that the doors to hell were still wide open, and admitting freely everyday, mercy or no mercy. Of course he's a saint now so it won't do to speak harshly of the pontificate that has witnessed the greatest exodus of Catholics since the days of Pope Pius IX. You can be personally holy and still somehow miss the ball like Pope Pius X when he was blindsided by the Great War in 1914. Popes aren't always men for all seasons. Neither are Jesuits. The ones who ran the Society of Jesus after Vatican II presided over a near dissolution of many provinces as tradition and good-will were supplanted by mistrust and confusion.

As if by magic "Summer Breeze" just started to play on Pandora and I am back in days gone by to 1975. I was looking desperately for something to give my life meaning then as now. I believed in the Jesuits and in America and, even with qualifications, in myself. Most of all I thought that we were on our way to a vastly better world as the last helicopters got dumped into the ocean off the coast of Viet Nam.

"We won't need these again. We know now better than to fight foreign wars where we aren't wanted."

A few years later in "The Deerhunter" and in "Apocalypse Now" this theme seemed to sum up all of the horror of the nineteen-sixties. But by then I was in Detroit, Michigan and working to get oil delivered to the GM assembly plants around Detroit and in Ohio and drawing-compounds to car-factories. Social justice meant primarily my own paycheck while still trying to think the right things, caring to read a book at the end of the day. By the late '70's I knew that no ligatures were holding America together, nothing besides our greed and the cheap cost-savings of using plastic over using metal. America was sentimental and tyrannical at the same time – the same deadly mix that led the Nazi storm-troopers to get misty when they heard "The Horst Wessel Song."

Little has changed since then; the sentimental Trump supporters are busy celebrating that the Second Amendment is now safe. They can keep their guns and sleep soundly with them beneath their pillows. No renegade Mexican or Syrian will disturb them in their patriotic slumbers. The Electoral College system has made it sure that the majority who voted for Hillary Clinton will not prevail. The Obama's will leave the Whitehouse and America can be great again; America, saved from socialism and lazy liberals looking for a handout. The true believers can afford to holster their weapons, for now. The spoiled college kids in Seattle and Portland can stop protesting because it won't do any good anyway. Upstanding conservatives out of the heartland won't have to shoot them down in a one-sided civil war. The liberals will leave the streets and go back to texting each other on their Smartphones.

The summer breezes of 1975 have long passed away. It is winter now. Donald Trump has just emerged as America's idea of a transformation. The country was ready in any case to draw down and take aim at all the traitors and immigrants, the same-sex perverts, and the Hollywood and media interventionists. There could now emerge a seamless web from government on down to the worthy, in-the-trenches conservatives who had been left behind with a pink-slip and an old pick-up truck to face a globalized world. The jobs would come flooding back just as the buffalo returned at the summons of the Ghost Dancers among the Plains Indians at the end of the 1880's. All we can do in the face of these great expectations is to wait and see. The real spiritual needs of people don't change though. Even now my friend has come to the church for comfort when someone is lying there dying in Seattle. She has come just as of old Catholics came to pray and to light a candle for the dying and the dead.

***

I finally ordered today Anthony Trollope's novel, "The Way We Live Now." I figured that I could compare how he handled his novel with the way that I was attempting to say something similar about this year of 2016. I wanted to see whether I was in tune with the contemporary world or whether, as I suspected, I was an anachronism. It was a little late in the day to try out the theme of Graham Greene when he wrote his novel, "A Burnt-out Case." I remember that I was reading it along with "Look Homeward Angel" in 1975. It was then that I had decided to become a writer rather than a social savior or even a Midwest industrial drone.

***

We may be entering an age of bluff and frivolity. My book might sell better if it is called, "Laughing Our Way to Oblivion" rather than the comparatively dull and placid title of, "Pacific End." What good is it anyway, this process of reconciling ourselves with the quietude of our eventual extinction? Why not mount a vain and useless protest instead? Why not ask for a meaningless election recount? Why not ask that the Electors follow the popular will this one time rather than allowing a prairie brush fire of delusion to prevail, anointing the popular loser with a win to a position of supreme power, one that could alienate America from the world by essentially giving it the finger from the top of the Trump Tower? Or should we liberals simply "stand down" as the saying goes, join the groups of the disappointed reformers from the Chartists of England to the Luddites. Donald Trump is as American as apple pie, a real success story; Americans will always love a winner. He read America's politics like a balance sheet and came out on top. Surely that kind of street-smarts is worth something, even to an obscure novelist.

***

If I could draw out every story so that nothing precious would ever be lost, I think I could be satisfied with these fleeting days and not blame myself if they remained without leaving some extract in the words I have recorded here. The days and nights grow increasingly swift with the years. They approach like waves and break into the rocky chasm of the lives that have vanished. The winter nights closed in about me and I didn't want to break away to see if the summer beaches I had known still existed after I left them in September. Maybe they just dissolve into mists. The ocean is one vast flood tide and Newport and its environs do not emerge again like Brigadoon until it is May and I am champing at the bit again to run into the pastures of summer. My energies reach the lowest ebb with the dying year. I want a quiet place where life can provide for me what no novel ever can...

I still loved her; that was the funny part. I was still caught in the kelp forest of her mermaid realm. I had given up trying years ago to return to the surface for that last breath of clear cold air. No one has returned yet from that subterranean world of shadow and light beneath the sea. I had ventured out in May and now I found myself beached on the shore with the whole world before me as it used to be, only it was bleached dry now like the driftwood that I had gathered for her.

✳✳✳

The German novelist, Thomas Mann, was sufficiently complex and contradictory that he required the same heavy and substantial security in his life as in his prose style in order to create his great novels. He could have pursued by other means this same burgerlich existence if he had been a sturdy German merchant and not a writer at all. Prosperity, fame, and honors are redemption of a sort for the successful novelist. But not all novels have the rounded and substantial quality that we look for in our classics; provisional efforts, short trial flights, and essays should be accommodated. In any case, it is late to start a writing career, or any career for that matter, after the age of sixty. But then again, maybe experimentalism is the wave of the future novel. We are living after all in a synthetic age where it is not uncommon to have to accept a generic substitute for the real thing. Still we all carve security. We can feel the cold just beyond the circle of firelight that keeps the snow-beasts at bay outside the cave.

As November turned to Thanksgiving and the liturgical year came to an end I reflected that December is still out there to provide material for my novel without questioning its initial presuppositions. It seems to be about the right length and I have built it in such a way that I can still insert various passages without the reader even knowing about the late-stage alterations. I can still correct any misperceptions and try to avoid any critique based on invalid points and not merely on the desire to add to the burdens of a poor novelist.

***

If Donald Trump gets bored and resigns Michael Pence gets to be President. It seems very likely to me that Donald may just get bored with a job that entails checks and balances. He is after all used to being a boss. On the other hand he appears to know how to say what some people need to hear and to confirm them in their illusions; this may just be the secret of success and power. Truth-tellers and unwelcome prophets on the other hand tend to end up with their heads served up on plates. We don't like leaders who chart difficult courses for us unless we are already primed and ready to go. It takes a lot of amps to jump-start the American people, but once they get moving in a certain direction it is hard to stop them. An example is our history of warfare.

The American Civil War was largely Mr. Lincoln's war. Many northerners opposed slavery being extended into the new western states but the new immigrant workers in the cities weren't that anxious to fight to keep the union together. After the carnage of war though Americans enjoyed all the glamour and drama of the battles and the defeated south was anxious to restore a sense of valor and victory. Stir into this brew thirty years to heal old wounds and enshrine dreams of glory and America was delighted to hear of the victory over Spain in 1898, in what was then called "a splendid little war." Americans were ready to join the mix again in 1917 when Wilson sent the doughboys off to France. It is not that Americans are particularly generous but we are a touchy people, sort of like a bull that knows when it is not being respected. This means that we are easily led by someone who knows our pet ideas and vanities. We tend to be jealous if we think that anyone is getting an edge on us or is taking us for a ride. America does not esteem an easy-mark and has a hidden esteem for a good con-man. We don't mind thieves as long as they are sufficiently cagey and never make the mistake of saying they are sorry. We prefer our scoundrels to remain impenitent. Americans substitute sentiment for ethics and this makes us a little scary to nations that form their policies on the basis of reason.

The nation's founders feared democracy as much as they feared tyranny and they feared religious enthusiasm more than both.

They designed what they hoped was a machine with plenteous capacity but not one that would speed up beyond control. So the question really is whether Donald Trump is a true demagogue or only a businessman, one who just likes to hear himself talk. We will have four years to find out.

***

It isn't as though our Presidents have been that estimable anyway. You won't find a lot of saints among them and those that you do find didn't always make the best choices. Selfishness and caution is a good substitute for prudence. Then again we sometimes need a man like John Kennedy who, accustomed to take calculated risks with serial adultery could risk a nuclear war rather than eave the country an indefinite hostage to a short missile flight from Cuba. One nervous Captain on a Soviet ship sailing under orders to Cuba could have started the first domino falling. We all hope that a general stand-down on nuclear arms will be possible soon. Until then, no accidents, please. Lots of tradeoffs between the big powers had better be our policy.

Looking for heroes, history usually ends up creating piles of the dead. Venality and a desire to be let alone to enjoy life have more to do with keeping the peace than principled pacifism. The best politicians and novelists have learned to leave idealism behind them substituting a sober but not somber disillusionment with all human affairs. Above all else these avoid looking for the one big win, whether at roulette or even by writing a bestseller. Yesterday's bestsellers are seldom even read in ten years. The best way to become a classic author is to be quiet, competent, and able to write to a sustained standard of excellence like Arnold Bennett, the author of "The Old Wives' Tale," or like Somerset Maugham in his novel, "Of Human Bondage." If your prose is exaggerated or fevered and your characters are chaotic or their motivations conflicted as are those that appear in the writings of Dostoyevsky you are running a great risk as a novelist. The novel is after all a rather formal exercise in discourse for all of its breadth and variety. There are many rules that aren't evident until the author breaks them. Even then it may be possible to make your mark if you are daring enough and refuse to ever apologize like D.H.

Lawrence or James Joyce. A little doubt and you end up walking into a river with stones in your pockets.

But to come back to Presidents as precedents: both chief executives and appellate decisions are honored most by those who have no knowledge of either. To know the law is to know how illusory its protections often are. We exist daily in a world at risk of annihilation and beset by change and as a result we look about us for anything that we can rely upon and...

(A Sudden Unaccountable Interruption)

"Giving another one of your great lectures?"

"I thought we weren't talking."

"We aren't. I just thought I would leave a little piece of me in your head to keep you from getting pompous and full of yourself."

"Well thanks, but I think that I know when to qualify my statements."

"Always keep an escape exit! You really identified with Arthur Miller didn't you in that biography you are reading about Marilyn Monroe. She led him a merry chase, the nice Jewish intellectual who thought he had to do the right thing all the time. Too bad he didn't love her enough to just screw up once and awhile. It would have given her room to breathe."

"She needed him to be solid so that she could be the mess that she was and know he'd still be there for her no matter what she did."

"She had that security with Joe DiMaggio and it bored her to death."

"Well she liked people who were involved with the theater; he couldn't share that with her. She wanted to be considered a good all-around character actress rather than just a comedy star with a good body. More than that, she wanted anything that she felt that she couldn't have. That's why she chased after the Kennedy boys.'"

"You're so judgmental."

"Just trying to get to the bottom and discover who she really was; what's so bad about that?"

"It doesn't leave anybody any room to surprise you. You always have to be in the one-up position, like with me. It drove me crazy. No matter what I said I would think, "He already probably knows this so why am I even talking?""

"That isn't true. I took my entire emotional tenor from you. If you were happy, I was happy. You had me just like Marilyn had Arthur Miller. She finally left him so drained that there are probably several great plays that we will never see because he was busy trying to write the perfect screen vehicle for her."

"Yes, one that was as he saw her, not as she really was. We know when people are relating to us as an illusion. Some of us are born to screen other people's projections of who they need us to be. Marilyn could be sweet but she was also a cunning social climber. Arthur Miller wanted her all new and shiny and unsullied, just the way you wanted me to be. You both would forgive us anything and that only made me feel worse. I wanted to rub your nose in it because I hated it that you thought you were so above me."

"I thought we were talking about Marilyn."

"Well I am Marilyn … at least you thought I was."

"I thought you were beautiful, but that wasn't what let you sink such deep roots into me."

"What was it then?"

"I appreciated that you would always understand what it is like to feel like the world was always about to dissolve beneath you because that's how I feel. I felt that between us we could hold on to a world that scared us both to death."

"You didn't look scared."

"Because I was trying to be what you needed me to be; you can't deny it that you wanted me to be perfect."

"Just like your mother; you think you are royalty and what did that make me?"

"Well you could have joined us in the castle."

"Don't try and make me smile. By the way, I don't like Arthur Miller. I think he's mannered and pretentious. "Death of a Salesman" is so phony."

"Now who is being judgmental? You never had a leg to stand on, yet you criticized everybody and whenever they tried to defend themselves you hung upon them. I watched you do it! You always take the easy way out, the cheap and gutless way, and let other people clean up your messes, just like Marilyn."

"Stop it! If you knew how that hurts!"

"And nothing that you ever say ever hurts anybody?"

"I tried to make it right; I was ready to kill myself for you!"

"That was always just one more missile in your arsenal; you bring in the heavy guns when you are in retreat. I knew if I let you get any traction there I would be rescuing you from suicide attempts for the rest of my life. No thanks baby! You can join me in life if you want to, but I'm not going to spend the rest of my life at a death-watch."

"You don't love me; you don't. You just needed material for a good novel like Arthur Miller needed Marilyn to make up for his cold heart and lack of imagination. Why wouldn't you ever make love to me?"

"Because I knew that to do so would be to place myself irrevocably in your power and because I knew that you would always be able to look back on anything that happened between us and make it into something that it wasn't. Show me a wound that you can resist opening just to see the blood flow!"

"See you *can* be cruel! I knew you hated me!"

"I never did, but you tore me up into little pieces just to see how they could fit together afterwards. Ow!"

"What is it?"

"My back again, just writing this down…"

"Well I would have rubbed your back any time but you never came over."

"You were drinking."

"That's no excuse. Everybody in your family drinks."

"And I don't want to live out their old scripts!"

"Now who's upset? See, is fighting like this really so bad?"

"I didn't want to say mean things to you."

"No, you would rather freeze me out like Arthur Miller writing his goddamn screenplay, "The Misfits." Well I'm a misfit and so are you. The difference is that you can hide behind all that writing and your degrees and make me feel unworthy in comparison."

"Why couldn't we be on the same team?"

"Because you are just like your Dad; you both suck all the oxygen out of the air."

"You know I needed to live up to him and…"

"You scare him too; that's why he puts you down all the time. You're a scary person."

"I'm only a novelist; we have no real power. You need to read "Pacific End." It's all about how lost I am without you. Where's the power in that?"

"The power is that you get the last word. You can shut me up by just failing to write down what I'm saying to you."

"I wouldn't do that. To do that would be to sacrifice artistic integrity. Artists like to be honest even if it costs them. We are answerable to our sense of the inner logic of events."

"Oh yeah, then try this one on for size. You don't know what I think. All of this has come out of your head, you talking for us both. Marilyn had to be dead for Arthur Miller to write, 'After the Fall.'"

"Well, I'm glad you aren't dead and … *Ow*, my back again."

"See, it's telling you that I speak the truth. You won't admit it but if I died you would write about me forever telling everybody how hard it was for a sensitive artist type like you to have loved a tramp. I thought you deserved for me to die. I figured that it was the least that I could do to advance your writing career."

"It would have killed me. You are wrong. I have always wanted life over art."

"No novelist does, that's why they are novelists…"

***

And just like that I was clear about the true relation of art to life. Maybe writing is too high a price to pay for failing to live. But then again, I must have loved her because she still lives inside of me. I always thought she was someone who deserved to be molded in marble, but I would have traded all of that for her smile and just to know now that she is alright. So maybe I'm not a novelist after all. Anyway, these are only notes for a novel so maybe there is still a way out! The book covers haven't closed. No proof copies exist. I could still revise and revise and revise. Rough drafts are the final refuge for the uncommitted.

***

So where do I look for an ending? How will I know when I have reached it? Has the climax of my life already occurred? Just how close am I to that graveyard in Newport? Maybe I have another twenty years and this experimental novel will be the way that I reattached to the life that I felt to be slipping away with the her loss. Maybe I can still find a simple, solid girl to stay by me as I slip gracefully away. After a few years will I look back on these years as my "Sturm und Drang" period, these years when I lived on the ocean and knew a girl who used to whistle from across the water and I would come out to call her name into the night wondering if she was really there. She was always magic for me, a creature half of myth, a phantom who asked me not to look at her, as though if I did I would be able to read her secrets and know why she kept a guard on the citadel of her heart. She used her beauty to keep people at bay because she didn't really believe in it any more than Marilyn had. She thought she was a monster.

It is only possible for some people to live with themselves if they can bail their vessel out by exporting the inner toxins that would otherwise overwhelm them. Even then, the stray items cast away always return to them with the tide. It isn't death that they seek but some means of reparation for the injuries that they alternately evoke and try to avoid. Caught in a whirlpool of contradictory perceptions and impulses they draw others into the spiral of their anguish and misfortunes. Women like these are irresistible to artists. We paint them. We sculpt them. We write novels about them. Books like, "Portrait of a Lady;" "Madame Bovary;" "Anna

Karenina;" "The Custom of the Country;" "Lady Audley's Secret;" and many more, all of them drawn from the same cauldron of pain. Novelists try and get at the dark secrets of their hearts and discover why they wrap them in pain and carry their secrets into death, out into the darkness, drowning them in the sea rather than taking the plunge into life that novelists really value above anything that appears on the printed page. If we do our job well then the reader can sense the beating hearts of she who cannot be named and of her spiritual sisters.

***

Normally this last section would have sufficed for an ending. It has that final feel that artists strive to attain. But life being life it still continues and therein is the trouble. Every novel has a beginning and a middle section of plot development, but endings are always contrived.

"I think I'll cut the thread just here."

This is why I oppose suicide because it is always arbitrary in the same way that novels are. Death by its very nature is not ours to bestow, even on ourselves. We owe something to the story-line. There needs more for an explanation of even anguish than that it is momentarily unsupportable. Redemption requires that we walk the way of the cross to the end and where that end may be is not a matter of knowledge or of feeling or of will. Death is simply too absolute to be courted, even by those who hope for an afterlife when all will finally fall into its proper place. All novelists are all in this regard like atheists because they demand that time finish what it has begun.

I have a feeling that writers seldom re-read their own works. The reason is that the desire to revise is so powerful. It is far better to just leave the poor thing alone as published. Nothing is worse than re-writing the portraits of the artist as a young man from the perceptive of an old man. We always think that what we know now present in a germinal state in the person that we once were. We are always in a position to gain or lose our souls. In a sense we only exist as we are in the present moment, but that present moment is always altering our sense of the whole as well so that any point of time can never be set aside as definitive and allowed to blossom into the dark flower of death. Even to refer to death as a dark flower is to distort the frigid vacancy of a corpse. Whatever is left in death is never the miracle of what once was.

Death is in the last analysis not the logical outcome of a life. It seems a blasphemy that death plucks people out of time at the end of what we hope has been the somewhat productive process of living, of meeting trials, of reaching higher levels of moral development. There is always something a little unfinished in even a long lifetime, an editorial conference, proof-sheets to review for errors, and of course to stand finally before an audience of admiring or hostile critics to attempt some lame explanation of how the actual story fell far short of what was initially intended.

"But I'm working on a little thing now that promises to be ... well, I think I have broken new ground as an author."

I think that every life should be somewhat like this with something always left untried. Any life that has been presumptuously judged by ourselves to have been worthless exceeds that very conception.

***

Resistance of the urge to make premature generalizations has been part of the legacy of novelists. There is always another book to write. The studio presided over by the head of production always has an option on our next four films. Even she who must remain unnamed may someday look back on these bitter days that have separated us and wonder if they were really essential to her story. If I can find elements of her in what I have written here, does no similar element of me exist speaking within her? And regarding her accusations, I despise death. Death for all of its inevitability is not foreseeable and I don't want it, not for me, and certainly not for her. The habit of living has trained me to tolerate incomplete drafts, so I am not stopping here.

An open-ended story never concludes and I don't believe that any life is not open-ended. Human beings are ontologically oriented to a tomorrow, one better than what can be described, but I'm in no great hurry to get there. Bodily death after all is rather prosaic. Most people look rather generic in their coffins like an old used tube of toothpaste. It takes a conscious attitude of resistance to be a star or even just any person. This is why my attitude to death has always been one of intense opposition. I may never be able as a result to reach a pacific attitude to death, but of course as in all else I will just have to wait and see what will happen next.

As for the larger world, I would like to live in a country of contentment and gratitude rather than one of fragmented and polarized attitudes. I would like a world that will bear my full weight without threatening to collapse like a weak scaffold each day. It would be fortunate if words could contain reality in a way that appeared to be better fitted to capture events and not be imposed upon them after the fact.

The Chinese in their book of changes explain how even chaos is finally governed by certain abiding patterns of transformation. We throw the yarrow sticks and look at the resultant hexagram. What I have written here is the pattern for the present hour but it is one that is already about to dissolve. For she who cannot be named an entirely new configuration may emerge without warning to erase all of the preceding days and nights. We are driven back into life to find our answers. Novels only give us hints of what may still be possible.

Conclusion:
Everything Returns

I heard a story once from a doctor that has never left me. It was about a young woman in advanced pregnancy who was brought in with shortness of breath and all the symptoms of a pulmonary embolus. She was about to be administered blood thinners when she cried out, "I am losing it" and the doctor told her quickly that if she coded he promised to bring her back.

The clot was too massive and she died. I have always wondered if as her spirit struggled to retain its hold on her body and the two lives that it contained whether that promise faded gradually away like a vanquished hope. Somewhere in some alternative universe she is certainly owed a second chance. This time her eyes will flicker open some time later and she will be assured that the clot-buster drugs worked and that she has been stabilized and the child is alright. There has to be a way that our legitimate expectations in this contingent world are covered somewhere by a parallel track through the bottle-necks of such horrible chance events so that this time it will all work out.

As a parallel thought, I know a man who is spending the last years of his life nourishing and embroidering a story that he tells with all the frequency of a nursery story, one that celebrates his life. Repetition has become over time the equivalent of a litany sung before a statue carved to celebrate his own particular rendition of a song otherwise of little relevance to the world at large.

These two stories are connected because in the first we have a life story that should have been prolonged to at least the point where a new life could be transmitted and in the latter we have a story that having outlived its relevance has been reduced to a private mythos and a shrine in the desert.

The question is whether the guillotine of chance shows any pattern as in Thornton Wilder's, "The Bridge of San Luis Rey," or whether some brute force crushes us as it rolls over in its sleep. Is it up to novelists to resolve questions such as these so as to assure us all that everything will be alright in the end and a moral will emerge that will not leave the demons laughing?

***

Even if we do get a second chance, not everyone can contemplate the prospect of a return with equanimity. The Buddhists for instance deplore the likelihood of rebirth; we will then have to face the prospect of living again with only the most vestigial karmic recall from our past lives to guide us. We are likely to repeat the same mistakes again and again. Progress is incremental if it even exists at all.

Those who fear complete extinction will welcome the idea that they may like Hailey's Comet come this way again. Novelists of course along with all those who desire vicarious immortality live in hope of multiple editions of their works. We would all like to keep company with Plutarch, Tacitus, and Plato although the very novelty of the novel appears to doom it to the ephemeral requirements of a particular age and sensibility.

Perhaps the best way of conceiving of a return to those who do not relish a boomerang existence is to frame a return as an opportunity to revise an incomplete text or to resolve various lingering ambiguities. Most lives appear to me to have a certain summary quality where what is most essential is deferred until some ideal future time when our onerous obligations will fall away at last and we will be free to go fishing, to let our hair down, or to tell the boss what we really think of him.

Novelists of course are irresponsible enough to use part of their lives engaged in writing down what others may dismiss as just so much pointless raving or as conclusions that they have reached cheaply through an intuitive gift rather than by dwelling in various libraries and reaching down the many heavy volumes by dead writers to outline the permutations of human choices. Some people, not satisfied with the vague promises of cryogenics, insist that their libraries should be similarly preserved along with their bodies, pages marked with bookmarks where they once left off reading in some distant century. Others will want their manuscripts buried with them so that should they ever be exhumed an enterprising agent in the future may (relying upon the publicity potential of the macabre) find some latter-day publisher willing to bring out a fresh edition. All of which is to say that writers contemplate an endless stream of future readers and who can blame them? Why should writers suffer the results of their unique malady alone when others are capable of threading the labyrinth of thoughts that they have initiated?

It is precisely here that the question of a universal human consciousness comes into play. Is it essential that one particular cranium contain the results of part of the collective experience of the human race? To the degree that what we write is significant at all it must appeal to others along a universal continuum while still possessing something particular to ourselves. It may be only in style and in our eccentric turns of phrase that we are recognizable, as is witnessed by the peculiar tonal qualities of Thomas Carlyle in his "Sartor Resartus" and of Thomas De Quincy in his "Confessions of an English Opium Eater." No one will fail to recognize a passage from "Finnegan's Wake" or confuse it with Samuel Johnson's, "Rasselas." The question is whether it is any comfort to the dying to know that others will love as they have loved, rejoice in the dawn as they have rejoiced, or enjoyed a glass of bourbon with sensations similar to their own.

We each have an inborn bias for personal survival and hence we covet a return if only to sample once again our favorite delights before resuming our residence among the silent dead. Here resides the appeal of a general resurrection when body and soul will resume their accustomed intimacy and looking about them will be happy to see that in their absence a vast improvement has been made in the moral stature of their fellow men and women. On that far distant day novels that were long allowed to vanish from the bookshelves only to be supplanted by far less worthy effusions by far less talented and enterprising writers will be issued once again, or so the pious novelist believes.

Decisions on such open issues of longstanding were forced upon me in the year 2016 and at precisely the time when I was most loathe to saying, "Goodbye." Everywhere I went I heard tales of unprepared partings. I came home only to hear that many friends had died, illnesses had returned, spouses had been lost, and everywhere there was change. I could see and appreciate the ways that people lose heart to continue. The quick re-shuffling of the deck of existence can scatter all that remains of even a winning hand back into randomness and chance.

I found as the year drew to a close that I clung to "Pacific End" for its obscure hints at life and was fearful lest my words should be pointlessly scattered like spilled Scrabble tiles on the floor. Within its circumference was at least one more approximation at formulating experience, preventing its bleed-off into meaninglessness and a train of mere temporal succession. I had wanted to get back those hours of untried confidence that everything would work itself out. My best comfort was that certain hints and guiding incidents kept re-occurring.

When I had returned home I opened a fortune cookie that read: *Fortune favors those who are in motion.* Perhaps that was the key to the security that I sought. Forget the building of citadels; stay ahead of the crack in the breaking ice. The old world I had known was indeed dissolving all about me. No parking! Stay off the grass! No stopping or standing! Revoke Obama Care! Don't come back! We never wanted you in the first place.

But I was running short on the time to exercise my options so suddenly I was back on the Oregon Coast and it occurred to me, as though it should not have been latent throughout this multifaceted discourse that I have tried to frame here, that redemption would be pointless without a return of sorts. To begin new lives without a prior framework of reverence and memory would be to be redeemed but unconscious that you had been given further ground into which to emerge, an old pattern continued, but on a higher level. The famous phrase that "at present we see things only through a glass darkly but then (and in that "then" is everything) we will see Him as He is and we will know Him, even as we are known" contains in compressed form all of the hope of Christianity as well as its radical openness to what still remains undisclosed. The outlines of heaven have been left ill-defined. We are given far closer analogues of hell than we are given of heaven: joy, bliss, paradise, or as the Muslims believe a garden of sensual delights. All of these fall short by being metaphors, analogues, or mere directional indicators towards a state that combines moral fixity on God as our direction with a perfect fulfillment and even enlargement of our present capacities to encompass new regions of delight and security. Compared to these descriptions of our possible future state most of the world's pleasures decrease our overall security because we know that they are subject to loss and ourselves subject to extinction in the only body that we have ever known. Once having come into existence our extinction becomes not only inconceivable and unfathomable but charged with a sense of injustice – we do not deserve to die!

Still, the fact remains that we do perish and thereafter, absent a few cases of the return of saints and the haunted rumors of various apparitions, we will remain dead. For this reason we place our trust in the idea that the souls of those who have preceded us are already engaged in the early tutelage of heaven that will reach its perfection in that vast reunion on the last day when the bodies that we once inhabited will join the souls retained and supported in that repository out of time's embrace where they concurrently dwell in God. The doctrine of the Communion of Saints explains that our present prayers, actions, and sacrifices have some causative and salutary effect upon the condition of the dead as they pursue their way through whatever purgative process may remain to them to adjust to the new conditions imposed upon them by dwelling in eternity. They are in us and we are in them and all are in Christ and by that very reason all are in God.

Of course phrases such as those just written here are by their very nature directional and not comprehensive. They are aspirations not cognitions or descriptions of what is already fully comprehended and as such cannot be cohesively verified in the usual ways, but neither can they be refuted by any customary means. To mock or degrade them is simply foolishness. They should be respected as means to describe elements of faith.

The burden of the present novel is to have given the reader the suggestion that transcendent solutions are not only credible but that to disbelieve is a sign of an emotional distemper based on a sense of pride and presumption and not on facts. Weariness with the pursuit of an inadequate life's course or because a particular instance of bereavement is held to be insupportable is not a disproof of a happier terminus and answer to the human equation. To compel hope is of course impossible and to that end we look to art to enhance whatever prosaic station we currently inhabit on our life's course. Some days and nights are certainly easier to bear than others but I am trying to take heart once again.

***

As I just mentioned I suddenly found myself returned to the very place where over the long summer of 2016 I had meditated a similar return to the place where she who cannot be named would no longer be with me. I am back in Newport and have only to look up from my table to look down the street and see the gulls circling over the regular pattern of white wave-breaks and the vast sky open to alternate sun-breaks and the ever advancing squall-lines over the sea. The antique streetlamps are not yet lit nor the Christmas lights that make December not only tolerable but joyful throughout the Northern Hemisphere where Christianity first took root. Before coming to my usual writing domicile I dropped in on the Newport Oracle. I showed her how much I had written since late spring and mentioned that she was in the book. As usual she responded in a way that was surprising at first but deeply meaningful and in character.

"It isn't important to me that I am preserved in a book. I am more concerned for the little ones who are coming into a land where people will rejoice in the exclusion of others. I am afraid for what the Americans have invited upon them. Trump has dementia you know; that is why he must look to others to tell him what is happening if the event exceeds his limited vocabulary and the four or five stock responses that his paranoia dictates. You must help me spread the word. Tell everyone that you know."

Of course I have been busy looking for minor comforts such as the separation of powers doctrine and the solid Democratic opposition to the Republican wish-list: of arms as salvation, women and men clearly divergent and sleeping in the right beds, and a Protestant revivalism enshrined in law. The Newport Oracle was as compassionate as ever, but for the first time she looked worried.

"You must help the young ones because it will be hardest for them. They have not had their lives yet. They will only know a time of divisions and hatred, of polarization as official policy, and suspicion as an endemic disease. I have seen what this can mean in other places. I didn't think to find it here."

I thought of pointing out to her that to a sizeable portion of Americans the Trump victory was disappointing because he was not conservative enough. These would much prefer the brown-shirt tactics of Germany in the nineteen-thirties. America was poised on a powder-keg of people who were convinced that they had somehow been cheated of their rightful heritage by Mexicans, Muslims, and various breeds of liberalism from the media to the newly married gays and lesbians. These would count their ammunition now and wonder if they had stockpiled enough to kill their neighbors if groceries became scarce after the Arabs stopped shipping us oil and the Chinese stopped underwriting the universal jurisdiction of American arms throughout the world. These are the people that the new President would now have to keep happy. In four years he might decide to return to the safety of his tower and let someone else carry the ball looking for that elusive first down that would carry the American Dream ten yards or closer to its goal.

"While I'm here I plan on meeting with the group at the Church," I said by way of changing the subject.

"That is good; you must help your people to survive."

As I left I realized that I couldn't tell her that my only advice for others is for them to look for a better security than I had ever been able to find.

I can see more clearly every day that the Saints had the best idea after all. We have nothing to cling to here. Even the land is dissolving around us and falling into the sea. I no longer look to politics, to the laws, to great artists, or to my own small efforts to hammer out of time and verbiage a general solution to the human condition. I find lately that I am just very sorry for everyone. I would like to yield at every intersection if it wasn't for the people behind me that would soon be honking their horns, delayed in getting to wherever they want to go. I don't know how to find an imprint small enough that it will not be seen as grounds for trespass. We stake out tiny spaces on the ocean reefs and hope that our mussel-shell existences will not be swept away by the next oncoming wave.

***

I look up from writing and already I can see that the sun is lost somewhere just behind the clouds, not yet set though because the tidal flats still have that silver sheen with just a touch of pink and yellow. The waves are grey but the winter sky with the sun positioned a mere ten degrees above the horizon is a pale clear blue. I wonder how things are at home, how does she fare as the year ends, she who must remain unnamed here? I returned and then departed once again and will soon return a second time, part of a cyclic life-form that seeks to experience and record all things passing.

Outside my window is a woman with a camera on a tri-pod. She stands with her husband and child and all alike are focused on her as she seeks to balance light, shadow, and moment for a perfect shot. Suddenly I know that the sun is gone because the tidal shallows are grey now also, old and grey as the saying goes. Only the zenith is still illumined by its unique angle to the sun. We must elevate our gaze from earth to see that it is still alive. Triggered by the advancing darkness the antique street lights are burning now. They will send their beams into the dark along with the ancient lighthouse on the battered headland north of here. I must refill my coffee while there is time before closing. Night will soon settle in along this coastal village. The storekeepers will close their shops and the few night-spots will receive those who are not yet ready to seek the solace of sleep. I will attend the meeting at the church with the other exiles before seeking out Circes with its colored lights and mostly empty tables to tell my friends there that I have returned. And somewhere, three hundred miles away, she who cannot be named will perhaps wonder what I am writing about now and whether doing so makes me feel any better.

***

Each day of the waning year back in the Oregon coast seemed to be taking away little chunks of me like the bottom of the beach path. Great ruts have been cut into the sand and soil as though the ocean, long impatient at the summer's delay, had doubled its efforts now that witnesses to its depredations were few. Each night the great waves of winter advanced upon the land renewed their assault. The beach looked like a grim battlefield, littered with logs and other nameless debris dragged up from the sea bottom. A great coil of kelp like a malevolent octopus lay at the bottom of the path, still and somnolent yet imbued with a sinister intent as though it was simply waiting for an unwary ankle to coil about it before swimming slowly out to sea again. My feet are perennially cold. Is it true that as we age we develop unusual sensitivities of body and of mind? The blood slows and is inadequate to properly feed the extremities. We die first like a rose petal that grows brown around the edges before rolling itself into a brown funnel and falling away from its source.

Out beyond the stampeding breakers the December sun shown, weary and bleak across the grey water as though its major energies were engaged elsewhere on the other side of the planet. The rich verdure on the slopes had been replaced by pale skeletal stems pointing at a sky that seemed to be making an accusation. The hillsides lay naked and shameless now, cut by shallow rivulets like the deep wrinkles on the face of a woman who had known passions in her youth but whose demands were now muted to the simple request not to be hurt when she is moved. I understand such women now and for that reason I am loathe to becoming one. Far better to travel along the level sunbeams of the setting sun to the person I had once been when I first came down to look at this very place on my father's instructions. It had seemed a paradise then and all things possible to my youthful and brave conceptions. Now I only heard as Matthew Arnold said in his poem, "Dover Beach," - its melancholy long withdrawing roar down the night-edges drear and naked shingles of the world."

✳✳✳

Americans are not accustomed to the decline and fall of empires if that drama is to be enacted on our native soil. Our appetite for heroes in America is an unending one. To speak as Thomas Wolfe once did of the bitter loneliness of Brooklyn is now to make readers uneasy. We read our authors to reassure us, to calm our fears that America is just another waning power and that the sun is moving westwards to the orient. We want a world that will embrace the inevitable return of spring but we want to still be alive to witness that renewal. It is little comfort to simply imagine what we cannot share. As a result we shift uneasily in our beds at night.

I want to go home now. I want to place my life in hands other than my own as I did last night when I woke at the deathly hour of four, the hour when many souls surrender to the all embracing clay. The night was still, unusually still, and yet the stars were all out and my feet were not cold although I wore no socks and only the light shoes that I had bought in August. I could feel within me the sum total of all of the year's losses and I felt that dark coming together of loneliness, shame, and regret that makes me wish I had made other choices, a feeling that I was unprepared in tensile strength to bear the weight of the misfortunes that were surfacing all around me like sharp granite spurs from the frozen earth.

I always said that authors are best summed up in their last works, but I was probably wrong. We write best when we have yet to test life's limits. We are still charged then, as Thomas Wolfe had been, with a hunger to find new places and to test our latent powers. I had once believed that if only I could live by the sea then I would mellow with time and become a worthy successor to that larger-than-life, bombastic, and rhetorical Thomas Wolfe who I adored. I would encase in deathless prose his valediction to a life that had met its end so early. I would be grateful and not spoil everything by caviling at every inconvenience and loss knowing that in the end all would be taken from me anyway. I would be grateful simply to have been here for the eye-glimpse of life that is allotted to each of us. I would possess the courage then for a graceful surrender when it was time and consider myself lucky in my one and individual fate whatever it was to be. I would say with Saint Ignatius Loyola the prayer I had said so often at the novitiate when I was only twenty-two:

Take and receive O Lord all my liberty

Take my memory, my understanding, and my entire will

Whatsoever I have or hold you have given to me

I give it all back to you and surrender it wholly to be governed by your will

Give me only your love and your grace

With these I am rich enough and ask for nothing more.
Amen.

Now awake on a December night so many years later, gazing out over the star-flung heavens at the white ribs of the breaking waves, I recalled that once years ago during a family reunion at Cannon Beach I had been caught up in a rip tide and barely made it back to shore. I recall thinking at the time that every day after that was in the nature of a bonus because for me it had all been over before I felt my grateful feet grasping at the first precious touch of the hard sands. I had regained the land and with the land, life. So now I knew that I would always gratefully return, no matter how closely at times I have walked along the knife-edge of despair. The cold salt waters will slide away from me and my mind will quicken and recover its pulse-beat of comfort and design. I will imagine the future once again and look around me to find comfort in the unfathomable miracle of existing at all.

✳✳✳

I went to attend the Saturday vigil mass tonight and as usual I felt the arms of the universal and apostolic Church curl about me there. God is always close to the poor and the He hears the cries of the brokenhearted.

It is not uncommon for people to come up to me and tell me their stories just as I in my turn go to the Newport Oracle. Tonight it was an ex-soldier who though he said was not a Catholic cared to remain like me after mass had ended to hear the Spanish mass as well. I stood in the back studying the various angles of the brick walls and the curving arch of the nave. I thought of how, if I had become a priest, I would hold my hands out to the scattered families and ask them to help me, because although the priest sets the tone of parish life he requires the warmth of every member of the Body of Christ to create a sense of Church and its life-blood of charity.

Why I thought, would I ever wish to go out alone into the December night?

***

Snow on the coast is an unusual occurrence but appropriate for one in my current fragile state of mind. I thought of how I had once imagined that people reach the time of death with no more regret or a sense that something is amiss than a red apple has when it is plump and full having fulfilled its destiny as an apple by being picked. Old people seemed vaguely picturesque then like visitors from a strange land where people always have sagging faces and benevolent jowls like pug dogs or boxers.

I was not selfish in presuming myself to be immune from age; I extended the same gift of immortality to my classmates and relatives. My magic and perfect parents would always be there to imbue their surroundings with glamour and good taste and to view me with the proper mixture of doubt and disapproval. Nothing abrupt or ugly could ever touch us. Squalor and penury were simply evidence that the poor we would have always with us as a separate species. The deaths of the famous and powerful simply made for good tabloid stories. Their dramas added spice and flavor to the roles they had played for the vast throng of Americans whose only function is to struggle each day and to labor until some far-off day when pensioned and beaming they would retire.

Then would come the time for long-deferred leisure pursuits: the late-night card games and the long talks on back porches. Eventually retirement would in its turn become exhausting and life would be surrendered gracefully and without any accompanying horrors. One day the shuffling grey creature would be taken to the church, lie in her coffin, and look remarkably like any other generic old lady, dusty and rouged and ready for her long siesta. But she would not be me; that is the point!

Applied to myself and those who were in any degree of my vintage years there would always be a summer day along the endless California beaches, the war would end with peace and honor, and life in its proper sense, pure and without menace, would begin again. I would not as in these last days of 2016 see the sun setting far to the south of where it should have plunged gloriously into the sea on the high summer days.

There would be no reason to periodically purge my phone tree of old names of those who would not be returning any messages. I could always be assured that someone older and wiser was at hand to tell my latest troubles to and before whom to bewail my errors. Best of all, the world would not be spinning merrily along a new orbit into endless space with neither chart nor policy to guide it. I wouldn't revisit old haunts with dismay at the changes or quail at the prospect of trying to begin again in a new place where no one knows my name.

When the chill days arrived with snow in the coastal mountains I thought of that immortal phrase of Sir Thomas Browne, "our sun makes but winter arches," and looked out over the December breakers to where the pale sun, just about to set, having failed to reach its proper zenith, like a bad golf drive leaving a long second shot to reach the green, was about to disappear. In the past I have fought fear with anger and even in the midst of panic I would have tried to retain a sense that a little more effort would always carry me through. It was all part of my individual mythos, one confirmed by no other devotees but only by me, the high priest or priestess of my cult of me, hero or prima-donna of the grand opera that would someday leave the provinces and open on Broadway to a long overdue acclaim.

✶✶✶

As the year began to diminish and fade around me it gradually became clear, through what process I cannot say, but perhaps simply as a result of the effort involved in writing, that there was a reason for my sense that everything had somehow been dislodged this year and come to rest again in a position that was off-center from where they should be. It was not that death or age or political misjudgments were a surprise to me; these things had always existed. The problem was that my particular narrative was based on the assumption that I could somehow always engineer the successive events of my life so that even reversals from many years ago would still be subject to change by being assimilated into my present actions where I still maintained control and the power of choice, because after all it is the general shape of the narrative taken as a whole that is responsible for that moment of aesthetic suspension where all of the parts come together to achieve their desired effect. I still expected that my life could be composed like a novel into a sense of trim completeness with nothing extraneous or unassimilated into the larger governing form. I had been perpetually seeking to do something on a much more humble scale analogous to what Proust had accomplished in his great novel sequence where he sought to recapturing the past in all of its uniqueness and sensibility and to make it live again in words.

But even Proust understood that the poignancy of his effort was due to the unalterable fact that the past is, I was about to say set in stone but that is wrong; the past is not set in stone at all, it is merely preserved in scattered artifacts and in the fragile memory traces of those who witnessed and were part of various events. Even then the past is construed differently, depending upon our desires and expectations, by the different people involved in each passing encounter. There is no way to get back to the ur-text of our lives because we each follow a different path of hermeneutics as we try and assemble the overall tale. The point of contention is not about what happened but about what meaning is to be derived from chains of daily experience and how they fit into the great web of expectation and design that we impose on our lives and our place within it from outside. The past cannot be altered but its place in the whole can be altered by subsequent events and in this way it is still subject to our forming consciousness.

***

Even having said this though I am beginning to realize that we would all have long since achieved mindfulness if we could approve our past even as we live the events that are falling away from us, but regret and discontent and even tragedy leave behind pieces of the puzzle that are bent, torn, or otherwise deformed. These pieces are difficult to fit into the larger design, yet they often occupy too central a place to be discarded. She who cannot be named was an essential part of a design we had both shared for years.

Radical relocations or spontaneous substitutions might suffice but there is the problem of the diminishing fund of time available. As we age our resource base is diminished so that our ability to distract or disguise the vast empty spaces and fatal lacunae of our lives cannot rely upon vast reversals of fortune and circumstances to remedy deficits. Our lives are likely to be finally what they already are and not something vastly different and improved. We are confined to the fragile and evanescent present moment to effect any changes. Even if we approve of our actions and they have surrounded us with material resources and acclaim we may still lament that they are only the residue of our triumphs, all that remains of our former lives.

The world effaces its slaughters and forgives its grim dictators; these are eventually seen as the blind forces of history. They have in some way served the common good, but usually at a much higher cost than the one that is considered to be generally acceptable to our humanitarian instincts. The memory of the saints is still preserved in statues and missals and we seek their intercession for our various needs. The rest of us simply join that vast parade of anonymous corpses in the unplumbed catacombs of forgetfulness and inconsequence. The beads and glass shift within the kaleidoscope and new patterns are formed. But it all happens so swiftly, this march of the generations in time's vast parade. So where is comfort to be found as I approach again the solstice and am launched upon another year? If the past cannot be regained and the future is diminished so that the comings and goings, the assemblages and the dispersals fail to cohere to the design that in my case was probably misconceived at the start, where shall I, the author of this singular text, find a sense of closure and completeness? Am I to be satisfied with only an incomplete and partial articulation here so that my text joins the many fragments of unfinished manuscripts that possess even less chance of survival than do finished works? Worse still will my life cycle down into unrecorded years with here and there a poem to capture a fleeting sense that my experiences have meaning? If my life will not conform to the dictates of a novel then where am I to look for an adequate form to contain it?

I could go on and on but further irony is as pointless as Shelley's lament, "I fall upon the thorns of life; I bleed." Instead I should be glad that to date I have yet to receive a terminal diagnosis and only a single tooth has preceded me to the grave. Where is my sense of humor? It is time to dig out my old volumes of P.G. Wodehouse or John Keane, time to rejoin the human race.

I suppose that my summation of the course followed by human lives in "Pacific End," and I owe my patient readers this much, has as its final affirmation this assurance; that for all of the seeming finality of persons and events, all things do return. We will see each other again.

The earth-circling sun will summon us forth again and the long sought answers will come unbidden to our long silent and earth-stopped tongues. So there is really nothing to worry about and I can be sure that my boxes at home of the volumes of great literature will be probed someday by my greedy eyes. Someday I will pull over to the side of the road on a throbbing motorcycle on a July day to read a message from she who cannot here be named saying, "Where are you wandering one? I hope you are enjoying Oregon. I can't wait to see you again. Love -----

✲✲✲

The deaths of others this year have shown me how vain it is for me to expect that a special dispensation would be made for me simply because as a writer I need to be here to see how everything connects to everything else. Each of these vanished ones had been like me accustomed to feeling that they inhabited a reserved realm of continuity; they played some essential role in other people's lives and consequently they must be preserved;

yet they had died. They were rushed in an unseemly manner from the stage with little time allotted to wind up their affairs and to make their last set of statements, heavy with significance and grim portent. These transient ones may not have known that upon their continuity depended my own sense of immunity. Each belonged secure and unaltered where I expected them to be should I wish to call or visit. Surviving was the least that they could do to advance the vast mural that was even now scrolling its way towards completion, the panorama turning on its great cylinder, powered by everyone who I ever came to know but most of all by my family and friends. Did they realize that all of the major roles had been cast and that we all might be called to perform at any time on a stage that had been long reserved for us?

(I trust that my readers can recognize irony when as in the above sentences it co-opts the narrative. How else can I express the sense of what it means when someone we know and care for becomes suddenly as irrecoverable as if he or she had died centuries ago and not merely yesterday? No sword however sharp severs as neatly the past from the present as is the case among the recently dead. They take parts of us with them. We bleed from their wounds).

✷✷✷

Of course the sentiments of desperation I have just recounted presume that I (and others as well) are the authors of our fate and not subject to the overriding currents of providence that alone can give any life its real and definitive form. Novels after all do not possess the status of sacred writings, those veiled yet meaningful sources of revelation. Transformation, redemption, and repetition cannot be achieved by our sole efforts to bring things together or to separate them and by so doing to create out of our lives a perfect and self-sustained whole. Perceptions are subject to delusions, hallucinations, and poor judgments. Texts become detached from their referents. The result is that neither life nor novel is ever complete, the realization of a perfect design. We are confined to the instant, the present hour, minute, and second. From this tiny immanence we must survey all that we have ever been, all that we are, and whatever may still be, and in fear and trembling make our choices.

✳✳✳

I knew after two weeks on the coast that I needed to get along home and see if next year could bring me some sense of restoration. I had finished my last tasks for 2016. So I sought out again the Newport Oracle to say my farewells before returning to Washington.

As usual we spoke of many things and she advised me to write less and to live more, advice that I intend to take. She tells me that she dreams of returning to India to volunteer, to do anything needed, to work off any residual karmic deficits so that she need not be reborn. I think that it would be a pity if future times were bereft of her soul, but I do not dispute her wish to move on to better things.

My sister tells me that sometimes people only enter our lives for a season. Everything is passing and some things are quite naturally passing away. I tell the Oracle that I hope she will remain where she is. Time is different in her presence and I find that comforting. I look up to find that the shops are closing. I see that it is too late now for coffee; it will soon be dark. The lights are coming up all over the beach district and the pale blue of a sunset's afterglow holds several vast cumulus clouds. I bid her farewell and look in the storefronts at the Christmas trees and other displays that speak of warmth and home.

Each additional day I have waited looking about me for a vanished summer and waiting for the current chill to pass. I am tired of deaths and threats of death. All year long I had been geared up for living – the Olympic competition in Rio, the drama of the Presidential election, trying to prove that I could get along without she who must not be named, and hoping to find the proper fundamental structure out of which novels emerge – beyond all of this shoreline cacophony the vast sea had moved in its unchanging rhythm. I had met so many people, gathered smiles like summer grain, and still the fundamental problems remained. I was still impatient for with the particulars of life. I wanted to discover the fundamental base chord to which all things vibrate the great droning hum of being. But we cannot give of what we do not first possess – happiness, peace, and some point from which to move out into the world.

All the phenomena happening around us: things coming together, things coming apart; they are being transformed, but not always for the better. The result is that we are all seeking redemption from some force or being that can comprehend the whole and attune the parts.

Some look to the Christ or fear the anti-Christ; others are unsure if the messiah will ever come. One thing is certain though: things recur, even if not always in the same form. We hope that our familiar world of things will return, but even if they did would we recognize them when we have already altered in so many ways since our last parting. We are always engaged in starting our lives over again, hoping this time to finally get it right.

***

"No," the Newport Oracle would say, "It is not about getting it right; it is about taking the time first to grasp what we are even talking about. If you can see anything clearly you will already be close to the heart of all things and you will know what to do because it will already be at your finger's ends. Total objectivity is impossible, but so is total subjectivity; there is only the ever-present now. The question is what will you do next? Will you try to swim back up the stream to its source when you are already at the point where the river empties itself into the ocean? It cannot be done!"

"You only have what you have made of your life and you must try and do something with it, something good something of love. There is no point to making some vast preliminary study – the world is already doing that and as a result the most appalling conditions prevail; people are cold and hungry and we still do not have peace. We turn away from what everyone already knows. We look our neighbor in the eye and do not see her. Worse still, we look in the mirror and do not recognize ourselves because we are not as we wish we could be. Happiness is always for tomorrow and we will get to it when we are finished with whatever we are doing to keep us from ever getting there. Why not just stop? Why not realize that this is the place and this is the time and that we will always only be our uncertain striving selves, but that is enough."

"If we did not spend so much effort to avoid the obvious we would already be making the world better by doing what is at hand, by loving the person who is asking right now for our help. I do not know what I will do tomorrow; I do know what I am doing right now."

"Writing is your way of always keeping the world at one remove. What if there was no new novel to compose or to revise? What if the dead-line for submission of proof-sheets was already past, the type was set, the presses rolling; would you yell STOP? It is too late to re-write your life and selectively cancel events. You simply are and that is all. But you are alive and because you are alive more living is being asked of you. Is that so dreadful? Maybe it isn't death that you fear but living with no guarantee of perfection."

I tell her that I want to be a good novelist and in order to be one I must know all things and know how to say them perfectly.

"And if you were so perfect, what then? You would be so wise that nobody could understand you. Isn't it better to simply join the rest of us who will leave no record behind us but the lives that we have touched? Why must you alone be immortal, and on your own terms? Aren't you trying to make up for what you have left undone in simply living? How do you think that others manage who will never know what you have already read who will never write what you have already written? Somehow they manage to find their lives, to raise their children, and to face death gracefully when it comes."

I tell her that I know this, but I need more. I want all of the options clearly defined and on the table. I need clarity in the contract before signing on for life.

"No one has had all the data since Adam and Eve. God made it very simple for them; eat this and do not eat that; and they still made a mess of everything. The rest of us just have to take our chances and hope for the best."

***

I leave her and try and catch the closing at the coffee bistro and to see the last light of this one day fade over the ocean's vast expanse. I gaze at the two tiny dollar-store Christmas snow-globes in the window and I hear the parting voices of the last patrons as they walk out into the night. I savor this final fifteen minutes before closing, minutes set aside to merely observe, to allow life to trickle past me like a single tear of rain on the windows. All events, precious, evanescent, unrelated in thought or theme, happen and then as swiftly, are no more. We novelists try and reconstruct life in print, but for all of our efforts the law of life is change followed by dispersal.

And I, like Melville's Ishmael before me, or like Thomas Wolfe's wanderer and his lost and bitter ghosts, alone remain to tell thee.

***

And then suddenly I was home again. I drove through the snow that had gathered in the passes of even the low coastal mountains. I drove through the driving rain squalls that seemed reluctant to leave me as though they would willingly draw me out again to sea where they had become saturated as the winds that track from untold miles across its vast surface just as I had canvassed this strange year of 2016 in "Pacific End," gathering material wherever I might. I crossed the Narrows Bridge and the rain stopped and the moon appeared, shining on the waters so that when I reached my boat on Liberty Bay I could see my home in the new light that only absence can bestow. The dull routine of my days now seemed to me to be a treasure beyond price because for one thing I was alive. I was not frightened of what would come with the new administration or appalled by the stale relics drawn from the long self-serving roll of Republican apparatchiks. I thought that the country would never be worse than its people and I thought that bad things would only happen to us if we surrendered in some unaccountable manner and gave our consent. Hard times can unite a country in ways that good fortune never can. I thought about what St. Ignatius Loyola, the founder of the Jesuits, had said about Holy Indifference, how we should be willing to part with anything if God's providence so decrees, that we should lose it or rid ourselves of it. He spoke of the danger of any affection that cannot contemplate loss. Ignatius was no cold stoic though; his emphasis upon indifference was an act of freedom given and received. To cling to anything is to be owned by it. He felt that we must be able if necessary to turn on a dime, to be flexible, to embrace change without a backward glance because adaptability is the key to virtue.

***

I still felt the need for aesthetic closure though, even having reached some degree of renewed sense of what life can and cannot give. But how to adapt when the world seems at times to be spiraling out of its accustomed orbit; that had been the question that had haunted me all year. Each day had brought its record of some new atrocity bred of competing absolutes and a failure to negotiate or to seek a common core of humanity that will bridge all divergences. I came to the end of the biography of Robert Lowell and thought that even with recognition and acclaim the life of poets is a grim one. Novelists in contrast are held to be made of sterner stuff because they are less involved with their own perceptions and the self-dictating mandates of language and form. The novel is assumed to be freer and more akin to life by virtue of possessing a story to tell. We expect more sanity and sagacity from our novelists than from our poets. The intuitions and leaps of reason may still be present, but cause and effect still rule the day in novels.

Even as I reflected in this way though I recalled how I had once become immersed in novels such as "The Notebooks of Malte Laurids Brigge" by Rainer Maria Rilke and "Against the Grain" by the French author, Huysmans, that like poetry had attained their best effects by an intense exploration of states of mind so that prose and poetry came quite close and story and plot in the traditional sense become secondary or even absent. Was it not in this genre that my own incessant probing belonged, in intentionality at least if not in achievement? Writers must believe in what they are doing and engage in a face-to-face relation with other authors, many of whom are long dead yet must serve as the closest thing to a mentor and guide that the writer possesses. The torch is passed even if the new writer can only carry it a short distance forward. The author's own awareness fades in and out like a light seen behind trees, the will-of-the-wisp of inspiration and insight. In making an end I realized that I was being brought again to that place of beginnings where we rummage through all that remains and mourn what has vanished, perhaps forever, the world that we once believe would always dance attendance according to our wishes and demands.

***

There was a time when I thought that I would always burn with what Walter Pater called a "hard gem-like flame" by virtue of the mere desire to do so. I loved the gargantuan confidence of Thomas Wolfe in his great masterpiece, "Of Time and the River," because I always felt that life was too precious to be allowed only its short trail of sparks across a midnight sky without leaving a trace in the imperfect medium of words. Brooding on the preciousness of all things is unfortunately not a universal pursuit with the result that we as a culture are becoming spendthrifts with this fragile world that we spoil, soil, and despoil without a sense of the delicacy of the human spirit or the tracery of our crystalline world. I think at times that we need to punch through the barriers raised by suffering and death to what lies beyond, but then I wonder if part of life is in the willingness to gently set events aside like an emptied salad plate so that the main course of human existence can finally be served. Where is the place for violence in this? Would an endless repletion of our past joys and sorrows be adequate to satisfy us for eternity?

As we age we draw what we have most valued around us to guard us against the coming chill. Human affection and alliances are proof to individual dissolution, but we require more than memory. As individuals we are flickering out each day like votive candles, one by one, or like drops of dew at dawn sublimated into mist. Stoics find comfort that the species at least will endure, but I am one who desires to hold out for a translation to a higher sphere. We have been condemned too long to a single lifetime, possessors of a calcified identity, one that serves as a wall of separation and the incomplete intuition of others that share our brief and bitter fate in this passing world. It is time to take the staircase of death to another level where the illustrious dead have preceded us. These have left without bitterness or regrets. Why may not what was adequate to them be adequate to us as well? Can we learn nothing from their status as conservators, as the absent landlords of our hearts, to know we have been loved, and that love was all that was ever essential to us? Whatever has been loved will always be loved. Time works no change on the diamond-hard core of having love appear for an hour or even an instant against the setting of our vast circuitous universe, one that touches us at every conceivable portal as we look upwards. Nothing can be remote that touches us at every point. The vastness of space and time contain us and having done so once we are irrevocably embedded here and thus recoverable at the will of whatever contains all being within itself. Even should image or metaphor or metaphysic fail us there remains the force of an urgent appeal, a prayer before the bar, a petition for clemency based upon having been grateful that we were ever here at all. Such is my trust and my hope that what has been by virtue of its mere transient actuality can be transformed but never extinguished.

✳✳✳

Even factoring in the economics of eternity though, we still hope for a life that can be meaningful on its own terms. So what has become of my hypothetical ideal life, the one where my book jacket says that I divide my time between Paris and New York City, the biographical blurb that says that I am paid to travel extensively to various hotspots in the world where history is being made, the one that says I have appeared in various magazines that span the major publications represented on every newsstand in America? Which universities are now bidding to add to their collections the letters and fragments and other memoranda of my life spent in the pursuit of literature? How many memoirs of the great movers and shakers of the past fifty years record conversations with me as the interviewer and I walked along the Seine or the Volga? Fans will look in vain for me in the index of the six hundred page definitive biographies of major literary figures, those whose witness has defined the sensibilities of our tumultuous age. I have played no part in any but a handful of lives. I am remarkable chiefly because I have skimmed over life leaving as little impact as a sparrow's wing or a passing shadow. My latter-day effusions into print notwithstanding, I will at best awaken a passing smile and a shake of the head if my name is mentioned to my field of acquaintance after I am gone, the usual tribute paid to harmless eccentrics who have left the world little different than it would have been had they never lived.

But it is precisely to these elements that I owe my everyman status. The more that I read biographies of those who have lived the life that I desire the more I realize that fame and renown are not kind and that obscurity may be among the greater gifts that the common man receives. The smallness of our part in the great human drama of every age spares us the culpability for the damage that might have ensued from our ill-considered sense that we possess all of the essential answers and deserve consequently to be served and obeyed. The world would have been a better place if Joseph Stalin for instance had simply owned a plumbing business in some village in his native Georgia. It takes lots of penance to offset the premature death of millions.

✳✳✳

The day after my birthday was a clear day with sunlight that was like milk diluted by spring water. It has been a year of changes and of deaths and I know that more are to come. How appropriate it is in the last analysis that America has manifested its own flaccid machismo and premature senility by having the Electoral College appoint a man as President who was not the popular choice but rather a legacy of the fears of the early founders of the nation for the undisciplined enthusiasms of the multitude. The electors, bound hand and foot to party allegiances, have appointed a man of bluff and bluster, of accusations and reprisals to the highest office in the land.

As a proper figurehead for our bloated empire he can best symbolize what we have collectively become and unite us around all that we have to offer to a spiritually starved world: our bombs, our baseless self-assurance, and our scorn of any higher culture than raw power. Crudity and obviousness is increasingly our national charism and who better to symbolize these than this man of the hour belched up by the sour stomach and resentment of the rural poor and from the wastelands of Midwest industrial America?

I will not be shocked by anything that will emerge in the coming year but rather see in it the fulfillment of a prophecy, the same that decreed the passing of every agglomeration of worldly glory since the Egyptians and the Persians. As for me, I desire only peace, to find again the simple sense that I and my generation once had, a true sense of the wonder that is inherent in being young, that the world would always lie green and pure before us, and that when we came at last to die it would be to have enjoyed hours of perfect sunlight and to perish in our innocence, a privilege unknown to any other age or place since we were first exiled from Eden.

***

The resources for entertainment in North Kitsap County are somewhat limited so it comes as no surprise that the local casinos run by the various native tribes provide that rare mixture of pseudo-glamour, good food, and the promise of labor-less money that are bound to appeal to the offspring of the pioneers. The lure of iced Dungeness crab and little-neck clams with melted butter was sufficient to draw me forth to walk through the smoke-tainted casino with its flashing lights and bewildered zombie-like habitués. This is the America that Trump will rule. A nation of maimed and decrepit aspirants to wealth and position with a declining base and little in the way of frontiers that have not long since been staked-out and claimed.

We live in a land of the canned glamour-squalor of media personalities, high-end sports figures, and the omnipresent militarism that is what remains of any indigenous ideas derived from an American culture. The reason that the Great American Novel eludes us is that we are unworthy of anything beyond a footnote in the tedious history of empires. Those who even care to visit Washington D.C. only encounter a drained swamp, a museum of monuments, and Masonic symbolism, tributes to the vanished Deist ideal of what reason without grace can accomplish.

The rest is a marketplace of political venality.

What better man to inherit all of this than a child of privilege and wealth, later a star of reality-television, a man known for glitzy wives of foreign extraction and for his readiness with insults and non sequiturs? The sudden screeching turn that has caused a minority of Americans to use the Electoral College to shift from its first black president to his polar opposite shows how desperate we are. At some primal level we all know that America is a vast and mindless creature of greed and instinctual gratification that is being sustained by a communist ally. The pending foreclosure sale on America is an omnipresent possibility and meanwhile we do what we can to grasp for the brass ring and eat ourselves sick with cotton-candy.

***

As is customary during the holidays I met with old friends. We talked about how high property taxes are and what we are doing to complete what were once our exaggerated ideas of a mission in this world, a proffered world of science where we could reach the stars. I think it is fair to say that we have each manifested in our own way the reality of the collective diminished expectations of our nation. My friends are all good sorts, honest, decent, and with good taste. Each of us is reluctant to think that our present condition at the dawn of our senior years may represent the high-point before we are whittled down one after the other by various illnesses. None of us at least will be caught on a weekday night running to the bank-machine for a stake at the casino. We have no children to call us at night and complain that the reason that they are wrecks is that we were insensitive and selfish and never understood them. None of us has cancer or multiple sclerosis. We cannot claim veteran's benefits, having all escaped the carnage of Viet Nam. We have dodged bullets whose impact on others we never heard. So I guess you can say that we were the lucky ones. But it isn't enough.

I told my friends that I had now established a residential beach-head on the Oregon Coast where I could recall better days along the same beaches where we had camped in the dunes thirty years ago. We agreed that we all meet too seldom and that we will make an effort to get together and compare notes more often, but then we are all so busy. We are still reaching for the laurel bough and the golden fruit.

With her usual grace the slim form of the Basque Princess came over to ask us if we needed a re-fill for our coffees. Our time together is passing swiftly and I don't know when we will all meet again. It is enough that we have managed to maintain a tenuous peace, holding together the fragile bond of our old associations. It is precisely those people who know us well who can point out the discrepancies between all that we once planned and what we ended up achieving. We tell ourselves that there is still time. We don't look our age at least and we have every expectation that a fortuitous genetic boost will help us over any rough places in the road ahead. I catch a passing wink from the Basque Princess and hope that this might be true. I recall that I used to tease my friends by saying that they could take comfort that long after they had gone I would see that daisies were planted on their graves. The whole point is that I am months older than each of them. Survival is the final triumph that comes to the rescue among old friends to equalize their fortunes.

"He was rich but now he's dead; too bad because he would have loved to see all the changes in the old neighborhood."

I tell them that I have been reading a biography of Joan Didion. None of them have ever heard of her. I tell them that she was an essayist who was in a great position to bear witness to the loss of the American dream over the past fifty years. I also tell them about how in my novel I have tried to express my fear of death and of time's haunting quality and to recall in it Thomas Wolfe. I explain that he was always pressing the envelope of experience to extract all the joy while always bearing in mind that we end with a stone above us that few people will ever care to read. The saga that once seemed so enviable and simple of achievement finally turns and mocks us. The closer we come to victory the harsher is the final knowledge that it must all be surrendered in the end.

We get up finally with smiles and good wishes all round and each of us goes his way to resume his quest for what remains, to merge again with associations and relations that the others do not share. The tidal drift has brought us each to shore at a different place. We shout at each other across the distance and hope that we are heard. We keep our disappointments to ourselves as part of the regimen for maintaining old friendships. When we die at last, it may be some time before the others hear of it. When we get the news we will shake our heads and try to recall the last thing that we said to the other and finally decide that it really doesn't matter anymore.

***

As the year dwindled down I felt as though I was left breathing the thin atmosphere of the cold that had settled over the whole Puget Sound region. The shortened days seemed to have left an unaccustomed vacuum. The sun seemed to barely clear the low horizon each day before being sucked back again leaving only night behind. The usual solidity of the world and my sense that certain essential connections would hold seemed suddenly as frail as isinglass. I saw how natural it was to speak of ghosts at such a time and how the ashes that coated the December embers symbolized all of the vanished times, places, and customs. It takes a base of rebellion and even anger to push aside these forces that would subdue us. To lose our ego seems to invite our extinction no matter how often we praise humility and resignation. However illusory it may be, we need to feel that we are laboring to complete a story, a version of our lives that we feel is presentable, not just to God but to the even stricter tribunal of our pride.

The deaths of others over the year seemed to be creating a whirlpool the lazy circles of which were pulling also on me. Even generating the required inner heat of the organism is not an easy task when we begin to feel the ebb-tide of age setting in. Too few novels speak of these dim feelings that seem almost to be an illusion until we compare notes with others and learn that they can also feel this shift in meanings and institutions, of relations and expectations, as things diminish and decline. There should be a single word that explains these things through long repetition, but I can't find it. I am reduced to simply saying that it takes more deliberation lately to force the world into focus each day. I understand now why the elderly tend to appear wrapped in scarves and hats and wearing gloves against the ever present chill. It isn't enough anymore to just kick the metabolism up by walking faster. Even the heart seems to run slower, burdened by the many disappointments that become harder to bear and more irremediable with every year. The querulous demeanor and bewilderment of age are a function of this sense that an entire world of lost associations is drifting away while the desire to adapt to changes is minimal. Why should *we* change? *We* came from that privileged generation that knew all of the answers. *We* were busy creating a new world that would last forever and suddenly we looked up and saw how sordid and foolish had been the last forty years.

Had we subsidized the forces that now threaten to overwhelm us with debt, inequality, and a world of menace and discord? Should we have protested more, made our voices better heard? Or had we always been helpless pawns, besotted by the heady liquor of progress and of post-war American prosperity? It wasn't that we could not go home again at all; the problem was that all the familiar places had altered. If we revisited them we would expect to find them as though they had been packed carefully away in our absence and would be just as we had left them. The images in our heads would not match what we found.

The past dimensions are changed and displacement is the rule. It is when ideas are first felt as perceptions that they become most real to us. Explanations are the way that we deal with what we first encounter somewhere along the blood. I guess I can say this best by saying that an air of defiance was always my ultimate resource. I always kept a reserve of energy that I could draw on as needed to refuse, to drag my feet, to demand that things be other than they are.

It is different now. I can feel more clearly than ever before how true were the words of Christ to Peter were, that when he was young he could go where he wished but that in age he would be bound and taken where he did not wish to go. I expect that what I am describing is less personal than I think it is. Writers hope to grasp the universal but are surprised when they actually do. Secretly we think that we are exceptions to the common lot, that we like King Lear can say, "Peace Kent! Stand not between the dragon and his wrath." We end by wandering over the moor with only a fool to be our guide, looking for our vanished daughter. The primary vice of age is the suspicion that others wish to push us aside and our fear of ridicule when we can no longer match the glories of our former days. Time and circumstance join forces against us with the same message that our ways and loyalties are already poor dead things. Only tyranny can delay the proper succession of role and custom.

We look up suddenly and find that our private list of the dead exceeds the living ones who remain. A few more years and it will not matter, because we will have joined them. It once seemed so natural to me to oppose death as a personal affront but we each carry it with us as the other side of the bright coin of living. Sooner or later the coin must be turned bright side down. Each pulse-beat kept at bay what was always as close to us as the next belated breath. We skated blithely over the black waters year after year sustained by what finally claims us. Death is not a late arrival then but the shadow-side of every form. All things define themselves in reference to their opposites. How could we have ever thought that life would be the one exception?

✳✳✳

The year of the arbitrary composition of "Pacific End" was dwindling down towards that hour when the Seattle Space Needle kindles with fireworks and the Emerald City shines in the waters of Puget Sound as the new year of 2017 begins. The new administration is already beginning to give the country a premonition of what is to come. Headlines include the need to rebuild our nuclear arsenal as a sort of national symbol. We place a premium on our ability to draw an equivalency between our national interests and the survival of the planet.

Israel at least is happy in our guarantee to risk our relations with the entire Muslim world to see that its re-colonization of Palestine is allowed to continue unabated. Americans will be happy in knowing that Mexican families are being broken up as parents are returned to Mexico without their children who are citizens by birth. The ranks of the newly insured can soon be purged so that we can join the nations that are not surprised that we have untouchables among us whose fate is to die in the streets because they are too old or sick or poor to do otherwise.

It's all part of being a Republic rather than a democracy. Why trust the majority to elect a President? Why not go with the vast sterile heartland of America and the proud traditions of the Old South to whom death, defeat, and slavery are part of their proud legacy? Wrap the young in flags and till the cotton-fields with the noble dead. The liberal generosity of the coastal suburbs and larger cities will never deserve to have mere numbers suffice to defeat American myths and the advent of the next Great American Novel will be kicked down the road for a member of the NRA to write.

***

Syria as the year ended was becoming the poster child for what ails the world as Russia backs Assad and his wife as part of what Putin believes will be the new Black Sea jet-set that will throng "the Russian Riviera" in the years to come.

On the local scene I kept on hearing of deaths, even while others have great dreams for new purchases in the coming year. In New Year's Day I ate from vast piles of iced crab-legs at the local casino and wondered if I felt lucky or whether I was simply gorging before famine as I try to forget. It was my first year in many years without receiving a card from she who cannot be named. The dam of regret and exile seems to be holding after all without a leak to tell me how she is doing and whether my silence was the gift that she most desired as she had requested.

My new home on the coast was established but was at least temporarily vacant. I felt only the temporary displacement that might be called moral syncope. These deaths during 2016, even if not my own, affected me in a way that had never been the case in previous years. It was just as a shark attack reminds surfers that the vast black waters always harbor these biological equivalents of cold actuarial probabilities. Thereafter the image of a fin slicing the water or a dark shape just below the surface seems an expectation and not a mere projection of a habitual neurotic tendency. Our survival lies beyond our ability to achieve it by sheer will, least of all simply so that an author can achieve a proper sense of closure to a work of art. The moving finger writes, the shears are poised to sever the thread, and much to his embarrassment the author keels over and falls, the coffee cup falls to the floor, and the line that seemed so promising is suspended over an uneasy and indefinitely suspended definite article.

Is this what death will be? Will my defiance or sense of ill-timing be adequate to secure a deferral of a sentence passed by sheer chance: a clot along the blood, a transient ischemia, or a momentary break in the smooth rhythm of the cardiac muscle? Suddenly, I will be reduced to an unfortunate medical event. Where then will be the august author of "Pacific End" with its many pronouncements and partial suggestions? Did it grasp the whole or only serve an indicative function to point to the unlived duration of a year shared with so many others who experienced more or greater things from it but were too busy to write about them? Does the writer finally come to realize that he was never more real than when he appeared in words? We fall silent one by one at last and our last book is pushed before an indifferent public or if still alive we finally decide to keep our thoughts to ourselves. After all, who has appointed us as arbiters of fate and keepers of the public conscience? We live in a world of billions of people not so very different from ourselves who must finally make their own choices and figure it all out on their own.

∗∗∗

Still, for all of my grim reflections, I was glad to be home again on my little peninsula after leaving the coast behind me, knowing that next summer I would probably return and take up the thread of life wherever it could be found. There were still reasons to rejoice; it was Christmastime after all. I recall thinking in the waning days of 2016 of one of Thomas Wolfe's final titles, "The Web and the Rock," and of the wisdom contained in that title. In our lives we are engaged in weaving patterns with our days and nights, our lives are grounded in associations and loyalties, commitments and investments in places, in people, and in ideas. For all of the importance that we not forget the ground of all being and the origin of things, our particular affections and loyalties are not without worth. We embody the eternal in the present by our every action. We leave a train of small but significant events behind us among people who we may never see again. The final design of our lives cannot be seen from only one vantage point. As for the loss of she who cannot be named I came to see that to love to exclusion is not to have loved at all. Love is a university and all are to be matriculated as occasion offers. We need never feel that we have loved in anyone in vain.

✶✶✶

As a novelist I try and remain open to the many faces, voices, and stories that surround me. So I took comfort in the waning days of 2016 that I was still alive, even if wounded and diminished by the year's losses. But at the same time I was never more aware of how much remained intact. Many of the bulwarks of my security had held firm. I ended the year, unsure of whether I would ever again encounter she who cannot be named. "Pacific End," at least lay solid and intact as a tribute, the best comfort that a novelist could wish. A transient impulse based on an encountered phrase had become an eddy and then a current. The current in turn had become part of time's great river, the same that is rushing all of us onward towards an end that exceeds our imaginations whether as wayfarers or at home.

Always there is a brooding marble angel holding the scale of our days and nights and fate or providence standing with shears in hand to sever the thread of our lives so that further change becomes impossible. Until then all things whirl about us like the fallen leaves forming patterns that are, as swiftly as they are gathered: severed, parted, and dispersed. In the end it is the private realm of private loyalties and associations that must sustain us. We now know enough, that for Americans at least a general solution is impossible. We stand behind barriers of mutual incomprehension, advanced polities without arbiters or prophets, to face the interminable questions of life and death, naked and alone.

✶✶✶

All endings have a certain arbitrary quality and the end of novels is no exception. There is always something left to say or some qualification to be made even to our most adamant assertions. The life of Thomas Wolfe was no exception. We will never know what he would have made of his own version of Pacific End; what we do know is that he wrote his former editor, Max Perkins, about a hunch that had come upon him as he lay in the hospital day after day. The hunch was that this time he wasn't going to make it out alive, that he had come to the end of his vast and endless wanderings. He began to realize that as we approach death the eternal begins to make inroads upon us so that it becomes natural to begin letting things go. This all too solid world begins to blur along the edges and to assume the contours of a dream, a dream from which it is high time that we were awoken. Why was it that we ever imagined that this dim region of shades was our natural home?

We begin as death takes hold upon us to merge with categories of thought that break down all dimensions and parameters. Other people are no longer strangers to our own emotions or we to theirs. At first our new conclusions are fragmentary and ill-defined. Sight fails us at last and hearing alone remains. Then suddenly we begin to glimpse a vast invitation to join what was planted in a hillside outside Jerusalem in a borrowed tomb years ago. The gospel narratives are like a mountain range behind which the dawn begins to rise. At first they are only like a jagged line held in silhouette against a greater light. Then the light begins to gather and the mountain snows blind us in their purity and perfection. As the day comes we see ourselves at last, not as we were bent under the burden of our days and nights, but with a purity towards which all of our desires have led, although we could neither define it nor grasp it without the aid of grace.

Beyond this point words themselves fail us and ideas shimmer into incandescence and we realize why the dead do not return to bear witness to us; it is because we would never understand. Even the novelist, ever confident that anything can be the subject of his text, can only fall silent at last and with the great river of time prepare to enter the sea.

Postscript

"Home-life of Great Authors"
by Hattie Tyng Griswold

Life allows amendments applied to the future but no re-writes of what has already been. Experience shows that life-scripts often end suddenly before even the most basic and justifiable expectations are met or any cohesive narrative can be completed while novels often continue long past the point where the patient reader may wish that the author had found a way to leap to the climax and then wind it all up in a tidy moral. My own arbitrary design: to confine events, my reflections on them, and even the composition of the book itself to a single year may leave the reader wondering whether certain unresolved strands will ever come together at some future time. Since one of the key points that I have attempted to make is that both life and novels resist closure it should come as no surprise that I have embodied this conclusion in the very narrative at issue here in "Pacific End." Still any conclusion can provide at least a different vantage point at the end than was present at the beginning of the text. So for those who cannot resist speculation regarding the future a few last words are appended here.

From a political point of view the year 2017 has begun with the inauguration of a man who evidently plans to carry into his four years as the President a goodly number of preconceived but untested ideas. It is unlikely that he will have time to read this book, particularly since it calls into question what are evidently many points essential to his political beliefs. On a more minor note, the subtle recurring theme of whether she who cannot be named will rescind her present posture and resume her position at the center of the anonymous author's regard is likewise unresolved. The year of 2017 in the brief sample that it has provided so far raises many questions about the fate of the program so bravely chosen by the citizens who dwell in America's vast inner heartland with their guns locked and loaded awaiting the Moslem hoards who will soon be sweeping through plain and prairie.

The narrative voice loosely identified with the author's own voice (how closely they match is left deliberately vague as is becoming in an aspiring novelist) has tried to impose some structure upon accidental happenings each of which has shown how loosely knit the underlying pattern of events is. This makes it less difficult to cast away any preconceptions we may have about how our lives will turn out. In the place of premature certitude a clear path to resignation and to trust begins to open. If we are to find a "happy ending" it is on the other side of what we know in our present state. Premature resignation is as much to be deplored as is a rigid insistence on getting our own way. Life is if nothing else a feast for our perceptions. I woke today to the rich golden color of the winter sun playing on the teak and mahogany of the place I currently call home. I left the security of bed and blanket behind me, said my morning offering, and set off once again on the thousand mundane and precarious tasks of living, awake and expectant for whatever lies ahead.

I like this description from a book now in the public domain about Johan Wolfgang von Goethe who lived a complete life in his age, if anyone ever has done so. I include it here by way of a parting word.

One by one the companions of his youth and his manhood were taken from him, until, upon the death of Carl August, he could truthfully exclaim, "Nothing now remains." It was well that the end drew near.

When one can say, "Nothing now remains," it is surely time for the angel with the brazen trumpet to proclaim, "For him let time be no more."

Lightly let the silver cord be loosed and the golden bowl broken, rather than that the lonely life linger on, with its eyes fixed only on the past, which has become but a dim mirage where ghostly figures are seen walking but from which all warmth and light have fled. Happy indeed is he who, when the allotted years have been passed, and he lingers waiting on the stage for the signal which shall cause the curtain to fall forever on his little life drama, has something which to him is real and tangible to look forward to in the near future. The bitterness of a lingering death must be in all old age without this hope.

Let us trust that after that last low cry of Goethe for "more light," the morning dawned upon the great intellect and great heart which had been watching for it so long. Let us hope, also, that the world may yet learn to see him as did Emerson, who found him "a piece of pure nature, like an oak or an apple, large as morning or night, and virtuous as a brier-rose."

The End